NORTH BELLMORE PUBLIC LIBRARY
1551 Newbridge Road
North Bellmore, NY 11710
Phone: 785-6260
DEC 1 0 2003

Bloom's Modern Critical Interpretations

The Adventures of
   Huckleberry Finn
All Quiet on the
   Western Front
Animal Farm
As You Like It
Beloved
Beowulf
Billy Budd, Benito
   Cereno, Bartleby the
   Scrivener, and Other
   Tales
The Bluest Eye
Brave New World
Cat on a Hot Tin
   Roof
The Catcher in the
   Rye
Catch-22
Cat's Cradle
The Color Purple
Crime and
   Punishment
The Crucible
Daisy Miller, The
   Turn of the Screw,
   and Other Tales
Darkness at Noon
David Copperfield
Death of a Salesman
The Divine Comedy
Don Quixote
Dracula
Dubliners
Emma
Fahrenheit 451
A Farewell to Arms
Frankenstein
The General Prologue
   to the Canterbury
   Tales
The Glass Menagerie
The Grapes of Wrath
Great Expectations
The Great Gatsby
Gulliver's Travels
Hamlet

The Handmaid's Tale
Heart of Darkness
I Know Why the
   Caged Bird Sings
The Iliad
The Interpretation of
   Dreams
Invisible Man
Jane Eyre
The Joy Luck Club
Julius Caesar
The Jungle
King Lear
Long Day's Journey
   Into Night
Lord of the Flies
The Lord of the Rings
Macbeth
The Merchant of
   Venice
The Metamorphosis
A Midsummer Night's
   Dream
Moby-Dick
My Ántonia
Native Son
Night
1984
The Odyssey
Oedipus Rex
The Old Man and the
   Sea
On the Road
One Flew Over the
   Cuckoo's Nest
One Hundred Years of
   Solitude
Othello
Paradise Lost
The Pardoner's Tale
A Passage to India
Persuasion
Portnoy's Complaint
A Portrait of the Artist
   as a Young Man
Pride and Prejudice
Ragtime

The Red Badge of
   Courage
The Rime of the
   Ancient Mariner
Romeo & Juliet
The Rubáiyát of Omar
   Khayyám
The Scarlet Letter
A Scholarly Look at
   The Diary of Anne
   Frank
A Separate Peace
Silas Marner
Slaughterhouse-Five
Song of Myself
Song of Solomon
The Sonnets of
   William Shakespeare
Sophie's Choice
The Sound and the
   Fury
The Stranger
A Streetcar Named
   Desire
Sula
The Sun Also Rises
A Tale of Two Cities
The Tale of Genji
The Tales of Poe
The Tempest
Tess of the
   D'Urbervilles
Their Eyes Were
   Watching God
Things Fall Apart
To Kill a Mockingbird
Ulysses
Waiting for Godot
Walden
The Waste Land
White Noise
Wuthering Heights

Bloom's Modern Critical Interpretations

E.M. Forster's
A PASSAGE TO INDIA

Edited and with an introduction by
Harold Bloom
Sterling Professor of the Humanities
Yale University

CHELSEA HOUSE
P U B L I S H E R S
A Haights Cross Communications ◆ Company
P h i l a d e l p h i a

Library of Congress Cataloging-in-Publication Data

A Passage to India /edited with an introduction by Harold Bloom.
    p. cm — (Bloom's modern critical interpretations) Includes
bibliographical references and index.
    ISBN 0-7910-7574-5
    1. Forster, E.M. (Edward Morgan), 1879–1970. Passage to India. 2.
India—In literature. I. Bloom, Harold. II. Series
    PR6011.O58P37 2003
    823'910—dc21

                                                    2003006755

Contributing editor: Camille-Yvette Welsch

Cover design by Terry Mallon

Layout by EJB Publishing Services

Chelsea House Publishers
1974 Sproul Road, Suite 400
Broomall, PA 19008-0914

www.chelseahouse.com

Contents

Editor's Note   vii

Introduction   1
    Harold Bloom

A Passage to India   11
    Lionel Trilling

Two Passages to India: Forster as Victorian and Modern   29
    Malcolm Bradbury

Language and Silence in *A Passage to India*   45
    Michael Orange

The Marabar Caves in the Light of Indian Thought   65
    Chaman L. Sahni

A Passage to India and the Limits of Certainty   73
    Wendy Moffat

Krishna at the Garden Party: Crises of Faith in *A Passage to India*   87
    Wilfrid R. Koponen

Apropos of Nothing: Chance and Narrative
in Forster's *A Passage to India*   99
    Leland Monk

Colonial Queer Something   111
    Yonatan Touval

Forster's *Passage to India*: Re-Envisioning Plato's Cave   129
    Debrah Raschke

Materiality and Mystification in *A Passage to India*   147
        Benita Parry

An Aristotelian Reading of the Feminine Voice-
as-Revolution in E. M. Forster's *A Passage to India*   171
        Elizabeth MacLeod Walls

Forster's Imperial Romance: Chivalry,
Motherhood, and Questing in *A Passage to India*   185
        Maria M. Davidis

Chronology   209

Contributors   213

Bibliography   215

Acknowledgments   221

Index   223

Editor's Note

My Introduction ponders the complexities of the novel's singular religious stance, and relates this to Forster's *Alexandria: A History and a Guide* and to his *The Hill of Devi*.

Lionel Trilling writes a generous appreciation of Forster's liberal imagination at work in the novel.

Close to Trilling's emphasis is that of Malcolm Bradbury, whose Forster is both Victorian and modern, an appeal to and for values, and yet as dark as Herman Melville in his cosmological implications.

Expounding the dialectics of language and silence in *A Passage to India*, Michael Orange ascribes the novel's aesthetic success to a stylistic delicacy that makes possible its high rhetorical self-consciousness.

Chaman L. Sahni, expounding the significance of the Marabar Caves, says that they embody a Brahman without attributes as contrasted to the personal Brahman of the Temple.

For Wendy Moffat, *A Passage to India* turns upon Forster's conviction that "the Hindu is concerned not with conduct, but with vision."

Wilfred R. Koponen mediates upon spiritual crises in the book, which are related to Forster's judgment of India: "She is not a promise, only an appeal."

Chance and nothingness are seen by Leland Monk as narrative principles in Forster's work, while Yonatan Touval intricately relates homoeroticism to colonialism in *A Passage to India*.

Plato's cave is summoned up by Debrah Raschke as the inversion of Adela's epiphany of the Marabar Caves, after which Benita Parry writes a critique of what she takes to be Forster's own mystification by India.

Elizabeth MacLeod Walls judges Forster's use of Adela's voice to be a sabotaging of Victorian morality, while Maria M. Davidis ends this volume by studying romance elements of quest in *A Passage to India*.

HAROLD BLOOM

Introduction

I

E. M. Forster's canonical critic was Lionel Trilling, who might have written Forster's novels had Forster not written them and had Trilling been English. Trilling ended his book on Forster (1924) with the tribute that forever exalts the author of *Howards End* and *A Passage to India* as one of those storytellers whose efforts "work without man's consciousness of them, and even against his conscious will." In Trilling's sympathetic interpretation (or identification), Forster was the true antithesis to the world of telegrams and anger:

> A world at war is necessarily a world of will; in a world at war Forster reminds us of a world where the will is not everything, of a world of true order, of the necessary connection of passion and prose, and of the strange paradoxes of being human. He is one of those who raise the shield of Achilles, which is the moral intelligence of art, against the panic and emptiness which make their onset when the will is tired from its own excess.

Trilling subtly echoed Forster's own response to World War I, a response which Forster recalled as an immersion in Blake, William Morris, the early T. S. Eliot, J. K. Huysmans, Yeats: "They took me into a country where the will was not everything." Yet one can wonder whether Forster and Trilling, prophets of the liberal imagination, did not yield to a vision where there was not quite enough conscious will. *A Passage to India*, Forster's most famous work, can sustain many rereadings, so intricate is its orchestration. It is one of only a few novels of this century that is *written-through*, in the musical sense of thorough composition. But reading it yet again, after twenty years away from it, I find it to be a narrative all of whose principal figures—Aziz, Fielding, Adela Quested, Mrs. Moore, Godbole—lack conscious will. Doubtless, this is Forster's deliberate art, but the consequence is curious; the characters do not sustain rereading so well as the novel does, because none is larger than the book. Poldy holds my imagination quite apart from Joyce's *Ulysses*, as Isabel Archer does in James's *The Portrait of a Lady*, or indeed as Mrs. Wilcox does in Forster's *Howards End*, at least while she is represented as being alive. The aesthetic puzzle of *A Passage to India* is why Aziz and Fielding could not have been stronger and more vivid beings than they are.

What matters most in *A Passage to India* is India, and not any Indians nor any English. But this assertion requires amendment, since Forster's India is not so much a social or cultural reality as it is an enigmatic vision of the Hindu religion, or rather of the Hindu religion as it is reimagined by the English liberal mind at its most sensitive and scrupulous. The largest surprise of a careful rereading of *A Passage to India* after so many years is that, in some aspects, it now seems a strikingly *religious* book. Forster shows us what we never ought to have forgotten, which is that any distinction between religious and secular literature is finally a mere political or societal polemic, but is neither a spiritual nor an aesthetic judgment. There is no sacred literature and no post-sacred literature, great or good. *A Passage to India* falls perhaps just short of greatness, in a strict aesthetic judgment, but spiritually it is an extraordinary achievement.

T. S. Eliot consciously strove to be a devotional poet, and certainly did become a Christian polemicist as a cultural and literary critic. Forster, an amiable freethinker and secular humanist, in his *Commonplace Book* admirably compared himself to Eliot:

> With Eliot? I feel now to be as far ahead of him as I was once behind. Always a distance—and a respectful one. How I dislike his homage to pain! What a mind except the human could have excogitated it? Of course there's pain on and off through each individual's life, and pain at the end of most lives. You can't shirk it and so on. But why should it be endorsed by the schoolmaster and sanctified by the priest until "the fire and the rose are one" when so much of it is caused by disease or by bullies? It is here that Eliot becomes unsatisfactory as a seer.

One could add: it is here that Forster becomes most satisfactory as a seer, for that is the peculiar excellence of *A Passage to India*. We are reminded that Forster is another of John Ruskin's heirs, together with Proust, whom Forster rightly admired above all other modern novelists. Forster too wishes *to make us see*, in the hope that by seeing we will learn to connect, with ourselves and with others, and like Ruskin, Forster knows that seeing in this strong sense is religious, but in a mode beyond dogmatism.

II

A Passage to India, published in 1924, reflects Forster's service as private secretary to the Maharajah of Dewas State Senior in 1921–22, which in turn issued from his Indian visit of 1912–13 with G. Lowes Dickinson. It was not until 1953 that Forster published *The Hill of Devi*, utilizing letters he had written home from India, both forty and thirty years before. *The Hill of Devi* celebrates Forster's Maharajah as a kind of saint, indeed as a religious genius, though Forster is anything but persuasive when he attempts to sustain his judgment of his friend and employer. What does come through is Forster's appreciation of certain elements in Hinduism, an appreciation that achieves its apotheosis in *A Passage to India*, and particularly in "Temple," the novel's foreshortened final part. Forster's ultimate tribute to his Maharajah, a muddler in practical matters and so one who died in disgrace, is a singular testimony for a freethinker. *The Hill of Devi* concludes with what must be called a mystical apprehension:

> His religion was the deepest thing in him. It ought to be studied—neither by the psychologist nor by the mythologist but by the individual who has experienced similar promptings. He penetrated in to rare regions and he was always hoping that others would follow him there.

What are those promptings? Where are those regions? Are these the questions fleshed out by *A Passage to India*? After observing the mystical Maharajah dance before the altar of the God Krishna, Forster quotes from a letter by the Maharajah describing the festival, and then attempts what replies seem possible:

> Such was his account. But what did he feel when he danced like King David before the altar? What were his religious opinions?
> The first question is easier to answer than the second. He felt

as King David and other mystics have felt when they are in the mystic state. He presented well-known characteristics. He was convinced that he was in touch with the reality he called Krishna. And he was unconscious of the world around him. "You can come in during my observances tomorrow and see me if you like, but I shall not know that you are there," he once told Malcolm. And he didn't know. He was in an abnormal but recognisable state; psychologists have studied it.

More interesting, and more elusive, are his religious opinions. The unseen was always close to him, even when he was joking or intriguing. Red paint on a stone could evoke it. Like most people, he implied beliefs and formulated rules for behaviour, and since he had a lively mind, he was often inconsistent. It was difficult to be sure what he did believe (outside the great mystic moments) or what he thought right or wrong. Indians are even more puzzling than Westerners here. Mr. Shastri, a spiritual and subtle Brahmin, once uttered a puzzler: "If the Gods do a thing, it is a reason for men not to do it." No doubt he was in a particular religious mood. In another mood he would have urged us to imitate the Gods. And the Maharajah was all moods. They played over his face, they agitated his delicate feet and hands. To get any pronouncement from so mercurial a creature on the subject, say, of asceticism, was impossible. As a boy, he had thought of retiring from the world, and it was an ideal which he cherished throughout his life, and which, at the end, he would have done well to practise. Yet he would condemn asceticism, declare that salvation could not be reached through it, that it might be Vedantic but it was not Vedic, and matter and spirit must both be given their due. Nothing too much! In such a mood he seemed Greek.

He believed in the heart, and here we reach firmer ground. "I stand for the heart. To the dogs with the head," cries Herman Melville, and he would have agreed. Affection, or the possibility of it, quivered through everything, from Gokul Ashtami down to daily human relationships. When I returned to England and he heard that I was worried because the post-war world of the '20's would not add up into sense, he sent me a message. "Tell him," it ran, "tell him from me to follow his heart, and his mind will see everything clear." The message as phrased is too facile: doors open into silliness at once. But to remember and respect and prefer the heart, to have the instinct which follows it wherever possible—what surer help than that could one have through life? What better hope of clarification? Melville goes on: "The reason that the mass of men fear God and at bottom dislike Him, is because they rather distrust His heart." With that too he would have agreed.

With all respect for Forster, neither he nor his prince is coherent here, and I suspect that Forster is weakly misreading Melville, who is both more ironic and more Gnostic than Forster chooses to realize. Melville, too, distrusts the heart of Jehovah, and consigns the head to the dogs precisely because he associates the head with Jehovah and identifies Jehovah with the Demiurge, the god of this world. More vital would be the question: what does Professor Godbole in *A Passage to India* believe? Is he more coherent than the Maharajah, and does Forster himself achieve a more unified vision there than he does in *The Hill of Devi*?

Criticism from Lionel Trilling on has evaded these questions, but such evasion is inevitable because Forster may be vulnerable to the indictment that he himself made against Joseph Conrad, to the effect that

he is misty in the middle as well as at the edges, that the secret casket of his genius contains a vapour rather than a jewel; and that we need not try to write him down philosophically, because there is, in this particular direction, nothing to write. No creed, in fact. Only opinions, and the right to throw them overboard when facts make them look absurd. Opinions held under the semblance of eternity, girt with the sea, crowned with the stars, and therefore easily mistaken for a creed.

Heart of Darkness sustains Forster's gentle wit, but *Nostromo* does not. Is there a vapor rather than a jewel in Forster's consciousness of Hinduism, at least as represented in *A Passage to India*? "Hinduism" may be the wrong word in that question; "religion" would be better, and "spirituality" better yet. For I do not read Forster as being either hungry for belief or skeptical of it. Rather, he seems to me an Alexandrian, of the third century before the common era, an age celebrated in his *Alexandria: A History and a Guide* (1922), a book that goes back to his happy years in Alexandria (1915–19). In some curious sense, Forster's India is Alexandrian, and his vision of Hinduism is Plotinean. *A Passage to India* is a narrative of Neo-Platonic spirituality, and the true heroine of that narrative, Mrs. Moore, is the Alexandrian figure of Wisdom, the Sophia, as set forth in the Hellenistic Jewish Wisdom of Solomon. Of Wisdom, or Sophia, Forster says: "She is a messenger who bridges the gulf and makes us friends of God," which is a useful description of the narrative function of Mrs. Moore. And after quoting Plotinus (in a passage that includes one of his book's epigraphs): "To any vision must be brought an eye adapted to what is to be seen," Forster comments:

> This sublime passage suggests three comments, with which our glance at Plotinus must close. In the first place its tone is religious, and in this it is typical of all Alexandrian philosophy. In the second place it lays stress on behaviour and training; the Supreme Vision cannot be acquired by magic tricks—only those will see it who are fit to see. And in the third place the vision of oneself and the vision of God are really the same, because each individual *is* God, if only he knew it. And here is the great difference between Plotinus and Christianity. The Christian promise is that a man shall see God, the Neo-Platonic—like the Indian—that he shall be God. Perhaps, on the quays of Alexandria, Plotinus talked with Hindu merchants who came to the town. At all events his system can be paralleled in the religious writings of India. He comes nearer than any other Greek philosopher to the thought of the East.

Forster's Alexandria is in the first place personal; he associated the city always with his sexual maturation as a homosexual. But, as the book *Alexandria* shrewdly shows, Forster finds his precursor culture in ancient Alexandria; indeed he helps to teach us that we are all Alexandrians, insofar as we now live in a literary culture. Forster's insight is massively supported by the historian F. E. Peters in the great study *The Harvest of Hellenism*, when he catalogs our debts to the Eastern Hellenism of Alexandria:

> Its monuments are gnosticism, the university, the catechetical school, pastoral poetry, monasticism, the romance, grammar, lexicography, city planning, theology, canon law, heresy, and scholasticism.

Forster would have added, thinking of the Ptolemaic Alexandria of 331–30 B.C.E., that the most relevant legacy was an eclectic and tolerant liberal humanism, scientific and scholarly, exalting the values of affection over those of belief. That is already the vision of *A Passage to India*, and it opens to the novel's central spiritual question: how are the divine and the human linked? In *Alexandria*, Forster presents us with a clue by his account of the Arian heresy:

Christ is the Son of God. Then is he not younger than God? Arius held that he was and that there was a period before time began when the First Person of the Trinity existed and the Second did not. A typical Alexandrian theologian, occupied with the favourite problem of linking human and divine, Arius thought to solve the problem by making the link predominately human. He did not deny the Godhead of Christ, but he did make him inferior to the Father—of *like* substance, not of the *same* substance, which was the view held by Athanasius, and stamped as orthodox by the Council of Nicaea. Moreover the Arian Christ, like the Gnostic Demiurge, made the world;—creation, an inferior activity, being entrusted to him by the Father, who had Himself created nothing but Christ.

It is easy to see why Arianism became popular. By making Christ younger and lower than God it brought him nearer to us—indeed it tended to level him into a mere good man and to forestall Unitarianism. It appealed to the untheologically minded, to emperors and even more to empresses. But St. Athanasius, who viewed the innovation with an expert eye, saw that while it popularised Christ it isolated God, and he fought it with vigour and venom. His success has been described. It was condemned as heretical in 325, and by the end of the century had been expelled from orthodox Christendom. Of the theatre of this ancient strife no trace remains at Alexandria; the church of St. Mark where Arius was presbyter has vanished: so have the churches where Athanasius thundered—St. Theonas and the Caesareum. Nor do we know in which street Arius died of epilepsy. But the strife still continues in the hearts of men, who always tend to magnify the human in the divine, and it is probable that many an individual Christian to-day is an Arian without knowing it.

To magnify the human in the divine is certainly Forster's quest, and appears to be his interpretation of Hinduism in *A Passage to India*:

Down in the sacred corridors, joy had seethed to jollity. It was their duty to play various games to amuse the newly born God, and to simulate his sports with the wanton dairymaids of Brindaban. Butter played a prominent part in these. When the cradle had been removed, the principal nobles of the state gathered together for an innocent frolic. They removed their turbans, and one put a lump of butter on his forehead, and waited for it to slide down his nose into his mouth. Before it could arrive, another stole up behind him, snatched the melting morsel, and swallowed it himself. All laughed exultantly at discovering that the divine sense of humour coincided with their own. "God si love!" There is fun in heaven. God can play practical jokes upon Himself, draw chairs away from beneath His own posteriors, set His own turbans on fire, and steal His own petticoats when He bathes. By sacrificing good taste, this worship achieved what Christianity has shirked: the inclusion of merriment. All spirit as well as all matter must participate in salvation, and if practical jokes are banned, the circle is incomplete. Having swallowed the butter, they played another game which chanced to be graceful: the fondling of Shri Krishna under the similitude of a child. A pretty red and gold ball is thrown, and he who catches it chooses a child from the crowd, raises it in his arms, and carries it round to be caressed. All stroke the darling creature for the Creator's sake, and murmur happy words. The child is restored to his parents, the ball thrown on, and another child becomes for a moment the World's desire. And the Lord bounds hither and thither through the aisles, chance, and the sport of chance, irradiating little mortals with His immortality.... When they had played this long enough—and being exempt from boredom, they played it again and again, they played it again and again—they took many sticks and hit them together, whack smack, as though they fought the Pandava wars, and threshed and churned with them, and later on they hung from the roof of the temple, in a net, a great black earthenware jar, which was painted here and there with red, and wreathed with dried figs. Now came a rousing sport. Springing up, they struck at the jar with their sticks. It cracked, broke, and a mass of greasy rice and milk poured on to their faces. They ate and smeared one another's mouths and dived between each other's legs for what had been pashed upon the carpet. This way and that spread the divine mess, until the line of schoolboys, who had somewhat fended off the crowd, broke for their share. The corridors, the courtyard, were filled with benign confusion. Also the flies awoke and claimed their share of God's bounty. There was no quarrelling, owing to the nature of the gift, for blessed is the man who confers it on another, he imitates God. And those "imitations," those "substitutions," continued to flicker through the assembly for many hours, awaking in each man, according to his capacity, an emotion that he would not have had otherwise. No definite image survived; at the Birth it was questionable whether a silver doll or a mud village, or a silk napkin, or an intangible spirit, or a pious resolution, had been born. Perhaps all these things! Perhaps none! Perhaps all birth is an allegory! Still, it was the main event of the religious year. It caused strange thoughts. Covered with grease and dust, Professor Godbole had once more developed the life of his spirit. He had, with increasing vividness, again seen Mrs. Moore, and round her faintly clinging forms of trouble. He was a Brahman, she Christian, but it made no difference, it made no difference whether she was a trick of his memory or a telepathic appeal. It was his duty, as it was his desire, to place himself in the position of the God and to love her, and to place himself in her position and to say to the God, "Come, come, come, come." This was all he could do. How inadequate! But each according to his own capacities, and he knew that his own were small. "One old Englishwoman and one little, little wasp," he thought, as he stepped out of the temple into the grey of a pouring wet morning. "It does not seem much, still it is more than I am myself."

Professor Godbole's epiphany, his linkage of Mrs. Moore's receptivity toward the wasp with his own receptivity toward Mrs. Moore, has been much admired by critics, deservedly so. In this moment-of-moments, Godbole receives Mrs. Moore into Forster's own faithless faith: a religion of love between equals, as opposed to Christianity, a religion of love between the incommensurate Jehovah and his creatures. But though beautifully executed, Forster's vision of Godbole and Mrs. Moore is spiritually a little too easy. Forster knew that, and the finest moment in *A Passage to India* encompasses this knowing. It comes in a sublime juxtaposition, in the crossing between the conclusion of part 2, "Caves," and the beginning of part 3, "Temple," where Godbole is seen standing in the presence of God. The brief and beautiful chapter 32 that concludes "Caves" returns Fielding to a Western and Ruskinian vision of form in Venice:

Egypt was charming—a green strip of carpet and walking up and down it four sorts of animals and one sort of man. Fielding's business took him there for a few days. He re-embarked at Alexandria—bright blue sky, constant wind, clean low coastline, as against the intricacies of Bombay. Crete welcomed him next with the long snowy ridge of its mountains, and then came Venice. As he landed on the piazzetta a cup of beauty was lifted to his lips, and he drank with a sense of disloyalty. The buildings of Venice, like the mountains of Crete and the fields of Egypt, stood in the right place, whereas in poor India everything was placed wrong. He had forgotten the beauty of form among idol temples and lumpy hills; indeed, without form, how can there be beauty? Form stammered here and there in a mosque, became rigid through nervousness even, but oh these Italian churches! San Giorgio standing on the island which could scarcely have risen from the waves without it, the Salute holding the entrance of a canal which, but for it, would not be the Grand Canal! In the old undergraduate days he had wrapped himself up in the many-coloured blanket of St. Mark's, but something more precious than mosaics and marbles was offered to him now: the harmony between the works of man and the earth that upholds them, the civilization that has escaped muddle, the spirit in a reasonable form, with flesh and blood subsisting. Writing picture post-cards to his Indian friends, he felt that all of them would miss the joys he experienced now, the joys of form, and that this constituted a serious barrier. They would see the sumptuousness of Venice, not its shape, and though Venice was not Europe, it was part of the Mediterranean harmony. The Mediterranean is the human norm. When men leave that exquisite lake, whether through the Bosphorus or the Pillars of Hercules, they approach the monstrous and extraordinary; and the southern exit leads to the strangest experience of all. Turning his back on it yet again, he took the train northward, and tender romantic fancies that he thought were dead for ever, flowered when he saw the buttercups and daisies of June.

After the muddle of India, where "everything was placed wrong," Fielding learns again "the beauty of form." Alexandria, like Venice, is part of the Mediterranean harmony, the human norm, but India is the cosmos of "the monstrous and extraordinary." Fielding confronting the Venetian churches has absolutely nothing in common with Professor Godbole confronting the God Krishna at the opposite end of the same strip of carpet upon which Godbole stands. Forster is too wise not to know that the passage to India is only a passage. A passage is a journey, or an occurrence between two persons. Fielding and Aziz do not quite make the passage together, do not exchange vows that bind. Perhaps that recognition of limits is the ultimate beauty of form in *A Passage to India*.

LIONEL TRILLING

A Passage to India

The years between 1910 and 1914 were the vestibule to what Forster has called "the sinister corridor of our age." *Howards End* records the sense of Germany's growing strength; Mr. Schlegel, father of Helen and Margaret, had voluntarily exiled himself from the old Germany of philosophers, musicians and little courts and he spoke bitterly of the new imperialism to which "money [was] supremely useful; intellect, rather useful; imagination, of no use at all."

Not many books of the time were so precisely sensitive to the situation, yet a kind of sultry premonitory hush comes over literature in these years. The hope of the first decade of the century has been checked. The athletic quality of intelligence which seemed to mark the work of even five years earlier has subsided.

In 1910, following the publication of *Howards End*, Forster projected two novels but wrote neither. The next year he finished a play, *The Heart Of Bosnia* which, by his own account, was not good, although it almost reached the stage in 1914; plans for its production were abandoned at the outbreak of war and the manuscript was lost by the producer. In 1912, Forster, in company with Dickinson and R. C. Trevelyan, sailed for India. Dickinson, travelling on one of the fellowships established by Albert Kahn in the interests of international understanding, had official visits and tours to make

From *E.M. Forster* by Lionel Trilling. © 1943, 1964 by New Directions Publishing Corp.

and the friends separated at Bombay. But their itineraries crossed several times and they spent a fortnight as guests of the Maharajah of Chhatarpur, who loved Dickinson and philosophy—"'Tell me, Mr. Dickinson, where is God?'" the Maharajah said. "'Can Herbert Spencer lead me to him, or should I prefer George Henry Lewes? Oh when will Krishna come and be my friend? Oh Mr. Dickinson!'"

The two travellers came away from India with widely different feelings. Dickinson, who was to love China, was not comfortable in India. Displeased as he was by her British rulers, he was not pleased with India itself. "There is no solution to the problem of governing India," he wrote. "Our presence is a curse both to them and to us. Our going away will be worse. I believe that to the last word. And *why* can't the races meet? Simply because the Indians *bore* the English. That is the simple adamantine fact." It is not an enlightening or even a serious view of the situation, and Forster, dissenting from it, speaks of the "peace and happiness" which he himself found in India in 1912 and again on his second visit ten years later.

The best fruit of the Indian journey was to be *A Passage To India*, but meanwhile Forster wrote several short pieces on Indian life of which two, "The Suppliant" and "Advance, India!" (both reprinted in *Abinger Harvest*) admirably depict the comic, sad confusion of a nation torn between two cultures.

He began to sketch the Indian novel, but the war postponed its completion for a decade. And the war quite destroyed the project for a critical study of Samuel Butler, with whose mind Forster's has community at so many points. But the war, which sent Forster to non-combatant service in Egypt, developed in him the interest in Imperial conduct and policy which the Indian tour had begun. Hitherto Forster's political concern had been intense but perhaps abstract; now it became increasingly immediate. The three Egyptian years gave him not only the material for two books and many essays, but also a firm position on the Imperial question.

The first of Forster's Egyptian books is the guidebook, *Alexandria*; its introductory account of the city's history gives Forster the opportunity to display his love of the Hellenic and naturalistic, his contempt for the Christian and theological; its second part arranges tours to points of interest, and the whole job is scholarly, attractive and efficient.[1] Much less can be said for *Pharos And Pharillon*, another venture into Alexandrian history and local color. The volume is infused with the archness which has been noted earlier as the fault of Forster's first historical essays; the years have but intensified it. Under Forster's implacable gentleness, the past becomes what it should never be, quaint, harmless and ridiculous. Menelaos, Alexander, the Ptolemies, the Jews, the Arabs, the Christian theologians, the very lighthouse itself, all become submerged in high irony. This desperately persistent fault of taste is all the more surprising because Forster has himself so rightly characterized it in one of his best essays, "The Consolations of History."

> It is pleasant to be transferred from an office where one is afraid of a sergeant-major into an office where one can intimidate generals, and perhaps that is why History is so attractive to the more timid among us. We can recover self-confidence by snubbing the dead.... Tight little faces from Oxford, fish-shaped faces from Cambridge,—we cannot help having our dreams.

The same fault of lofty whimsicality inheres in other of the sketches which in *Abinger Harvest* are collected under the rubric of "The Past." Sufficiently objectionable in "Captain Edward Gibbon" and in "Voltaire's Laboratory," it becomes really bad in "Trooper Silas Tompkyns Comberbacke" and in "The Abbeys' Difficulties," the first of which dramatically reveals the open secret that the Trooper's real name was Samuel Taylor Coleridge, the second that the young people with whom the Abbeys had difficulty were Fanny and John Keats.

A single sentence of *Pharos And Pharillon* points away from this slim, feasting antiquarianism; speaking of Fort Kait Bey, Forster mentions the holes in it "made by Admiral Seymour when he bombarded the Fort in 1882 and laid the basis of our intercourse with modern Egypt." In 1920 Forster wrote his note for *The Government Of Egypt*, a pamphlet of the International Section of the Labour Research Department, a Fabian organization. Although it does little save support the Committee's recommendation that Egypt be given either dominion status or autonomy and although it is scarcely interesting in itself, it indicates Forster's increasing interest in public affairs.

It was an angry interest. In 1934 Forster was to publish his biography of Dickinson, who had died two years before. Perhaps because Dickinson's life lacked tension or tone, perhaps because Forster wrote under some reserve, the biography is not a work of high distinction, but it serves to suggest the political atmosphere in which Forster lived. The crown of Dickinson's political life was his fight against what he called International Anarchy; his weapon, soon taken from his hands, was the League of Nations. He hoped to raise the minds of men above "the fighting attitude" of practical politics, but he could never, he confessed, formulate clearly "the great problem of the relation of ideals to passion and interest." This is, of course, Forster's own insistent question, but Forster's is an angrier mind than Dickinson's and any uncertainty he feels about the ultimate problems of politics does not prevent him from speaking out on matters of the moment.

England after the war was tense with class antagonism. In 1920 Forster became for a year the literary editor of the *Daily Herald*, a Labor paper to whose weekly literary page many well-known writers of liberal leanings contributed reviews. In the following years the amount of Forster's literary and political journalism, collected and uncollected, was considerable.

The political pieces are suffused with disillusionment about the war, a foreboding that a new war is imminent, a hatred of the stupidities of class rule. They pretend neither to originality of sentiment nor to practical perspicacity; they express, sometimes with anger, sometimes with bitterness, sometimes only with a kind of salutary irritation and disgust, the old emotions—the 19th century emotions, we almost feel, and we salute their directness—of a rational democrat confronting foolishness and pretense. Perhaps the most successful of these pieces is the essay "Me, Them and You." It is a review of the Sargent exhibition of 1925 in which, among all the aristocratic portraits, Sargent's pleasant, fanciful war picture, "Gassed," was hung. The situation was made for the satirist and Forster takes advantage of it in one of the truly successful Pieces of modern invective.

> The portraits dominated. Gazing at each other over our heads, they said, "What would the country do without us? We have got the decorations and the pearls, we make fashions and wars, we have the largest houses and eat the best food, and control the most important industries, and breed the most valuable children, and ours is the Kingdom and the Power and the Glory." And, listening to their chorus, I felt this was so, and my clothes fitted worse and worse, and there seemed in all the universe no gulf wider than the gulf between Them and Me—no wider gulf, until I encountered You.
>
> You had been plentiful enough in the snow outside (your proper place) but I had not expected to find You here in the place of honour, too. Yours was by far the largest picture in the show. You were hung between Lady Cowdray and the Hon. Mrs. Langman, and You were entitled "Gassed." You were of godlike beauty—for the upper classes only allow the lower classes to appear in art on condition that they wash themselves and have classical features. These conditions you fulfilled. A line of golden-haired Apollos moved along a duck-board from left to right with bandages over their eyes. They had been blinded by mustard gas. Others sat peacefully in the foreground, others approached through the middle distance. The battlefield was sad but tidy. No one complained, no one looked lousy or overtired, and the

aeroplanes overhead struck the necessary note of the majesty of England. It was all that a great war picture should be, and it was modern because it managed to tell a new sort of lie. Many ladies and gentlemen fear that Romance is passing out of war with the sabres and the chargers. Sargent's masterpiece reassures them. He shows them that it is possible to suffer with a quiet grace under the new conditions, and Lady Cowdray and the Hon. Mrs. Langman, as they looked over the twenty feet of canvas that divided them, were able to say, "How touching," instead of "How obscene."

Less remarkable but filled with a fine irritation is the piece on the British Empire Exhibition at Wembley ("An Empire Is Born") and another on the Queen's Doll House ("The Doll Souse"). Forster's old antipathy to the clergy turns up again in political form in the verses which answer Bishop Welldon's public complaint of the profanity of the Labor members of Parliament. One of the best of his essays, "My Wood," describes the growth of the property sense in himself after the purchase of a new tract of wood— "The other day I heard a twig snap in [my wood]. I was annoyed at first, for I thought that someone was blackberrying, and depreciating the value of the undergrowth. On coming nearer, I saw it was not a man who had trodden on the twig and snapped it, but a bird, and I felt pleased. My bird." The essay is especially to be noted because it states with almost startling explicitness a view of life which has been implicit in the novels:

> Our life on earth is, and ought to be, material and carnal. But we have not yet learned to manage our materialism and carnality properly; they are still entangled with the desire for ownership; where (in the words of Dante) "Possession is one with loss."

Over the anomalies of literary censorship Forster had long been exercised.[2] In 1939 he was appointed by the Lord Chancellor to the Committee to examine the Law of Defamatory Libel. His 1935 address to the Paris *Congrès International des Ecrivains* on the subject of literary freedom constitutes a declaration of political faith.

> It seems to me that if nations keep on amassing armaments, they can no more help discharging their filth than an animal which keeps on eating can stop itself from excreting. This being so, my job and the job of those who feel with me is an interim job. We have just to go on tinkering as well as we can with our old

tools until the crash comes. When the crash comes, nothing is any good. After it—if there is an after—the task of civilization will be carried on by people whose training has been different from my own.

I am worried by thoughts of a war oftener than by thoughts of my own death, yet the line to be adopted over both these nuisances is the same. One must behave as if one is immortal, and as if civilization is eternal. Both statements are false—I shall not survive, no more will the great globe itself—both of them must be assumed to be true if we are to go on eating and working and travelling, and keep open a few breathing holes for the human spirit.

In 1922 Forster made a second journey to India and took up again the Indian story he had projected. *A Passage To India* appeared with great success in 1924.

A Passage To India is Forster's best known and most widely read novel. Public and political reasons no doubt account for this; in England the book was a matter for controversy and its success in America, as Forster himself explains it, was due to the superiority Americans could feel at the English botch of India. But the public, political nature of the book is not extraneous; it inheres in the novel's very shape and texture.

By many standards of criticism, this public, political quality works for good. *A Passage To India* is the most comfortable and even the most conventional of Forster's novels. It is under the control not only of the author's insight; a huge, hulking physical fact which he is not alone in seeing, requires that the author submit to its veto-power. Consequently, this is the least surprising of Forster's novels, the least capricious and, indeed, the least personal. It quickly establishes the pattern for our emotions and keeps to it. We are at once taught to withhold our sympathies from the English officials, to give them to Mrs. Moore and to the "renegade" Fielding, to regard Adela Quested with remote interest and Aziz and his Indian friends with affectionate understanding.

Within this pattern we have, to be sure, all the quick, subtle modifications, the sudden strictnesses or relentings of judgment which are the best stuff of Forster's social imagination. But always the pattern remains public, simple and entirely easy to grasp. What distinguishes it from the patterns of similarly public and political novels is the rigor of its objectivity; it deals with unjust, hysterical emotion and it leads us, not to intense emotions about justice, but to cool poise and judgment—if we do not relent in our contempt for Ronny, we are at least forced to be aware that he is capable of noble, if stupid, feelings; the English girl who has the hallucination of an attempted rape by a native has engaged our sympathy by her rather dull decency; we are permitted no easy response to the benign Mrs. Moore, or to Fielding, who stands out against his own people, or to the native physician who is wrongly accused. This restraint of our emotions is an important element in the book's greatness.

With the public nature of the story goes a chastened and somewhat more public style than is usual with Forster, and a less arbitrary manner. Forster does not abandon his right to intrude into the novel, but his manner of intrusion is more circumspect than ever before. Perhaps this is because here, far less than in the English and Italian stories, he is in possession of truth; the Indian gods are not his gods, they are not genial and comprehensible. So far as the old Mediterranean deities of wise impulse and loving intelligence can go in India, Forster is at home; he thinks they can go far but not all the way, and a certain retraction of the intimacy of his style reflects his uncertainty. The acts of imagination by which Forster conveys the sense of the Indian gods are truly wonderful; they are, nevertheless, the acts of imagination not of a master of the truth but of an intelligent neophyte, still baffled.

So the public nature of the novel cannot be said to work wholly for good. For the first time Forster has put himself to the test of verisimilitude. Is this the truth about India? Is this the way the English act?—always? sometimes? never? Are Indians like this?—all of them? some of them? Why so many Moslems and so few Hindus? Why so much Hindu religion and so little Moslem? And then, finally, the disintegrating question, What is to be done?

Forster's gallery of English officials has of course been disputed in England; there have been many to say that the English are not like that. Even without knowledge we must suppose that the Indian Civil Service has its quota of decent, devoted and humble officials. But if Forster's portraits are perhaps angry exaggerations, anger can be illuminating—the English of Forster's Chandrapore are the limits toward which the English in India must approach, for Lord Acton was right, power does corrupt, absolute power does corrupt absolutely.

As for the representation of the Indians, that too can be judged here only on *a priori* grounds. Although the Indians are conceived in sympathy and affection, they are conceived with these emotions alone, and although all of them have charm, none of them has dignity; they touch our hearts but they never impress us. Once, at his vindication feast, Aziz is represented as "full of civilization ... complete, dignified, rather hard" and for the first time Fielding treats him "with diffidence," but this only serves to remind us how lacking in dignity Aziz usually is. Very possibly this is the effect that Indians make upon even sensitive Westerners; Dickinson, as we have seen, was bored by them, and generations of subjection can diminish the habit of dignity and teach grown men the strategy of the little child.

These are not matters that we can settle; that they should have arisen at all is no doubt a fault of the novel. Quite apart from the fact that questions of verisimilitude diminish illusion, they indicate a certain inadequacy in the conception of the story. To represent the official English as so unremittingly bad and the Indians as so unremittingly feeble is to prevent the story from being sufficiently worked out in terms of the characters; the characters, that is, are in the events, the events are not in them: we want a larger Englishman than Fielding, a weightier Indian than Aziz.

These are faults, it is true, and Forster is the one novelist who could commit them and yet transcend and even put them to use. The relation of the characters to the events, for example, is the result of a severe imbalance in the relation of plot to story. Plot and story in this novel are not coextensive as they are in all Forster's other novels.[3] The plot is precise, hard, crystallized and far simpler than any Forster has previously conceived. The story is beneath and above the plot and continues beyond it in time. It is, to be sure, created by the plot, it is the plot's manifold reverberation, but it is greater than the plot and contains it. The plot is as decisive as a judicial opinion; the story is an impulse, a tendency, a perception. The suspension of plot in the large circumambient sphere of story, the expansion of the story from the center of plot, requires some of the subtlest manipulation that any novel has ever had. This relation of plot and story tells us that we are dealing with a political novel of an unusual kind. The characters are of sufficient size for the plot; they are not large enough for the story—and that indeed is the point of the story.

This, in outline, is the plot: Adela Quested arrives in India under the chaperonage of the elderly Mrs. Moore with whose son by a first marriage Adela has an "understanding." Both ladies are humane and Adela is liberal and they have an intense desire to "know India." This is a matter of some annoyance to Ronny, Mrs. Moore's son and Adela's fiancé, and of amused condescension to the dull people at the station who try to satisfy the ladies with elephant rides—only very *new* people try to *know* India. Both Mrs. Moore and Adela are chilled by Ronny; he has entirely adopted the point of view of the ruling race and has become a heavy-minded young judge with his dull dignity as his chief recognized asset. But despite Ronny's fussy certainty about what is and is not proper, Mrs. Moore steps into a mosque one evening and there makes the acquaintance of Aziz, a young Moslem doctor. Aziz is hurt and miserable, for he has just been snubbed; Mrs. Moore's kindness and simplicity soothe him. Between the two a friendship develops which politely includes Adela Quested. At last, by knowing Indians, the travellers will know India, and Aziz is even more delighted than they at the prospect of the relationship. To express his feelings he organizes a fantastically elaborate jaunt to the Marabar Caves. Fielding, the principal of the local college, and Professor Godbole, a Hindu teacher, were also to have been of the party but they miss the train and Aziz goes ahead with the ladies and his absurd retinue. In one of the eaves Mrs. Moore has a disturbing psychic experience and sends Aziz and Adela to continue the exploration without her. Adela, not a very attractive girl, has had her doubts about her engagement to Ronny, not a very attractive man, and now she ventures to speak of love to Aziz, quite abstractly but in a way both to offend him and disturb herself. In the cave the strap of her field-glasses is pulled and broken by someone in the darkness and she rushes out in a frenzy of hallucination that Aziz has attempted to rape her. The accusation makes the English of the station hysterical with noble rage. In every English mind there is the certainty that Aziz is guilty and the verdict is foregone. Only Fielding and Mrs. Moore do not share this certainty. Fielding, because of his liking for the young doctor, and Mrs. Moore, because of an intuition, are sure that the event could not have happened and that Adela is the victim of illusion. Fielding, who openly declares his partisanship, is ostracized, and Mrs. Moore, who only hints her opinion, is sent out of the country by her son; the journey in the terrible heat of the Indian May exhausts her and she dies on shipboard. At the trial Adela's illusion, fostered by the mass-hysteria of the English, becomes suddenly dispelled, she recants, Aziz is cleared, Fielding is vindicated and promoted, the Indians are happy, the English furious.

Thus the plot. And no doubt it is too much a plot of event, too easily open and shut. Nevertheless it is an admirable if obvious device for organizing an enormous amount of observation of both English and native society; it brings to spectacular virulence the latent antagonisms between rulers and ruled.

Of the Anglo-Indian society it is perhaps enough to say that, "more than it can hope to do in England," it lives by the beliefs of the English public school. It is arrogant, ignorant, insensitive—intelligent natives estimate that a year in India makes the pleasantest Englishman rude. And of all the English it is the women who insist most strongly on their superiority, who are the rawest and crudest in their manner. The men have a certain rough liking for the men of the subject race; for instance, Turton, Collector of the district, has "a contemptuous affection for the pawns he had moved about for so many years; they must be worth his pains." But the women, unchecked by any professional necessity or pride, think wholly in terms of the most elementary social prestige and Turton's wife lives for nothing else. "'After all,'" Turton thinks but never dares say, "'it's our women who make everything more difficult out here.'" This is the result of the undeveloped heart. *A Passage To India* is not a radical novel; its data were gathered in 1912 and 1922, before the full spate of Indian nationalism; it is not concerned to show that the English should not be in India at all. Indeed, not until the end of the book is the question of the expulsion of the English mentioned, and the novel proceeds on an imperialistic premise—ironically, for it is not actually Forster's own—its chief point being that by reason of the undeveloped heart the English have thrown away the possibility of holding India. For want of a smile an Empire is to be lost.[4] Not even justice is enough. "'Indians know whether they are liked or not,'" Fielding says, "'—they cannot be fooled here. Justice never satisfies them, and that is why the British Empire rests on sand.'" Mrs. Moore listens to Ronny defending the British attitude; "his words without his voice might have impressed her, but when she heard the self-satisfied lilt of them, when she saw the mouth moving so complacently and competently beneath the little red nose, she felt, quite illogically, that this was not the last word on India. One touch of regret—not the canny substitute but the true regret—would have made him a different man, and the British Empire a different institution."

Justice is not enough then, but in the end neither are liking and goodwill enough. For although Fielding and Aziz reach out to each other in friendship, a thousand little tricks of speech, a thousand different assumptions and different tempi keep them apart. They do not understand each other's *amounts* of emotion, let alone kinds of emotion. "'Your emotions never seem in proportion to their objects, Aziz,'" Fielding says, and Aziz answers, "'Is emotion a sack of potatoes, so much the pound, to be measured out?'"

The theme of separateness, of fences and barriers, the old theme of the Pauline epistles, which runs through all Forster's novels, is, in *A Passage To India*, hugely expanded and everywhere dominant. The separation of race from race, sex from sex, culture from culture, even of man from himself, is what underlies every relationship. The separation of the English from the Indians is merely the most dramatic of the chasms in this novel. Hindu and Moslem cannot really approach each other; Aziz, speaking in all friendliness to Mr. Das, the Magistrate, wishes that Hindus did not remind him of cow-dung, and the Hindu Mr. Das thinks, "'Some Moslems are very violent'"—"Between people of distant climes there is always the possibility of romance, but the various branches of Indians know too much about each other to surmount the unknowable easily." Adela and Ronny cannot meet in sexuality, and when, after the trial, Adela and Fielding meet in an idea, "a friendliness, as of dwarfs shaking hands, was in the air." Fielding, when he marries Mrs.

Moore's daughter Stella, will soon find himself apart from his young wife. And Mrs. Moore is separated from her son, from all people, from God, from the universe.

This sense of separateness broods over the book, pervasive, symbolic—at the end the very earth requires, and the sky approves, the parting of Aziz and Fielding—and perhaps accounts for the remoteness of the characters: they are so far from each other that they cannot reach us. But the isolation is not merely adumbrated; in certain of its aspects it is very precisely analyzed and some of the most brilliant and virtuose parts of the novel are devoted to the delineation of Aziz and his friends, to the investigation of the cultural differences that keep Indian and Englishman apart.

The mould for Aziz is Gino Carella of the first novel. It is the mould of unEnglishness, that is to say, of volatility, tenderness, sensibility, a hint of cruelty, much warmth, a love of pathos, the desire to please even at the cost of insincerity. Like Gino's, Aziz's nature is in many ways child-like, in many ways mature: it is mature in its acceptance of child-like inconsistency. Although eager to measure up to English standards of puritan rectitude, Aziz lives closer to the literal facts of his emotions; for good or bad, he is more human. He, like his friends, is not prompt, not efficient, not neat, not really convinced of Western ideas even in science—when he retires to a native state he slips back to mix a little magic with his medicine and he, like them, is aware of his faults. He is hyper-sensitive, imagining slights even when there are none because there have actually been so many; he is full of humility and full of contempt and desperately wants to be liked. He is not heroic but his heroes are the great chivalrous emperors, Babur and Alamgir. In short, Aziz is a member of a subject race. A rising nationalism in India may by now have thrust him aside in favor of a more militant type; but we can be sure that if the new type has repudiated Aziz emotional contradictions it has not resolved them.

Aziz and his friends are Moslems, and with Moslems of the business and professional class the plot of the novel deals almost entirely. But the story is suffused with Hinduism.[5] It is Mrs. Moore who carries the Hindu theme; it is Mrs. Moore, indeed, who is the story. The theme is first introduced by Mrs. Moore observing a wasp.

> Going to hang up her cloak she found that the tip of the peg was occupied by a small wasp.... There he clung, asleep, while jackals in the plain bayed their desires and mingled with the percussion of drums.
>
> "Pretty dear," said Mrs. Moore to the wasp. He did not wake, but her voice floated out, to swell the night's uneasiness.

This wasp is to recur in Professor Godbole's consciousness when he has left Chandrapore and taken service as director of education in a Hindu native state. He stands, his school quite forgotten—turned into a granary, indeed—and celebrates the birth of Krishna in the great religious festival that dominates the third part of the novel.[6] The wasp is mixed up in his mind—he does not know how it got there! in the first place, nor do we—with a recollection of Mrs. Moore.

> He was a Brahman, she a Christian, but it made no difference, it made no difference whether she was a trick of his memory or a telepathic appeal. It was his duty, as it was his desire, to place himself in the position of the God and to love her, and to place himself in her position and say to the God: "Come, come, come, come." This was all he could do. How inadequate! But each according to his own capacities, and he knew that his own were small. "One old Englishwoman and one little, little wasp," he thought, as he stepped out of the temple into the grey of a pouring wet morning. "It does not seem much, still it is more than I am myself."

The presence of the wasp, first in Mrs. Moore's consciousness, then in Godbole's, Mrs. Moore's acceptance of the wasp, Godbole's acceptance of Mrs. Moore—in some symbolic fashion, this is the thread of the story of the novel as distinguished from its plot. For the story is essentially concerned with Mrs. Moore's discovery that Christianity is not adequate. In a quiet way, Mrs. Moore is a religious woman; at any rate, as she has grown older she has found it "increasingly difficult to avoid" mentioning God's name "as the greatest she knew." Yet in India God's name becomes less and less efficacious—"outside the arch there seemed always another arch, beyond the remotest echo a silence."

And so, unwittingly, Mrs. Moore has moved closer and closer to Indian ways of feeling. When Ronny and Adela go for an automobile ride with the Nawab Bahadur and the chauffeur swerves at something in the path and wrecks the car, Mrs. Moore, when she is told of the incident, remarks without thinking, "'A ghost!'" And a ghost it was, or so the Nawab believed, for he had run over and killed a drunken man at that spot nine years before. "None of the English knew of this, nor did the chauffeur; it was a racial secret communicable more by blood than by speech." This "racial secret" has somehow been acquired by Mrs. Moore. And the movement away from European feeling continues: "She felt increasingly (vision or nightmare?) that, though people are important, the relations between them are not, and that in particular too much fuss has been made over marriage; centuries of carnal embracement, yet man is no nearer to understanding man." The occasion of her visit to the Marabar Caves is merely the climax of change, although a sufficiently terrible one.

What so frightened Mrs. Moore in the cave was an echo. It is but one echo in a book which is contrived of echoes. Not merely does Adela Quested's delusion go in company with a disturbing echo in her head which only ceases when she masters her delusion, but the very texture of the story is a reticulation of echoes. Actions and speeches return, sometimes in a better, sometimes in a worse form, given back by the perplexing "arch" of the Indian universe. The recurrence of the wasp is a prime example, but there are many more. If Aziz plays a scratch game of polo with a subaltern who comes to think well of this particular anonymous native, the same subaltern will be particularly virulent in his denunciation of Aziz the rapist, never knowing that the liked and the detested native are the same. If the natives talk about their inability to catch trains, an Englishman's missing a train will make all the trouble of the story. Mrs. Moore will act with bad temper to Adela and with surly indifference to Aziz, but her action will somehow have a good echo; and her children will be her further echo. However we may interpret Forster's intention in this web of reverberation, it gives his book a cohesion and intricacy usually only found in music. And of all the many echoes, the dominant one is the echo that booms through the Marabar cave.

> A Marabar cave had been horrid as far as Mrs. Moore was concerned, for she had nearly fainted in it, and had some difficulty in preventing herself from saying so as soon as she got into the air again. It was natural enough; she had always suffered from faintness, and the cave had become too full, because all their retinue followed them. Crammed with villagers and servants, the circular chamber began to smell. She lost Aziz and Adela in the dark, didn't know who touched her, couldn't breathe, and some vile naked thing struck her face and settled on her mouth like a pad. She tried to regain the entrance tunnel, but an influx of villagers swept her back. She hit her head. For an instant she went mad, hitting and gasping like a fanatic. For not only did the crush and stench alarm her; there was also a terrifying echo.
>
> Professor Godbole had never mentioned an echo; it never impressed him, perhaps. There are some exquisite echoes in India; ... The echo in a Marabar cave is not like these, it is entirely devoid of distinction. Whatever is said, the same monotonous noise replies, and quivers up and down the walls until it is

absorbed in the roof. "Boum" is the sound as far as the human alphabet can express it, or "bou-oum," or "ou-boum"—utterly dull. Hope, politeness, the blowing of a nose, the squeal of a boot, all produce "boum."

Panic and emptiness—Mrs. Moore's panic had been at the emptiness of the universe. And one goes back beyond Helen Schlegel's experience of the Fifth Symphony in *Howards End*: the negating mess of the cave reminds us of and utterly denies the mess of that room in which Caroline Abbott saw Gino with his child. For then the mess had been the source of life and hope, and in it the little child had blossomed; Caroline had looked into it from the "charnel chamber" of the reception room and the "light in it was soft and large, as from some gracious, noble opening." It is, one might say, a representation of the womb and a promise of life. There is also a child in the mess of the Marabar cave for the "vile, naked thing" that settles "like a pad" on Mrs. Moore's mouth is "a poor little baby, astride its mother's hip." The cave's opening is behind Mrs. Moore, she is facing into the grave; light from the world does not enter, and the universe of death makes all things alike, even life and death, even good and evil.

> The echo began in some indescribable way to undermine her hold on life.... It had managed to murmur: "Pathos, piety, courage—they exist, but are identical, and so is filth. Everything exists, nothing has value." If one had spoken vileness in that place, or quoted lofty poetry, the comment would have been the same—"ou-boum." If one had spoken with the tongues of angels and pleaded for all the unhappiness and misunderstanding in the world, past, present, and to come; for all the misery men must undergo whatever their opinion and position, and however much they dodge or bluff—it would amount to the same.... Devils are of the north, and poems can be written about them, but no one could romanticize the Marabar because it robbed infinity and eternity of their vastness, the only quality that accommodates them to mankind.... But suddenly at the edge of her mind, religion reappeared, poor little talkative Christianity, and she knew that all its divine words from "Let there be Light" to "it is finished" only amounted to "boum."

"Something snub-nosed, incapable of generosity" had spoken to her— "the undying worm itself." Converse with God, her children, Aziz, is repugnant to her. She wants attention for her sorrow and rejects it when given. Knowing Aziz to be innocent, she says nothing in his behalf except a few sour words that upset Adela's certainty, and though she knows that her testimony will be useful to Aziz, she allows Ronny to send her away. She has had the beginning of the Hindu vision of things and it has crushed her. What the Hindu vision is, is expressed by Professor Godbole to Fielding:

> Good and evil are different, as their names imply. But, in my own humble opinion, they are both of them aspects of my Lord. He is present in the one, absent in the other, and the difference between presence and absence is great, as great as my feeble mind can grasp. Yet absence implies presence, absence is not non-existence, and we are therefore entitled to repeat: "Come, come, come, come."

Although Mrs. Moore abandons everything, even moral duty, she dominates the subsequent action. As "Esmiss Esmoor" she becomes, to the crowd around the courthouse, a Hindu goddess who was to save Aziz. And, we are vaguely given to understand, it is her influence that brings Adela to her senses and the truth. She recurs again, together with the wasp, in the mind of Professor Godbole in that wonderful scene of religious muddlement with which the book draws to its conclusion. She remains everlastingly in the mind of Aziz who hates—or tries to hate—all the other English. She continues into the future in her daughter Stella, who marries Fielding and returns to India, and in her son Ralph. Both Stella and Ralph "like Hinduism, though they take no interest in its forms" and are shy of Fielding because he thinks they are mistaken. Despite the sullen disillusionment in which Mrs. Moore died, she had been right when she had said to Ronny that there are many kinds of failure, some of which succeed. No thought, no deed in this book of echoes, is ever lost.

It is not easy to know what to make of the dominant Hinduism of the third section of the novel. The last part of the story is frankly a coda to the plot, a series of resolutions and separations which comment on what has gone before—in it Fielding and Aziz meet and part, this time forever; Aziz forgives Adela Quested and finds a friend in Ralph Moore; Fielding, we learn, is not really at one with his young wife; Hindu and Moslem, Brahman and non-Brahman are shown to be as far apart as Indian and English, yet English and Moslem meet in the flooded river, in a flow of Hindu religious fervor; and everything is encompassed in the spirit of Mrs. Moore, mixed up with a vision of the ultimate nullity, with the birth of Krishna and with joy in the fertile rains.

Certainly it is not to be supposed that Forster finds in Hinduism an answer to the problem of India; and its dangers have been amply demonstrated in the case of Mrs. Moore herself. But here at least is the vision in which the arbitrary human barriers sink before the extinction of all things. About seventy-five years before *A Passage To India*, Matthew Arnold's brother, William Delafield Arnold, went out to India as Director of Public Education of the Punjab. From his experiences he wrote a novel, *Oakfield: Or, Fellowship In The East*; it was a bitter work which denounced the English for making India a "rupee mine" and it declared that the "grand work" of civilizing India was all humbug. William Arnold thought that perhaps socialism, but more likely the Church of England, could bring about some change. This good and pious man felt it "grievous to live among men"—the Indians—"and feel the idea of fraternity thwarted by facts;" he believed that "we must not resign ourselves, without a struggle, to calling the Indians brutes." To such a pass has Christianity come, we can suppose Forster to be saying. We must suffer a vision even as dreadful as Mrs. Moore's if by it the separations can be wiped out. But meanwhile the separations exist and Aziz in an hysteria of affirmation declares to Fielding on their last ride that the British must go, even at the cost of internal strife, even if it means a Japanese conquest. Only with the British gone can he and Fielding be friends. Fielding offers friendship now: "'It's what I want. It's what you want.'" But the horses, following the path the earth lays for them, swerve apart; earth and sky seem to say that the time for friendship has not come, and leave its possibility to events.

The disintegrating question, What, then, must be done? which many readers have raised is of course never answered—or not answered in the language in which the question has been asked. The book simply involves the question in ultimates. This, obviously, is no answer; still, it defines the scope of a possible answer, and thus restates the question. For the answer can never again temporize, because the question, after it has been involved in the moods and visions of the story, turns out to be the most enormous question that has ever been asked, requiring an answer of enormous magnanimity. Great as the problem of India is, Forster's book is not about India alone; it is about all of human life.

NOTES

1. The historical part of the book is a model of popularization without condescension. Especially notable are the lucid pages on the Alexandrian mystics, the exposition of Plotinus has the quality of creative insight into mystical thought that makes *A Passage To India* so remarkable. It is worth noting that Dickinson in his youth was an enthusiastic student of Plotinus.

2. He deals with censorship in "Mrs. Grundy at the Parkers"' (*Abinger Harvest*) and in his introduction to Alec Craig's *The Banned Books Of England* (1937).

3. I am not using plot and story in exactly the same sense that Forster uses them in *Aspects Of The Novel*.

4. H. N. Brailsford in his *Rebel India* (1931) deals at some length with the brutality with which demonstrations were put down in 1930. "Here and there," he says, "mildness and good-temper disarmed the local agitation. I heard of one magistrate, very popular with the people, who successfully treated the defiance of the Salt Monopoly as a joke. The local Congress leaders made salt openly in front of his bungalow. He came out: bought some of the contraband salt: laughed at its bad quality: chaffed the bystanders, and went quietly back to his house. The crowd melted away, and no second attempt was made to defy this genial bureaucrat. On the other hand, any exceptional severity, especially if physical brutality accompanied it, usually raised the temper of the local movement and roused it to fresh daring and further sacrifices." p. 7, footnote.

5. The Indian masses appear only as crowds in the novel; they have no individualized representative except the silent, unthinking figure of the man who pulls the *punkah* in the courtroom scene. He is one of the "untouchables" though he has the figure of a god, and in Adela's mind, just before the crisis of the trial, he raises doubts of the "suburban Jehovah" who sanctifies her opinions, and he makes her think of Mrs. Moore.

6. The novel is divided: I. Mosque II. Caves III. Temple. In his notes to the Everyman edition Forster points out that the three parts correspond to the three Indian seasons.

MALCOLM BRADBURY

Two Passages to India:
Forster as Victorian and Modern

There are major writers whose work seems to us important as a contribution to the distinctive powers and dimensions of art; there are others whose work represents almost a personal appeal to value, and who therefore live—for certain of their readers, at least—with a singular force. There have not been many English novelists of our own time who have established with us the second function, but E. M. Forster is certainly one of them. He has served as an embodiment of the virtues he writes about; he has shown us their function and their destiny; he has left, for other writers and other men, a workable inheritance. Partly this is because he has always regarded art as a matter of intelligence as well as passion, honesty as well as imagination. In making such alliances he has given us a contemporary version of a once-familiar belief—that art can be a species of active virtue as well as a form of magic—and has thus sharply appealed to our sense of what man can be. Literary humanist qualities of this sort are not always easy to express today within the impersonal context of modern literary criticism—which tends, more and more, to ascribe virtue to structural performance within the text and to neglect what lies beyond. In fact, they are crucial virtues, and we fortunately have enough personal testimony—particularly from writers like Christopher Isherwood and Angus Wilson—to see the kind of inheritance he has left. At the same time, what Tony Tanner has called the "trace of

From *Aspects of E. M. Forster*, © 1969 by Harcourt.

totemism"[1] with which Forster has been and is still regarded—and I must assert here my own sense of indebtedness, intellectual, moral, and literary—has its dangers, and to his role and his influence may be ascribed certain slightly odd and uneasy features of Forster's present reputation. That he is a major writer I have no doubt, yet criticism has repeatedly expressed an unsureness about him, has wondered, time and time again, whether he really stands with the other great writers of the century we feel sure of—with Joyce or Conrad or Lawrence.

Why is this? One reason is surely that Forster stands much exposed to our modern predilection for historicist thinking—our inclination to substitute, in Karl Popper's phrase, "historical prophecy for conscience". Forster once told us that he belongs to "the fag-end of Victorian liberalism" (TC, 67), and the phrase is often taken with complete literalness and applied against him. As a result his intellectual and his literary destiny has been too readily linked with that strange death of liberal England which historians have dated around 1914, when the equation of economic individualism with social progress lost political force. Since it is easy to explain the exhaustion of political liberalism as a historical necessity, as the inevitable failure of a synthesis proven unworkable by the new social conditions of the second-stage Industrial Revolution, then it is also possible to see Forster's ideas and faith as historically superannuated, too. This view, indeed, has taken root—even though Forster recognises the ironies of the situation and works with them, even though he raises all the crucial questions about elevating social determinism above value; and we often overlook the fact that the liberalism he speaks for so obliquely has had a longer history as a moral conviction than as a political force, that it has as much to do with our idea of man and culture as with our political solutions, that it speaks for a recurrent need for the criticism of institutions and collectivities from the standpoint of the claims of human wholeness. But coupled with this there has been another distrust: distrust of the entire idea of art and culture as Forster suggests or expresses it.

In this century critics have increasingly accepted modernist norms for the judgement of literature, even though, of course, many of our writers have not been modernists in the strict sense. Forster is a paradox here; he is, and he is not. There is in his work the appeal to art as transcendence, art as the one orderly product, a view that makes for modernism; and there is the view of art as a responsible power, a force for belief, a means of judgement, an impulse to spiritual control as well as spiritual curiosity. The point perhaps is that Forster is not, in the conventional sense, a modernist, but rather a central figure of the transition into modernism; and that is surely his interest, the force of his claim. He is, indeed, to a remarkable degree, the representative of two kinds of mind, two versions of literary possibility, and of the tensions of consciousness that exist between them. He stands at the beginning of the age of the new, speaking through it and against it. In this way his five novels—and particularly his last two—can be taken as reflecting the advantages and disadvantages of the humanist literary mind in an environment half hostile to it; they clearly and often painfully carry the strain of a direct encounter with new experience. Forster has been, by training and temperament, sufficiently the historian to see the irony: that culture itself is in history, that a humanist view of the arts as a way of sanely perceiving and evaluating is itself conditioned, for it has its own social environment and limits. So Forster is at once the spokesman for the transcendent symbol, the luminous wholeness of the work of art, out of time and in infinity, and for its obverse—the view that a proper part of art's responsibility is to know and live in the contingent world of history.

If Forster is indeed a Victorian liberal, as some of his critics charge, he is also deeply marked by the encounters that the moralised romantic inheritance must make with those environments which challenge it in matters of belief, technique, and aesthetics. Of course, Forster's confession that he belongs to the fag-end of Victorian liberalism does express a real inheritance; but that end is also the beginning of new forms of belief and of new literary postures and procedures. My point is that he emerges not as a conventionally modernist writer, but rather as a writer who has experienced the full impact of what modernism means—a hope for transcendence, a sense of apocalypse, and *avant-garde* posture, a sense of detachment, a feeling that a new phase of history has emerged—while retaining (with tentative balance that turns often to the ironic mode) much that modernism would affront.

Forster's traditional literary inheritance, which reaches back through the Victorian period to roots in English romanticism, is something which he himself has sketched clearly and well in books like *Marianne Thornton*. He has shown us the formative influence of the world of the Victorian upper-middle-class intelligentsia in its liberal radical mode—that world of "philanthropists, bishops, clergy, members of parliament, Miss Hannah More"[2] which reached into evangelical Christianity and into agnostic enlightenment, that world which he draws upon and values, and against which he also reacts. To the cultural historian, its interest lies in its unconditioned spirit, its sense of disinterestedness, its capacity to act beyond both self and class interest and to transcend its economic roots without losing its social standing. Its view of the critical intelligence working in society is therefore accompanied by no strong sense of disjunction, and it takes many of its terms from the moralised line of English romantic thought. What Forster inherits from it is apparent—something of the flavour of that engaging marriage made by the most influential English romantics,

Wordsworth and Coleridge in particular, between the claims on the one hand of the imagination and the poet's transcendent vision, and on the other of right reason and moral duty; something of its power, therefore, to make a vision of Wholeness which embraces the social world in all its contingency. So the personal connection between inner and outer worlds—a connection forged through the powers of passion and imagination—has its social equivalent, in the notion of an obligation on society that it, too, be whole; that it grant, as Mill stresses, "the absolute and essential importance of human development in its richest diversity",[3] that it sees, in Arnold's terms, that perfection can be both an *inward* condition of mind and spirit and a *general* expansion of the human family. Forster draws on the full equation for his fiction, taking as his proper field the social realm of action as well as the life of individuals in their personal relations, and criticising his characters and their society now from the standpoint of right reason and culture, now from that of the heart, the passions, the power of visionary imagination that can testify, however inadequately, to the claims of the infinite. Thus there come under fire "the vast armies of the benighted, who follow neither the heart nor the brain" (RV, 214); and the connective impulses embrace not only man and man, and man and infinity, but the social order, too.

But if Forster is undoubtedly an inheritor of that world of value, he inherits with a due sense of difficulty. In *Howards End* he touches in with deep force those powers and forces in history which are process, and can't be gainsaid; the pastoral and vividly felt landscape of England is turned by the demanding processes of urbanisation and industrialism into a civilisation of luggage; while the very economics of the intelligentsia he belongs to become a matter for ironic exposure. In *A Passage to India* the final nullity of romanticism is exposed in the cave, where the worlds within us and without echo together the sound of *boum*; this is the extreme beyond Coleridgean dejection, for the visionary hope is lost in the face of an unspeaking and utterly alien nature, a nature only self-reflecting. The will to vision and the liberal thrust to right reason, the desire to connect both with infinity and all mankind, are placed against unyielding forces in nature and history—obstructing the movement of Forster's visionary themes and producing, particularly in these two last novels, a countervailing, ironic reaction. This countervailing sense, this sense of historical apocalypse coupled with spiritual abyss, is surely recognisably modernist. And what in the early novels appears as a species of social comedy—a comedy exercising the claims of moral realism against the liberal wish to draw clear lines between good and bad action—emerges in these latter novels as an essential irony of structure: indeed, as a direct challenge to the values Forster is so often supposed to represent. If, to cite Lionel Trilling (who writes so well of this ironic aspect of Forster), there is an ironic counterpart in the early work whereby while "the plot speaks of clear certainties, the manner resolutely insists that nothing can be quite so simple",[4] these complexities increase in the later work into the mental and aesthetic possession of two colliding views of the world.

Forster's way of assimilating two modes of thought—one an inheritance, the other an urgent group of ideas about contemporary necessity—is matched by the curious aesthetic implications of his techniques in fiction. He is often considered as a writer technically a coeval of his Victorian predecessors (Walter Allen calls him "a throwback"),[5] and in asserting his own debts has particularly named three writers: Jane Austen, Samuel Butler, and Marcel Proust. The indebtedness to the first two of his species of moralised social irony hardly needs elaborating; it is the third name which suggests that the "traditionalist" account of his technique is misleading. Of course, in his novels the omniscient author mediates, with the voice of the guide-book or essay or sermon, the proffered material—though as much to sustain fiction's place in the field of intelligence and thought as to establish the authenticity of fact. But at the same time he offers his work as the symbolist or autotelic artefact; a work of art is "the only material object in the universe which may possess internal harmony" (TC, 101). What is so fascinating about his most extended aesthetic statement, *Aspects of the Novel*, is its attempt to place the modes of symbolism and post-impressionism in the context of what might be considered the more "traditional" story-telling function; the novel *tells* (rather than *is*) a story, and it lives in the conditioned world of stuff, of event, of history. (So, finally, Forster puts Tolstoy above Proust.) Yet it has transcendent purposes; art, "the one orderly product which our muddling race has produced" (*ibid.*), has Platonic powers to touch infinity, reach to the unity behind all things, prophesy (in the Shelleyan sense).

In this respect Forster is as post-impressionist or post-Paterian as anyone else in Bloomsbury, and the ultimate field of action for the arts is that of the "unseen". Procedurally this symbolist power seems to lie in the analogue with music, and is gained from aspects of the novel outside and beyond story, in thematic recurrences, leitmotifs, pattern and rhythm, prophetic song. The problem of whether art can redeem life by transcending it is crucial to modernism; the encounter between the formally transcendent—the epiphany, the unitary symbol—and the world of history recurs throughout its works. And Forster's view is, like that of most modernism, dualistic: art may reach beyond the world of men and things—the world of "story"—but it can never leave that world behind, and must seek meanings and connections in it. What distinguishes Forster is the faint hope which he entertains on behalf of history: the hope that by understanding and right relationship men may win for it a limited redemption.

I have suggested that Forster is deeply involved in some of the largest intellectual, cultural, and aesthetic collisions that occur in the transition into this century; and it is his sharp sense of the contingent, of the powers that rule the world of men, that makes him so. The result is a complex version of modern literary disquiet. An intermediary between those two literary traditions of "moderns" and "contemporaries" that Stephen Spender[6] sees as the two main lines of modern English writing, he bears these burdens so as to expose the crucial choices that a writer of this transitional period might make. Divided as he is between infinite and contingent, he is none the less more available to the offered pressures than most of the more confirmed modernists. This is because his sense of the "crisis" of infinity is so much bound up with his sense of the divisive and changing forces of the world of time. For he is increasingly concerned with the problems of the infinite view within the cultural movements of the modernising world; and in his growing sense of the need to synthesise an ever more eclectic experience he testifies to the new multiverse, the chaotic welter of values, which has confounded the modern mind. Hence his visions, though they may suggest an order or unity in the universe, are defined, increasingly from novel to novel, in terms of an anarchy that they must always comprehend. Thus they are never fully redemptive, since the world of time persistently enlarges our feelings of intellectual, moral, social, and spiritual relativism, creating a world in which no one philosophy or cosmology accounts for the world order—where it is possible to believe with Mrs. Moore that "Everything exists; nothing has value" (PI, 156). This, with its suggestion that in seeing life whole one may see nothing except multiplicity, is the obverse of the unitary vision; and in *A Passage to India*, his fullest and most eclectic book, Forster gives us in full that possibility—and its sources in social relations, personal relations, and the realm of spirit.

Forster may have an ideal of unity, a will to a whole solution, but we mistake him if we see only that in him. For he is characteristically not a novelist of solutions, but rather of reservations, of the contingencies and powers which inhibit spirit. The power of sympathy, understanding, and community with all things is for him an overriding power; but its claim to wholeness is always conditioned, and mystery, to which we must yield, co-exists with muddle, which we must try to redeem, or even accept in its nullity. Indeed, it is because Forster is so attentive to the forces in our culture and world-order which induce the vision of anarchy—and threaten through its very real powers not only the will to but the very insights of the whole vision—that he seems so central a writer; a novelist whom we in our turn have not always seen whole.

Forster is a difficult and ambiguous writer, a writer who has often made his critics uneasy and caused them to feel how strangely elusive his work is. His observation of his materials, and his way of making his structures, usually involves two tones that come into perplexing relationship. There is the instinct towards "poetry", which goes with the view of art as a symbolist unity; and there is the comedy and the irony, the belittling aspect of his tone, which brings in the problems and difficulties of the contingent world. Because of this it is often possible simultaneously to interpret his work positively and negatively, depending on the kind of critical attentiveness one gives.

Thus for some critics, like Wilfred Stone, *A Passage to India* is Forster's most affirmative and optimistic novel, the one which most suggests, as Stone puts it, that "unity and harmony are the ultimate promises of life."[7] "The theme which this book hammers home," says Stone, "is that, for all our differences, we are in fact *one*.... Physically of one environment, we are also psychically one, and it is reason's denial of our commonality, the repression of that *participation mystique*, which has caused man to rule his Indias and himself with such futility and blindness."[8] But other critics like James McConkey and Alan Wilde have come to precisely the opposite view, seeing the work as a novel of the final dissociation between the chaotic life of man and an intractable eternal reality. In part the decision depends upon whether one insists, like Trilling, on a relatively realistic reading of the book, or whether, as E. K. Brown does, one reads it as a "symbolist" novel. If the world of men and manners, of politics and human behaviour, which it depicts suggests divisiveness, the world of the work itself as single "orderly product" suggests profound correspondences within it, a power to resolve its meanings which lies beyond any given character. Of this aspect of the book, Frank Kermode has remarked that it depends upon faking—faking a universe of promised wholeness, of rhetorical and structural unity, of a testing of the world of men from the standpoint of total coherence: "All that civilisation excepts or disconnects has to be got in for meaning to subsist."[9] What this means is that the world of men and the world of order must exist in paradoxical relationship, and this is what Lionel Trilling seems to imply, too, when he remarks that the novel has an unusual imbalance between plot and story: "The characters are of sufficient size for the plot; they are not large enough for the story—and that indeed is the point of the story."[10] But it is typically in such contrasts of time and transcendence that Forster deals, and to clarify the relationship between them one needs to look very closely at the overall working of the novel.

To a considerable extent, the book deals in themes and matters we have learned to associate with Forster from his previous novels. Here again are those rival claims upon men and nature which dichotomise the universe—the claims of the seen and the unseen, the public and the private, the powers of human activities and institutions and of the ultimate mysteries for which the right institutions and activities have yet to be found. And here again Forster's own sympathies are relatively apparent. The book is focused upon the testing-field of human relationships, with their various possibilities and disasters; on the "good will plus culture and intelligence" (p. 65) which are the necessary conditions of honest intercourse; on the clashes of interest and custom which divide men but which the liberal mind must hope, as Fielding hopes, to transcend. Its modes of presentation are familiarly complex—moving between a "poetic" evocation of the world of mystery and a "comic" evocation of the world of muddle, which is in a sense its obverse and refers to the normal state of men.

But what is unmistakable, I think, is that in this book Forster reveals new powers and resources—of a kind not previously achieved in his fiction—and that this extension of resource is linked with an extension of his sensibility, and above all with a new sense of complexity. For instance, *A Passage to India* is not simply an international novel—in the Jamesian sense of attempting to resolve contrasting value-systems by means of a cosmopolitan scale of value—but a global novel. The contrast of England and India is not the end of the issue, since India is schismatic within itself; India's challenge is the challenge of the multiverse, a new version of the challenge that Henry Adams faced on looking at the dynamo. What the city is as metaphor in *Howards End*, India is in *Passage*; it is a metaphor of contingency. Forster is not simply interested in raising the social-comic irony of confronting one social world with the standards of another; he stretches through the social and political implications to religious and mystical ones, and finally to the most basic question of all—how, in the face of such contingency, one structures meaning.

The geographical scale of the novel is, in short, supported by a vast scale of standpoint. Forster attempts a structure inclusive of the range of India, and the judgements of the book are reinforced by the festivals and rituals of three religions, by the heterodoxy—racial, political, cultural, religious, and mystical—of this multiple nation, and by the physical landscape of a country which both invites meaning ("Come, come") and denies any. "Nothing embraces the whole of India, nothing, nothing," says Aziz (PI, 151); the landscape and the spirit of the earth divide men ("Trouble after trouble encountered him [Aziz], because he had challenged the spirit of the Indian earth, which tries to keep men in compartments" (p. 133); and even the sects are divided within themselves just as the earth is:

> The fissures in the Indian soil are infinite: Hinduism, so solid
> from a distance, is riven into sects and clans, which radiate and

join, and change their names according to the aspect from which they are approached. (p. 304.)

Forster's social comedy works to provoke, among a variety of different and sympathetically viewed groups, those ironic international and intra-national encounters that come when one value-system meets another and confusion and muddle ensue. But his other aim is to call up, by a poetic irradiation, the ironies lying within the forces of mystery and muddle in the constituted universe of nature itself. For here, too, are deceptions, above all in the absence of Beauty, which is traditionally a form for infinity, so that the very discourse of Romanticism becomes negative under the hot sun—who is "not the unattainable friend, either of men or birds or other suns, [who] was not the eternal promise, the never-withdrawn suggestion that haunts our consciousness; he was merely a creature, like the rest, and so debarred from glory" (p. 120). There is much in India that invites a cosmic meaning, but it places both man and infinity:

> Trees of a poor quality bordered the road, indeed the whole scene was inferior, and suggested that the countryside was too vast to admit of excellence. In vain did each item in it call out, "Come, come." There was not enough god to go round. The two young people conversed feebly and felt unimportant. (p. 92.)

All this stretches the Whitmanesque enterprise called up by the title to a vast level of inclusiveness. It also involves Forster in a placing of the social and human world of his novel in a way he has never approached before. One way of putting the situation is to say that the human plot of the novel is set into singular relation to the verbal plot, with its radiating expansiveness of language. The human plot of the novel is essentially a story hinging on Adela Quested, who comes to India to marry, has doubts about her marriage when she sees what India has made of her fiancé, and tries herself to create a more reasonable relationship between British and Indians. She takes part in an expedition, arranged by an Indian, to the Marabar caves, in one of which she believes she is attacked by him. She accuses him of attempted rape, and, although at the trial she retracts her accusation, the incident has sown dissent and discord, and has exposed the political and institutional tensions of the country.

The plot moves us from the world of personal relationships to the social world (which in this case involves political relationships), and is set largely in and around the city of Chandrapore, at a time not stated but evidently intended to be in the 1920s.[11] The dense social world that Forster delineates so skilfully consists primarily of racial or religious groups with their own customs and patterns. The English, whom we see largely through the eyes of Adela Quested and Mrs. Moore, visiting India together, are identified with their institutional functions. Mostly professional middle-class people, they have gone through a process of adaptation to their duties, which are, as Ronnie says, "to do justice and keep the peace" (p. 53). They have learned the importance of solidarity, conventions, rank, and standoffishness; and their judgements and their social order are those of a particular class in a particular situation. Their ethics are dutiful and serious; they have a deep sense of rational justice; they are distrustful of mysticism and lethargy; their deep Englishness has been reinforced by their situation. They operate at the level of political and social duty, and their relationships—the ties that bind the characters together and enable Forster to thread the way from one to another—are those of the political and social roles they play.

The other group, which we see first largely through the eyes of Aziz, consists of Indians, though these are themselves divided by religions and castes. Here again what we see are primarily the professional classes, linked to the British by their duties and to their own people by their familial and friendly relationships. The two main groupings that emerge here are, of course, the Hindus and the Moslems, and Forster differentiates carefully between them, and their respective versions of India. Where they differ radically from the English is in their long and adaptive response to the confusions of their country, a response which obscures the firm lines of value that the British in their isolation can protect, and permits lethargy, emotionalism, and mysticism. Forster explores Indian custom and faith in great detail, noting its own patterns of classification, its own way of making and not making social and moral distinctions, above all recognising that Indians have adapted to a different physical environment by being comprehensive or passive rather than orderly or rationalistic.

These worlds—Anglo-Indian (to use the phrase of the day), Hindu, Moslem—are given us in full as they connect and draw apart, and Forster enters imaginatively into each of them. And to a large extent what interests him is not the relations between people, the normal matter for the novelist, but their separation. In the novel's social scenes we are always conscious of those who are absent, and much of the discussion in the early part of the novel is devoted to those not present—the whites are talked of by the Indians, the Indians by the whites. And this suggests the vast social inclusiveness of the novel, which spreads beyond the communities established for the sake of the action into a cast of thousands: nameless marginal characters who appear for a moment and are gone, like the punkah wallah or the voice out of the darkness at the club, and the inhabitants of Chandrapore who seem made "of mud moving" (p. 9).

Out of this complex social world derives a complex moral world, in which the values of no one group are given total virtue. The English may have thrown the net of rationalism and "civilisation" over the country, but India's resistance to this—"The triumphant machine of civilisation may suddenly hitch and be immobilised into a car of stone" (p. 220)—puts them in ironic relation to Indian reality; they scratch only the surface of its life, and theirs is a feeble invasion. On the other hand, the passive comprehensiveness of India is seen as itself a kind of social decay, debased as well as spiritual, leading to a potential neglect of man. The traditional repositories of Forsterian virtue—goodwill plus culture and intelligence—function only incompletely in this universe; and Forster's own liberal passion for social connection motivates a large section of the action, but does not contain its chief interest. In the deceptively guide-bookish opening chapter Forster establishes an appeal beyond the social world, to the overarching sky; it looks, at first, like a figure for the potential unity of man, the redemption that might come through breaking out of the social institutions and classifications that segregate them into their closed groupings, but the gesture has an ambiguous quality. The civil station "shares nothing with the city except the overarching sky" (p. 10), but the sky itself is an infinite mystery, and reaching away into its "farther distance, ... beyond colour, last freed itself from blue" (p. 11). Certainly, beyond the world of social organisation is that world of "the secret understanding of the heart" (p. 22) to which Aziz appeals; this is the world that is damaged when Ronnie and Mrs. Moore discuss Aziz and she finds: "Yes, it was all true, but how false as a summary of the man; the essential life of him had been slain." (p. 37.)

Forster is, as usual, superb at creating that "essential life" and showing what threatens it, and much of the book deals with its virtues and its triumphs. So at one level the social world is redeemed by those who resist its classifications—by Adela and Mrs. Moore, Fielding, Aziz, Godbole. Forster does not belittle their victories directly except in so far as he sees their comedy. But he does place beyond them a world of infinitude which is not, here, to be won through the personal. For this is not the entire realm of moral victory in the novel; indeed, these acts of resistance, which provide the book's lineal structure, are usually marked by failure. Adela's is a conventional disaster; she makes the moral mistake of exposing the personal to the social. Fielding's is more complicated; he is an agent of liberal contact through goodwill plus culture and intelligence, but he, like Mrs. Moore, meets an echo:

> "In the old eighteenth century, when cruelty and injustice raged,
> an invisible power repaired their ravages. Everything echoes now;
> there's no stopping the echo. The original sound may be

harmless, but the echo is always evil." This reflection about an echo lay at the verge of Fielding's mind. He could never develop it. It belonged to the universe that he had missed or rejected. And the mosque missed it too. Like himself, those shallow arcades provided but a limited asylum. (pp. 286–7.)

As for Mrs. Moore, who does touch it, she encounters another force still—the moral nihilism that comes when the boundary walls are down. Her disaster dominates the novel, for it places even moral and mystical virtue within the sphere of contingency; it, too, is subject to spiritual anarchy. Beyond the world of the plot, the lineal world of consequences and relationships, there lies a second universe of fictional structure, which links spiritual events, and then a third, which in turn places these in history and appeals to the infinite recession of the universe beyond any human structure that seeks to comprehend it.

This we may see by noting that in this novel, as compared with the earlier ones, the world of men is clearly granted reduced powers. The universe of time and contingency is made smaller, by the nature that surrounds man, by the scale of the continent on which man's presence is a feeble invasion, by the sky which overarches him and his works. It is a world of dwarfs and of dwarfed relationships, in which the familiar forces of romantic redemption in Forster's work—personal relationships as mirrors to infinity, a willingness to confront the unseen—undertake their movements toward connection without the full support of the universe. The theme recurs, but Mrs. Moore expresses it most strongly in Chapter XIV, when she reflects on her situation and grows towards her state of spiritual nullity in the cave:

> She felt increasingly (vision or nightmare?) that, though people are important, the relations between them are not, and that in particular too much fuss has been made over marriage; centuries of carnal embracement, yet man is no nearer to understanding man. And today she felt this with such force that it seemed itself a relationship, itself a person who was trying to take hold of her hand. (p. 141.)

The negative withdrawal is, of course, an aspect of that "twilight of the double vision in which so many elderly people are involved" (p. 216), and it is not the only meaning in the book. But it is the dominant one. It is by seeking its obverse that Adela compounds her basic moral error:

It was Adela's faith that the whole stream of events is important and interesting, and if she grew bored she blamed herself severely and compelled her lips to utter enthusiasms. This was the only insincerity in a character otherwise sincere, and it was indeed the intellectual protest of her youth. She was particularly vexed now because she was both in India and engaged to be married, which double event should have made every instant sublime. (p. 139.)

Human relationships are dwarfed not only by the scale of the historical and social world, which is potentially redeemable, but by the natural world, which is not.

Of course, intimations of transcendence are present throughout the novel. Structurally they run through the seasonal cycle, from divisive hot sun to the benedictive healing water at the end, and from Mosque to Caves to Temple. By taking that as his order, Forster is able poetically to sustain the hope of a spiritual possibility, a prefiguring of the world beyond in the world below. The climax of this theme is Godbole's attempt at "completeness, not reconstruction" (p. 298). But what happens here is that divine revelation is shifted to the level of the comic sublime; Forster's rhetoric now puts what has been spiritually perplexing—the webs, nets, and prisons that divide spirit as well as society—back into the comic universe of muddle. The Mau festival is the celebration of the formlessness of the Indian multiverse, seen for a moment inclusively. The poetic realm of the novel, in which above all Mrs. Moore and Godbole have participated, and which has dominated the book's primary art, is reconciled with the muddle of the world of men, in an emotional cataract that momentarily repairs the divisions of the spiritual world (through Godbole's revelation) and the social world (through the festival itself). It satisfies much of the passion for inclusiveness that has been one thread in the novel, the desire that heaven should include all because India *is* all. Earlier the two Christian missionaries have disagreed: Mr. Sorley, the more advanced,

> admitted that the mercy of God, being infinite, may well embrace all mammals. And the wasps? He became uneasy during the descent to wasps, and was apt to change the conversation. And oranges, cactuses, crystals and mud? and the bacteria inside Mr. Sorley? No, no, this is going too far. We must exclude someone from our gathering, or we shall be left with nothing. (p. 41.)

Godbole's universe of spirit is much more inclusive:

> Godbole consulted the music-book, said a word to the drummer,
> who broke rhythm, made a thick little blur of sound, and
> produced a new rhythm. This was more exciting, the inner
> images it evoked more definite, and the singers' expressions
> became fatuous and languid. They loved all men, the whole
> universe, and scraps of their past, tiny splinters of detail, emerged
> for a moment to melt into the universal warmth. Thus Godbole,
> though she was not important to him, remembered an old woman
> he had met in Chandrapore days. Chance brought her into his
> mind while it was in this heated state, he did not select her, she
> happened to occur among the throng of soliciting images, a tiny
> splinter, and he impelled her by his spiritual force to that place
> where completeness can be found. Completeness, not
> reconstruction. His senses grew thinner, he remembered a wasp
> seen he forgot where, perhaps on a stone. He loved the wasp
> equally, he impelled it likewise, he was imitating God. And the
> stone where the wasp clung—could he … no, he could not, he had
> been wrong to attempt the stone, logic and conscious effort had
> seduced, he came back to the strip of red carpet and discovered
> that he was dancing upon it. (p. 298.)

His doctrine—"completeness, not reconstruction"—is, of course, a species of
transcendence, a momentary vision of the whole, the invocation of a universe
invested with spirit. It links up with the symbolist plot of the novel, its power
as a radiant image, rather than with plot in the linear sense, with its world of
"and then … and then …" Threading its way through the novel, to an old
woman and a wasp, it takes these "soliciting images" and puts them in new
association—not with all things, but with each other and with what else
comes almost unbidden into the world of spirit. But the stone is left, and
equally spirit may or may not invest the universe in any of its day-to-day
affairs: "Perhaps all these things! Perhaps none!" (p. 302.) Things, in freeing
themselves from their traditional associations, social and historical, form a
new order, beyond dialogue, beyond human plot, in the realm where poetic
figures function on their own order of consciousness. Yet here, too, irony is
at work: mystery is sometimes muddle, completeness is sometimes the
universe where "everything exists, nothing has value" (p. 156). If history
ultimately obstructs, and does not give us a final, rounded structure in terms
of human events, if the horses, the earth, the clutter of human institutions

say, "No, not yet," then like obstructions dwell in the realm of spirit and symbol, too: the sky says, "No, not there". (p. 336.)

The linear, social plot, then, has stretched a long way in search of a structure of its own that will provide coherence in the world, but if it finds one it is in the form of an oblique, doubtful and ironic promise; personal relations only go so far to solve the muddle of history. As for the symbolist plot, it transcends but it does not redeem; it is there but "neglects to come" (p. 84). The power of the novel lies, of course, in the Whitmanesque ambition to include multitudes, to find eternity in some order in the given world. But is this ambition realised? Intimations of eternity may have their symbols in the world of men (in love and relationship) and in the world of nature (in the force of mystery that resides in things); the social and the natural worlds have in them touches that promise wholeness. But they do not of themselves have unity; they are themselves afflicted by the double vision which is all that man can bring to them, grounded as he is in history and hope at once. The world stretches infinitely about us, and there is infinity beyond us. But questions bring us only to the unyielding hostility of the soil and the unyielding ambiguity of the sky.

The universe, then, is less intimation than cipher; a mask rather than a revelation in the romantic sense. Does love meet with love? Do we receive but what we give? The answer is surely a paradox, the paradox that there are Platonic universals beyond, but that the glass is too dark to see them. Is there a light beyond the glass, or is it a mirror only to the self? The Platonic cave is even darker than Plato made it, for it introduces the echo, and so leaves us back in the world of men, which does not carry total meaning, is just a story of events. The Platonic romantic gesture of the match in the cave is the dominating ambiguity of the book. Does it see *itself* in the polished wall of stone, or is the glimmer of radiance a promise?

> There is little to see, and no eye to see it, until the visitor arrives for his five minutes, and strikes a match. Immediately another flame rises in the depths of the rock and moves towards the surface like an imprisoned spirit: the walls of the circular chamber have been most marvellously polished. The two flames approach and strive to unite, but cannot, because one of them breathes air, the other stone. A mirror inlaid with lovely colours divides the lovers, delicate stars of pink and grey interpose, exquisite nebulae, shadings fainter than the tail of a comet or the midday moon, all the evanescent life of the granite, only here visible. Fists and fingers thrust above the advancing soil—here at last is

their skin, finer than any covering acquired by the animals, smoother than windless water, more voluptuous than love. The radiance increases, the flames touch one another, kiss, expire. The cave is dark again, like all the caves. (pp. 130–1.)

Isn't it less the transcendence of a Whitman, uniting all things through the self and the ongoing lines of history, than the ambiguous and narcissistic transcendence of Melville, where the universe is a diabolical cipher, where the desire to penetrate meaning ends only in our being swallowed up in the meaning we have conferred? Isn't the novel not Forster's "Passage to India", but rather, in the end, Forster's *Moby Dick*?

NOTES

1. Review of *The Cave and the Mountain* by Wilfred Stone, *London Magazine*, new series, VI, 5 (Aug. 1966), 102.

2. Macaulay, *op. cit.* (p. 45), p. 9.

3. This phrase from Wilhelm von Humboldt, *Sphere and Duties of Government*, was used by J. S. Mill as his epigraph for *On Liberty* (1859).

4. *E. M. Forster* (Hogarth Press, London, 1944), p. 13.

5. *The English Novel* (Phoenix, London, 1954), p. 319.

6. *The Struggle of the Modern* (Hamish Hamilton, London, 1963).

7. Stone, *op. cit.* (p. 19), p. 344.

8. *ibid.*, p. 339.

9. "The One Orderly Product (E. M. Forster)", *Puzzles and Epiphanies* (Routledge, London, 1962), p. 84.

10. Trilling, *op. cit.*, p. 126.

11. Rose Macaulay finds it to be earlier: "the date of the novel is apparently approximately that of the earlier visit.... The European war is still ahead." (*Op. cit.*, pp. 176, 186.) Forster disagrees: the war Aziz foresees is the Second World War (pi, Everyman's Library ed., Dent, London, repr. 1957, p. ix). But Rose Macaulay's point has an imaginative truth: the book comes out of two phases of Imperial India.

MICHAEL ORANGE

Language and Silence in A Passage to India

Wovon man nicht sprechen kann, darüber muss man schweigen.
—Wittgenstein, *Tractatus*

I

Forster's delicacy of style in the novels that precede *A Passage to India* almost guarantees the rectitude of his attempt to understand the alien worlds of Islam, Hinduism and 'British India'. Elements of potential condescension or of patronising naïveté in the class attitudes of some of the characters of *Howards End* are carefully noted by the novelist, a useful starting-point for one whose last-written novel will share their position of attempted understanding.[1x] Over fifty years after the first publication of *A Passage to India* it is possible to measure the success of that book in the context of renewed attempts at discovering the relevance for the industrialised nations of cultures whose assumptions have been so different. Forster goes incomparably further than the instinctive refusal to articulate that has often accompanied the quest. Yet *A Passage to India* justifies this disengagement with language. More, it explains, while enacting, the strategy behind such refusals to communicate.

'The Ganges happens not to be holy here' (PI i, 2). The novel's third sentence thus quietly registers and assimilates a phenomenon unfamiliar

From *E. M. Forster: A Human Exploration*. G.K. Das and John Beer, eds. © 1979 New York University Press.

except in classical mythology to Western readers. The concept that a river may be 'holy' coincides, however, with the further understanding that in India, apparently, the same river is, in different locations, religiously speaking 'neutral'. Yet the phrase's undemonstratively parenthetical tone insinuates that this is not remarkable. The sense of wonder will be exercised more fully later. In the scale *A Passage to India* plays upon, such differentiation from Western values is scarcely noticed. None the less, it is crucial. As an index of the gap between Oriental and Western culture the phrase asserts, quite literally, a world of difference: wholly divergent concepts of the universe.

However, even with this abyss confronting Western consciousness so early in the novel, a converging movement can be detected. Classical mythology and Forster's unemphatic tone combine to imply that such an alien world-view may be assimilated at least conceptually. In the act of reading a bridge of some kind has been thrown across. By the third section of the novel, when this continual verbal oscillation between alien and familiar has become a conditioning medium of response, Forster can spin the coin almost carelessly to reveal the common metal on which two different cultures are stamped:

> a Brahman brought forth a model of the village of Gokul (the Bethlehem in that nebulous story) and placed it in front of the altar ... Here, upon a chair too small for him and with a head too large, sat King Kansa, who is Herod, directing the murder of some Innocents, and in a corner, similarly proportioned, stood the father and mother of the Lord, warned to depart in a dream.
>
> (xxxiii, 277–8)

But this is the limit to Forster's cultural parallelism. For *A Passage to India* continually asserts, despite some initiation into concepts of unity, that the images are firmly embedded in history; that the coin is diamond-faceted; and that language itself is powerless to convey the central experience to which the novel leads.

The success of *A Passage to India* depends acutely upon its pervasive sensitivity to its own verbal medium. In this novel the language of cognition, as the expression of thought and feeling in hierarchy subject to ordering by time, is avowedly insufficient as a means of incarnating mystical experience which exists outside time and is subversive of hierarchical order. In translating private, inward experience into public, shared understanding, the writer commits himself to materials crudely subject to history, hierarchy and consciousness. Where language encounters the silence beyond 'liberal humanism' or conceptualisation itself, it must settle for being sign-post rather than analogue. At the point of silence the alternatives for the artist are to retreat into the crudity of words again, or to fail to create at all. Forster's interest in musical expression underlines the point.[2] The conclusion to the biography of Dickinson provides an interesting commentary on the problem which has special relevance to *A Passage to India*:

> He was an indescribably rare being, he was rare without being enigmatic, he was rare in the only direction which seems to be infinite: the direction of the Chorus Mysticus. He did not merely increase our experience: he left us more alert for what has not yet been experienced and more hopeful about other men because he had lived. And a biography of him, if it succeeded, would resemble him; it would achieve the unattainable, express the inexpressible, turn the passing into the everlasting. Have I done that? *Das Unbeschreibliche hier ist's getan?* No. And perhaps it only could be done through music. But that is what has lured me on.[3]

Such contemporary examples as Eliot's choice of ending for *The Waste Land* and the experimental fictions of Virginia Woolf, Gertrude Stein and Aldous Huxley illuminate Forster's patient understanding of his craft. His achievement in *A Passage to India* is measured in part by his considerable success in transcending those limitations while preserving fidelity to traditional means of expression: the passage is to India, but the importance of the return ticket is not minimised. While the novel is a supremely graceful farewell to Forster's art, it is by no means a leave-taking imposed by insufficiency in his manipulation of the form, which proves flexible enough to focus both on the mystery of the tunnel of the stars and on the rigours of 'Cousin Kate' as performed in Central India.

This flexibility is paramount in the novel. Forster quietly but insistently induces belief in his verbal structures while disavowing their efficacy. The persistent muting of his ironic tones disinfects the prose of any trace of self-seeking virtuosity and directs attention outwards to the ostensible subject-matter—which necessarily resides, of course, within the words themselves. This controlling irony at the expense of the fiction itself functions as a continual reminder that any commitment to values expressed through words and based upon the hierarchies that they express must contend with functional limitations. Much experience is resolutely non-verbal. Non-verbal values become progressively and necessarily more remote in proportion to the persuasiveness of the language employed to embody them. The more felicitously they are expressed, the more readily they induce assent to propositions they set out to counter. This fundamental paradox is the source of the novel's classic consequent tension. While language eternally asserts its own reality, one of hierarchy, reason, time, and the logic of emotion, India itself represents a mysterious, sempiternal, mystical reality. Joseph Campbell makes this general point about Eastern culture:

> Throughout the Orient the idea prevails that the ultimate ground of being transcends thought, imaging, and definition. It cannot be qualified. Hence, to argue that God, Man, or Nature is good, just, merciful, or benign, is to fall short of the question. One could as appropriately—or inappropriately—have argued, evil, unjust, merciless, or malignant. All such anthropomorphic predications screen or mask the actual enigma, which is absolutely beyond rational consideration; and yet, according to this view, precisely that enigma is the ultimate ground of being of each and every one of us—and of all things.

> Prayers and chants, images, temples, gods, sages, definitions, and cosmologies are but ferries to a shore of experience beyond the categories of thought, to be abandoned on arrival.[4]

The resolution of the dichotomy between language and enigma represents the most complex aspect of Forster's success in the novel. He reconciles an adept manipulation of his verbal structures to the complete insufficiency of language itself, without finding it necessary to rely upon crudity of utterance to make the crucial disavowal of literary expression's congruence to mystical experience. This confident belief in the elastic power of his medium to work in opposed directions at the same time is the hallmark of *A Passage to India*. (It is pertinent to recall in this context that the British established their hegemony in India largely through the imposition of their language.) The power to reconcile disparity, to unify without sacrificing particularity, which the sensitive manipulation of language can command, establishes *A Passage to India's* status as a still-breathing masterpiece, rather than as a sad but exquisite register of failures.

II

The conflict dramatised and partly resolved in *Howards End*, between the worlds of 'telegrams and anger' represented by the Wilcox family and that of sensitive personal relationships incarnated by the Schlegels, is considerably more complicated in *A Passage to India*. The simple plea 'only connect' is applicable fundamentally to the abyss between the efficient English and the sensitive Indians they govern. None the less, Aziz's sensitivity is matched (despite the latter's evident limitations) by Fielding. British devotion to rigid class distinction is more than echoed in the triumph of caste represented by the Nawab Bahadur (cf. iv, 30–1). Aziz, despite his eventual decision to reside in a Hindu native state, is dismayed to find that after all he feels closer to Fielding than to Professor Godbole. Evidently the precarious bridge thrown across to an alien realm of experience by Margaret Schlegel is metaphorically insufficient to the complexity of *A Passage to India*. The very idea is ridiculed in the unsuccessful 'Bridge Party' convened to cater to Miss Quested's desire to know the 'real' India: 'a party to bridge the gulf between East and West; the expression was [the Collector's] own invention, and amused all who heard it' (iii, 222). At the end of the novel there is no 'marriage' between Aziz and Fielding. Forster's ironic tones, which effectively qualify the sense of kinship expressed in the banter at the Club, hint at the necessity of acknowledging such reservation. It appears that the sole means of attempting to communicate securely with others takes place from within the solipsistic shell of the individual personality. Mrs Moore is no befuddled sentimentalist, but because of, rather than despite her sharpness, is sufficiently sure of herself to reach out to Aziz.

On the level of plot, too, as well as of language, this kind of irony is maintained. The subaltern who baits Fielding for his championship of Aziz (xx, 177–8) unknowingly uses the example of his own brief meeting with Aziz to censure the latter's typical presumption (xx, 175). This restates in slightly different fashion Heaslop's mistaken initial pleasure and subsequent shock at his mother's first encounter at the mosque with the Indian. Yet the subaltern's earlier meeting with Aziz on the Maidan is the most graceful bridging of the racial abyss that the novel offers:

> They reined up again, the fire of good fellowship in their eyes. But it cooled with their bodies, for athletics can only raise a temporary glow. Nationality was returning, but before it could exert its poison they parted, saluting each other. 'If only they were all like that,' each thought.
>
> (vi, 51–2)

It is an episode whose comprehensive irony only becomes apparent at the novel's close. Aziz's and Fielding's last ride together painfully echoes this earlier one but expresses no more, despite all their efforts. Guarded friendliness, goodwill allied to circumspection remain after the vistas of instinctive communication and reciprocal affection close off. It seems scant reward.

The language which describes the polo-practice on the Maidan is crisply adequate to its purpose. The metaphors of temperature neatly register both exercise and passion, while the placing and choice of 'poison' conveys the disquietingly jarring note which characterises the relationship between the different races implicit in the scene, assimilated at the same time to the placid rhythm of the sentence which acknowledges the weary normalcy of such diseased relations. The passion for clarity and dispassionate observation harmonises with sensitivity to the subtleties of relationships: metaphor and plain-speaking cohere in this unemphatic idiom. Yet the ironies created by the tone of the narration tend disquietingly to subvert the assurance derived from any sense of confederacy with the latter's congenially sceptical outlook. For example, the Nawab Bahadur's social distance from his co–religionists (iv, 30-1) partly endorses the toughly self-protective realism of the general British aloofness from the natives. Switching to the missionaries Graysford and Sorley, this attitude is more directly, if regretfully, sponsored: 'perhaps it is futile for men to initiate their own unity, they do but widen the gulfs between them by the attempt' (iv, 32). In following the quotation through to the animal, insect and bacteriological kingdoms, the narrator's tone becomes gradually less respectful, more sardonic:

> Consider, with all reverence, the monkeys. May there not be a mansion for the monkeys also? Old Mr Graysford said No, but young Mr Sorley, who was advanced, said Yes; he saw no reason why monkeys should not have their collateral share of bliss, and he had sympathetic discussions about them with his Hindu friends.

The culmination of the enquiry is as brutally full of good sense as the rulers at the Club, and the narration mimics their voice:

> And oranges, cactuses, crystals and mud? and the bacteria inside, Mr Sorley? No, no, this is going too fat. We must exclude someone from our gathering, or we shall be left with nothing.
>
> (iv, 32)

It is, however, only much later in the novel, at Mau, that it appears possible that these tones, for all their practical good sense, are themselves subject to contextual irony. Mr Sorley joins Mrs Moore and Ralph with Professor Godbole, possessors of some fundamental knowledge or instinct which renders Fielding and Miss Quested liable to seem as crass as the Collector.

The very success of Forster's presentation of the two latter demonstrates both the shortcomings of language as an instrument fit to enact religious revelation and of the development of a civilisation whose achievement is consonant with verbal expression. The unobtrusive confidence of the account of Aziz's encounter in the Maidan with the subaltern attends the presentation of the schoolmaster and the young woman. The reasoned good sense of the narration is wholly appropriate to these vintage liberal humanists. Like the narrator, Miss Quested understands clearly, if not at first her own limitations, at least those attendant on marriage to Heaslop and the British in India: 'she would see India always as a frieze, never as a spirit, and she assumed that it was a spirit of which Mrs Moore had had a glimpse' (v, 41). This elusive 'spirit' holds her interest, as it does the narrator's, and alienates her from her compatriots. Yet her charity and sympathy draw her back to them. In announcing to Heaslop that they are not to be married, her intellectual and morally scrupulous nature is infused with the flow of feeling:

> She felt ashamed. How decent he was! He might force his opinions down her throat, but did not press her to an 'engagement', because he believed, like herself, in the sanctity of personal relationships.
>
> (viii, 76)

> ... a wave of relief passed through them both, and then transformed itself into a wave of tenderness, and passed back. They were softened by their own honesty, and began to feel lonely and unwise.
>
> (viii, 77)

The explicit metaphor is appropriate to the conceptions that Miss Quested and Heaslop entertain of themselves, in which personal relations, work, religious feeling and duty are readily understood as separate entities, and personality conceived in terms of 'dryness' or 'damp' does not necessarily appear ludicrous. Characteristically, the narrator, by drawing attention to the apparently irrelevant detail of the Indian bird that they see, disclaims their typical ordering of experience in this fashion, without insisting on its insufficiency. 'Nothing in India is identifiable, the mere asking of a question causes it to disappear or to merge in something else' (viii, 78): the comment reflects as much upon the genesis of *A Passage to India* as upon the characters it describes. Miss Quested's dissatisfied longing for a verbal absolute—"'Mrs Moore, if one isn't absolutely honest, what is the use of existing?'" (viii, 89)—is similarly pertinent to the novelist's sense of his vocation and the problems posed by the subject-matter of India.

Fielding, while less naïve than Miss Quested, shares her limitations as well as her virtues. The latter include most obviously an attempt to ignore the racial barrier: 'the world, he believed, is a globe of men who are trying to reach one another and can best do so by the help of good will plus culture and intelligence' (vii, 56). Once again the aspiration's Schlegelian overtones reveal in how close a relationship this character stands to Forster's central preoccupations as a novelist, while the critique of his shortcomings shows the direction in which this novel develops by comparison with the rest of Forster's fiction.

Forster defined the humanist as possessing 'four leading characteristics—curiosity, a free mind, belief in good taste, and belief in the human race',[5] characteristics which Fielding shares. His humanism derives from personal conviction without philosophical or religious sanction. His disavowal of religious conviction scandalises his Moslem friends, but Forster admires the 'zeal for honesty' (ix, 102) that inspires his plain-speaking and his refusal to indulge in the easy, acceptable answers. Yet as the novel proceeds, Fielding's lack of spiritual development is shown as a disabling limitation. It accompanies a circumscription of spontaneous feeling similar to Miss Quested's: 'he felt old. He wished that he too could be carried away on waves of emotion' (xi, 109). Fielding's honesty has its price: 'experience can do much, and all that he had learnt in England and Europe was an assistance to him, and helped him towards clarity, but clarity prevented him from experiencing something else' (ibid.). The virtues of clarity and honesty do not compensate for the fundamental commitment to instinct crucial to an understanding of Aziz, nor are they adequate to a concept as far beyond their range as the sense of evil:

> He felt that a mass of madness had arisen and tried to overwhelm them all; it had to be shoved back into its pit somehow, and he didn't know how to do it, because he did not understand madness: he had always gone about sensibly and quietly until a difficulty came right.
>
> (xvii, 154)

The metaphor of the pit dramatises the separation of conscious volition, which exercises the capacity for integrity and directness of address, from the unconscious, which prompts the entrapping of Aziz and the subsequent drama of Miss Quested's accusation and retraction: the latter demands response from a different source than that which regulates conduct, morality and justice. It is to Fielding's great credit (and a tribute to Forster's faith in the profundity of instincts for truth and decency) that he instinctively believes in Aziz, despite a personal philosophy which repudiates faith. The insistently spiritual context of the novel forces the realisation that this belief in Aziz is a quasi-religious affirmation:

> Fielding, too, had his anxieties ... but he relegated them to the edge of his mind, and forbade them to infect its core. Aziz *was* innocent, and all action must be based on that, and the people who said he was guilty were wrong, and it was hopeless to try to propitiate them.
>
> (xix, 164)

Yet despite the instinctive quality of Fielding's avowal, it rests on experience and the capacity to form workable judgements of people. Fielding's knowledge of his man is at stake, his sense of outrage located in the same area drawn upon by the novelist who offers an understanding of 'character'. Fielding's sense of limitation bears directly upon Forster's struggle with his art in *A Passage to India*. He reaches towards new understanding similar to that undertaken by the novelist, but unlike Forster it appears to elude him. At the moment of his great triumph over himself, when his dignified championship of Aziz withstands the insult of the Club's sneering disparagement, Fielding becomes aware of dimensions of experience foreign to his doggedly decent mentality. The Marabar Hills 'leap into beauty', but the mythical associations (Monsalvat, Walhalla) conjured by the novelist do not touch the schoolmaster. Legal justice, due process of law, the bricks and mortar of civilisation occupy his interest: 'who was the guide, and had he been found yet? What was the "echo" of which the girl complained? He did not know, but presently he would know. Great is information, and she shall prevail.' Forster, by confronting justice with beauty, denies Fielding the enjoyment of his dignified triumph over pettiness and malice. While the latter has fought with great moral courage, it appears that he was entered in the wrong lists. His sense of discouragement derives not from the degrading spectacle of the British herding together under a banner that parodies his own, nor from the regrettable insult to Heaslop, but from an apprehension of inadequacy that short-circuits his usual channels of communication with himself. Justice, morality and decency at their best ignore too much of human aspiration and potential, and of forms of being that transcend the merely human. This central, beautifully controlled passage deserves full quotation:

It was the last moment of the light, and as he gazed at the Marabar Hills they seemed to move graciously towards him like a queen, and their charm became the sky's. At the moment they vanished they were everywhere, the cool benediction of the night descended, the stars sparkled, and the whole universe was a hill. Lovely, exquisite moment—but passing the Englishman with averted face and on swift wings. He experienced nothing himself; it was as if someone had told him there was such a moment, and he was obliged to believe. And he felt dubious and discontented suddenly, and wondered whether he was really and truly successful as a human being. After forty years' experience, he had learnt to manage his life and make the best of it on advanced European lines, had developed his personality, explored his limitations, controlled his passions—and he had done it all without becoming either pedantic or worldly. A creditable achievement, but as the moment passed, he felt he ought to have been working at something else the whole time,—he didn't know at what, never would know, never could know, and that was why he felt sad.

(xx, 181)

The centre of experience appears to be mystical rather than ethical. Forster's prose contrives unemphatically the oppositions between the majesty of hills, starlight and universe, and the restrained evocation of Fielding's decency and self-dissatisfaction. The silence is felt, not remarked. The description indicates its presence in the phrase 'lovely, exquisite moment' without allowing it to expand, because Fielding fills it with words directed inwards. Unlike Godbole later, he does not resist the impulse to conceptualise: the difference is stressed by the comparison 'as if someone had *told* him'. Silence, *A Passage to India* insists, must be felt. The superb, gently deflating phrase 'wondered whether he was really and truly successful as a human being' rings achingly hollow in this context of physical beauty, mythology and eternity. Despite his concern for the oppressed, the wrongfully accused, despite even his awareness of his own circumscription, Fielding at such a moment is locked within the prison of the self. And despite her hostility towards him at this point in the novel, Miss Quested shares Fielding's nihilistic dissatisfaction, pointed by the quasi-religious context of her statement to Heaslop:

'How can one repay when one has nothing to give? What is the use of personal relationships when everyone brings less and less to them? I feel we ought all to go back into the desert for centuries and try and get good. I want to begin at the beginning. All the things I thought I'd learnt are just a hindrance, they're not knowledge at all. I'm not fit for personal relationships.'

(xx, 188)

By this recognition of their limitations, both Fielding and Miss Quested begin in some degree to 'inhabit the desert', to withdraw from their compatriots and from intercourse itself into inner contemplative silence. But although they can go so far, they are incapable of greater self-transcendence. Miss Quested's resumption of her 'morning kneel to Christianity ... the shortest and easiest cut to the unseen' (xxiv, 201) is the product of temporary distress rather than a sign of new understanding. She confesses wryly to Fielding her own sense of the shortcomings of honesty as a code (xxvi, 228–9), which parallels his own dissatisfaction. Immediately afterwards, however, they reassert their religious scepticism, explicitly disavowing any belief in an after-life: 'there was a moment's silence, such as often follows the triumph of rationalism' (xxvi, 229). This silence differs qualitatively from that experienced and then consciously sought by Mrs Moore, Aziz and Godbole. The sceptics' is, rather, a spiritual emptiness, the internal desert which clears the path to spiritual understanding but should never be confused with it. Hamidullah's lack of sympathy with Miss Quested after the trial examines the latter's valuable personal qualities in the light of a culture whose central emphases differ fundamentally:

> her behaviour rested on cold justice and honesty; she had felt, while she recanted, no passion of love for those whom she had wronged. Truth is not truth in that exacting land unless there go with it kindness and more kindness and kindness again, unless the Word that was with God also is God.
>
> (xxvi, 233)

Miss Quested's triumph over herself by sticking to her principles in preference to not letting down her friends remains insufficient even judged from the standpoint of her own culture, as the culminating phrases of this description insinuate. Integrity and fairmindedness are shown to be just the rump of religion, admirable qualities indeed but spiritually speaking negligible. At the end of this scene at the College, when Miss Quested's lodging after the trial has been under consideration, Fielding in weariness is visited once again by the displacing vision of love crucial to Hamidullah's philosophy:

fatigued by the merciless and enormous day, he lost his usual sane view of human intercourse, and felt that we exist not in ourselves, but in terms of each others' minds—a notion for which logic offers no support and which had attacked him only once before, the evening after the catastrophe, when from the verandah of the club he saw the fists and fingers of the Marabar swell until they included the whole night sky.

(xxvi, 237)

Once again the insufficiency of developing personality, exploring limitation and controlling passion (xx, 181) as a goal of the whole man (rather than the civilised social being) has become apparent. Hamidullah's tone is taken up by the narration, when Fielding and Miss Quested offer their inadequate explanations of the experience in the cave and of Mrs Moore's intuitive understanding: 'they had not the apparatus for judging' (xxix, 251). In condemning the inadequacy of their prose world, the narration adopts for purposes of judgement the idiom of Professor Godbole:

When they agreed, 'I want to go on living a bit,' or, 'I don't believe in God,' the words were followed by a curious backwash as though the universe had displaced itself to fill up a tiny void, or as though they had seen their own gestures from an immense height—dwarfs talking, shaking hands and assuring each other that they stood on the same footing of insight ... Not for them was an infinite goal behind the stars, and they never sought it.

(xxix, 252)

At the end of the novel, Fielding's slightly regretful curiosity about Hindu religion confirms this Godbolian deployment of phrase, as he attempts to question Aziz about Ralph's and Stella's affinity (obviously transmitted by Mrs Moore) with Hinduism. Aziz is silent. The silence is entirely consonant with the subject that occasions it, as Mrs Moore has demonstrated earlier: '"Say, say, say," said the old lady bitterly. "As if anything can be said! I have spent my life in saying or in listening to sayings: I have listened too much. It is time I was left in peace"' (xxii, 190–1). The explicit attack upon language from Mrs Moore becomes vicious in its rejection of the novel's sole form of expression: '"Oh, how tedious ... trivial ... Was he in the cave and were you in the cave and on and on ... and Unto us a Son is born, unto us a Child is given ..."' This develops more explicitly than the example cited earlier into a questioning of the idea of 'character' as customarily understood by the novelist: '"One knows people's characters, as you call them," she retorted disdainfully, as if she really knew more than character but could not impart it' (xxii, 196). The 'character' of Aziz only becomes available as we understand the silences of his religion and poetry. The narrator partly explains Mrs Moore's disillusion and feeling of displacement in the chapter which follows, but her own refusal to trust words is more significant as evidence of her capacity for in-dwelling, in such contrast to the eternally public world of the Club, and particularly of Fielding's and Miss Quested's best efforts.

The blend of sympathy and irony with which Aziz is presented illuminates the status of the latter tone in the novel. Irony in an important sense is equivalent to silence because it represents an implicit rather than externalised attitude to its subject. Yet irony is insufficient to Forster's purposes in presenting Aziz, who will increasingly command the narrator's sympathy as the novel progresses. In order to encompass the alien quality of this man's culture, Forster adopts a more tentative idiom than that used to portray the British: 'Here was Islam, his own country, more than a Faith, more than a battle-cry, more, much more ... Islam, an attitude towards life both exquisite and durable, where his body and his thoughts found their home' (ii, 13). Lionel Trilling remarks that 'so far as the old Mediterranean deities of wise impulse and loving intelligence can go in India, Forster is at home; he thinks they can go far but not all the way, and a certain retraction of the intimacy of his style reflects his uncertainty. The acts of imagination by which Forster conveys the sense of the Indian gods are truly wonderful; they are, nevertheless, the acts of imagination not of a master of the truth but of an intelligent neophyte, still baffled.'[6] However, it might be argued against this view that the narration's faltering into silence in the preceding quotation matches precisely the inarticulate nature of Aziz's own indefinite aspiration. Moreover, this willingness to trust to silence rather than more direct expression marks a primary strategy in Forster's attempt to penetrate Eastern culture. The phrase 'Islam, an attitude towards life both exquisite and durable' slackly generalises a sensation that exists in the blank space preceding it. Unless the reader links these words to the description of the mosque open to the moonlight, to the aspiration of Aziz which transcends patriotism, religion and valour, and then attempts to empathise with the silent crescendo of longing, the comment on Islam remains meaningless. In the description of the Bridge Party, for the most part incisively rendered in tones of English social comedy, the language again retreats from arenas to which speech is inappropriate. The contrast with the prevailing idiom in that scene makes the insufficiency of verbalisation quite overt:

There was a silence when he had finished speaking, on both sides
of the court; at least, more ladies joined the English group, but
their words seemed to die as soon as uttered. Some kites hovered
overhead, impartial, over the kites passed the mass of a vulture,
and with an impartiality exceeding all, the sky, not deeply
coloured but translucent, poured light from its whole
circumference. It seemed unlikely that the series stopped here.
Beyond the sky must not there be something that overarches all
the skies, more impartial even than they? Beyond which again ...
    They spoke of *Cousin Kate*.

                                                                     (v, 34)

As the novel progresses, the distrust of verbalisation becomes absolute.
Fielding refuses to point out to Aziz that water will not run uphill: 'he had
dulled his craving for verbal truth and cared chiefly for truth of mood' (vii,
65). Mrs Moore refuses to accept her son's words alone as an unimpeachable
index of his state of mind and feeling: 'his words without his voice might have
impressed her' (v, 44). Her own invocation of the deity is subject to the same
qualification: 'She must needs pronounce his name frequently, as the greatest
she knew, yet she had never found it less efficacious. Outside the arch there
seemed always an arch, beyond the remotest echo a silence' (v, 45–6). And
this point of view is enlarged on at the Caves in the reference to 'poor little
talkative Christianity' (xiv, 141). None the less, Aziz's susceptibility to the
poetry of religion fails to exempt his feelings from the strictures made by
silence on words. Aziz's religion is scarcely closer to that reality than
Fielding's ethical philosophy: '"there is no God but God" doesn't carry us far
through the complexities of matter and spirit; it is only a game with words,
really, a religious pun, not a religious truth' (xxxi, 264).
    The clarity of Forster's probing analysis of the interaction between
matter in the shape of language and the elusive spirit is a gauge of his own
sensitivity to what his medium can, and, more importantly, cannot perform.
The nagging uncertainty about the significance of the 'echo' in the Caves
measures the novelist's refusal to accede to his form's propensity for
continual explication. Only by attending to the breakdown of language
accompanying the presentation of Godbole and the Hindu religion does the
echo release its (strictly incomprehensible) 'meaning'. To begin with,
Godbole refuses to 'explain' the secret of the caves to Aziz and the English
ladies: 'the comparatively simple mind of the Mohammedan was
encountering Ancient Night' (vii, 68). Godbole preserves the enigma. Yet his
singing transcends the petty temper which accompanies the ending of
Fielding's tea-party. The explanation of the song of the milkmaiden to Shri

Krishna insinuates a possible reconciliation of eternity to time, by drawing futurity into the present:

> 'But He comes in some other song, I hope?' said Mrs Moore gently.
> 'Oh no, he refuses to come,' repeated Godbole, perhaps not understanding her question. 'I say to Him, Come, come, come, come, come, come. He neglects to come.'
>
> (vii, 72)

Expectancy has been celebrated. This heralds the crucial understanding that the moment itself (rather than the structures of potential realisation and futurity built upon it), when prolonged, absorbs eternity. Significance resides in waiting. That is the condition on which insight and understanding become available.

Yet the point is not made explicit, because Godbole initiates his audience into participation rather than partial understanding. With the departure of the intrusive Heaslop the meaning of the song infuses the entire scene: 'Ronny's steps had died away, and there was a moment of absolute silence. No ripple disturbed the water, no leaf stirred' (vii, 72). Forster finishes the chapter on this (non) note of silence, prolonging its effect without attempting explanation. The words do not approach enactment but figure as sign-posts to a condition of feeling that is the antithesis of ratiocination, and therefore of language.

At the Caves, Godbole's absence forms part of the atmosphere of doom that attends the expedition: 'a new quality occurred, a spiritual silence which invaded more senses than the ear' (xiv, 132). Aziz's inadequacy to interpret the Caves is related to the Hindu: 'he had no notion how to treat this particular aspect of India; he was lost in it without Professor Godbole' (xiv, 133). Mrs Moore, shattered by the experience of the Caves, can only respond to her feelings with direct honesty. She is unable to assimilate silence in Godbole's manner, to accept it fully. But she does register the totality of the silence and the apprehension of eternity:

> ... the echo, began in some indescribable way to undermine her hold on life. Coming at a moment when she chanced to be fatigued, it had managed to murmur, 'Pathos, piety, courage—they exist, but are identical, and so is filth. Everything exists, nothing has value.' If one had spoken vileness in that place, or quoted lofty poetry, the comment would have been the same—'ou-boum'. If one had spoken with the tongues of angels and

pleaded for all the unhappiness and misunderstanding in the world, past, present, and to come, for all the misery men must undergo whatever their opinion and position, and however much they dodge or bluff—it would amount to the same ...

... suddenly, at the edge of her mind, Religion appeared, poor little talkative Christianity, and she knew that all its divine words from 'Let there be Light' to 'It is finished' only amounted to 'boum'. Then she was terrified over an area larger than usual; the universe, never comprehensible to her intellect, offered no repose to her soul, the mood of the last two months took definite form at last, and she realized that she didn't want to write to her children, didn't want to communicate with anyone, not even with God.

(xiv, 140–1)

Where Mrs Moore approaches the obliteration of mental, spiritual and emotional distinctiveness that preludes the experience of totality or oneness, Godbole's culture, typically, enables him to make the necessary lesser distinctions between suffering and evil. His religious philosophy embodies acceptance, totality, reconciliation. His explanation to Fielding of Hindu concepts of good and evil strains Forster's prose style with its unwonted abstraction:

'Good and evil are different, as their names imply. But, in my own humble opinion, they are both of them aspects of my Lord. He is present in the one, absent in the other, and the difference between presence and absence is great, as great as my feeble mind can grasp. Yet absence implies presence, absence is not non-existence, and we are therefore entitled to repeat, "Come, come, come, come."'

(xix, 169)

This difficult explanation of Hin du morality opposes Fielding's ethical philosophy, which remains determinedly secular. The certainty of Godbole's faith dissolves the sort of self-doubt to which Fielding is liable. Nevertheless, a noticeable feature of Godbole's explanation is Forster's satirical framing of it by Fielding's impatience, tiredness and boredom, and—to be anachronistic—the insistence on Godbole's Peter Sellers brand of near-fatuity and inconsequentiality. The result is not, of course, to deprecate the Hindu's faith, but the process of explanation itself. The enactment at Mau is accorded almost sacred respect.[7x]

To convey the intricate feeling of the Shri Krishna ceremonies, Forster stands his language on its head:

> ... Professor Narayan Godbole stands in the presence of God. God is not born yet—that will occur at midnight—but He has also been born centuries ago, nor can He ever be born, because He is the Lord of the Universe, who transcends human processes. He is, was not, is not, was. He and Professor Godbole stood at opposite ends of the same strip of carpet.
>
> (xxxiii, 274)

'Stands' in the course of three sentences becomes 'stood'. The change of tense indicates the co-presence of time and eternity. The antitheses 'is, was not, is not, was', which further interfuse history and the present, are syntactically without meaning: Forster has exchanged the prose of reason and understanding for language as mystery, which modulates naturally into chant, '"Tukaram, Tukaram"'. 'Nonsense' becomes truth that lies beyond sense. Yet the language which is so effective at creating Fielding and Miss Quested is also capable of registering a range of feeling which is impossible to recreate more directly:

> When the villagers broke cordon for a glimpse of the silver image, a most beautiful and radiant expression came into their faces, a beauty in which there was nothing personal, for it caused them all to resemble one another during the moment of its indwelling, and only when it was withdrawn did they revert to individual clods.
>
> (xxxiii, 275)

The sign of divine presence and the language which records it are both inadequate to the state of feeling created by the ceremony, a failure transmitted again by Forster's ironic tones: 'the God to be born was largely a silver image the size of a teaspoon' (xxxiii, 274) Yet his sign partakes, like the Cross, of the reality it represents, is, more properly, the symbol of 'God Himself' (xxxiii, 275). Likewise, language transcends sign in the act of reading and becomes itself symbol, the chant:

> 'Tukaram, Tukaram,
> Thou art my father and mother and everybody.'
>
> (xxxiii, 275)

The necessary shortcomings of language, insisted upon throughout the novel, are transcended by the spirit of Hinduism which fleetingly gathers all mortal expression into a single communion: 'God si Love' (xxxiii, 276). The fractured proclamation of Mrs Moore's hesitant insight much earlier in the novel (v, 45), now repeated in a significant but unimportant abuse of language, heralds the spirit's attempt by 'a desperate contortion to ravish the unknown' (xxxiii, 278).

Yet afterwards language once again must submit to its syntactical, hierarchical, time-ridden status:

> how, if there is such an event, can it be remembered afterwards? How can it be expressed in anything but itself? Not only from the unbeliever are mysteries hid, but the adept himself cannot retain them. He may think, if he chooses, that he has been with God, but as soon as he thinks it, it becomes history, and falls under the rules of time.
>
> (xxxiii, 278)

The clash of rowing-boats and the dialectical exchange between Fielding and Aziz prevent a simplistic reading of the closing Hindu section as any kind of solution for problems of mortality, separation, racialism, or straightforward human cross-purposes. At the novel's end the syntax recovers its confident tones confronting a reality to which it is fully adequate, and bangs shut like a gate: 'no, not yet ... no, not there' (xxxvii, 312).

Forster's language makes no pretence of dissolving the intractable difficulties it has created. Yet while it imposes its linear conception of time and its rational order upon the timeless, chaotic diversity of experience, language itself strives also to accommodate the twin sensations of flux and stasis. It forms a central communication with both aspects of our experience. Forster's language in *A Passage to India* possesses an essentially moral dimension—the only morality of art apart from subject, as Conrad avowed[8]—manifest in the scrupulosity it consistently displays towards its own status even as it shows a willingness to trust to experience beyond language. As such, rather than further perpetrate problems of inevitable alienation, Forster's stylistic delicacy recreates the complex interaction between certain individual, social and spiritual conditions of being in permanent but fluid form.

NOTES

1x. As far as non-fiction is concerned, *The Hill of Devi: being Letters from Dewas State Senior* (1953) demonstrates how intelligently Forster confronted the limitations of the role of an observer, and how consistently his imaginative sympathy enabled him to transcend them.

2. Cf. Benjamin Britten's essay 'Some Notes on Forster and Music', in *Aspects of E. M. Forster: Essays and Recollections written for his Ninetieth Birthday 1st January 1969*, ed. Oliver Stallybrass (1969) 81–6.

3. Epilogue, GLD 201.

4. Joseph Campbell, *The Masks of God: Occidental Mythology* (1965) p. 3.

5. 'Gide and George', TCD 220.

6. *E. M. Forster: A Study* (1944) pp. 124–5.

7x. The descriptions of the Gokul Ashtami Festival in *The Hill of Devi* are more irreverent—Forster uses the word 'facetious'—than in *A Passage to India*: which is not to say that Forster doesn't permit a spirit of levity in the novel, but that it is subsumed into more serious explorations which the novel's contexts co-operate to render revelatory at points such as this.

8. G. Jean-Aubry, *Joseph Conrad: Life & Letters*, 2 vols (1927) I, 280.

CHAMAN L. SAHNI

The Marabar Caves in the Light of Indian Thought

The latent mythology evident in [cosmic-egg motif and] the unconditioned potential of the Marabar Caves has been brought out by various critics of the novel.[1] The present essay will complement their discussion by expounding the significance of the cave symbology from the Indian standpoint. It will first seek to establish that the Marabar Caves represent the complex variety of Indian thought, and then demonstrate the religious, mythological, and conceptual concentration that takes place in these caves. Further, an attempt will be made to illuminate the nature of Mrs Moore's experience in the cave in the light of Indian thought.

The history of Indian architecture reveals that the Marabar Hills, near Gaya, in Bihar, contain the most ancient rock-cut cave-temples of India.[2]

From inscriptions of later date we also learn that the caves were for centuries occupied by Brahmanical ascetics. On the highest peak of Barabar, there is still a Siva temple with a lingam sacred to Siddheswar.

The history of the Barabar caves clearly indicates that although they were originally associated with the three non-Vedic monastic schools of thought—Buddhism, Jainism, and the Ajivika doctrine—they are now known by names connected with Brahmanism and later Hinduism. It seems to me that Forster uses the symbol of the caves in the plural to suggest the various off-shoots of Indian thought, echoing the Impersonal Absolute. The Marabar Hills, containing these "extraordinary caves", symbolize the ancient

From *Focus on Forster's* "A Passage to India": *Indian Essays in Criticism*, ed. V.A. Shahane. © 1975 by Orient Longman.

mythical past and the mystical heritage of India, which has always been a great attraction for the foreigner but at the same time a source of great bafflement also.

"The incredible antiquity of these hills" (p. 123) is testified by geology. Geologically, they are part of the Deccan plateau which is certainly older than the Himalayas and much more so than the Indo-Gangetic plain from which it is separated by the Vindhya and the Satpura mountains. In the novel Forster uses the phrase "the high places of Dravidia" (p. 123), for what he calls "the Vindhya and Satpura hills, the plateau of Deccan" in the manuscript.[3] In Hindu mythology, "the Vindhya Mountains, at one time, in an excess of pride, so enlarged themselves that they fairly eclipsed the sun and even blocked its path."[4] Their pride was humbled by a mighty ascetic, Agastya, the patron saint of South India, who is also associated with the myth of the Descent of the Ganges. Since Forster starts the "Caves" section with the myth of the Descent of the Ganges, probably he might have read about the myth of saint Agastya who is said to have swallowed the entire ocean, depriving the earth of its life-sustaining waters, and thus making it imperative for another ascetic Bhagiratha to exercise his yogic powers to release the celestial Ganges from heaven and bring it down to earth. It seems to me that Forster is recounting the myth of Agastya and the Vindhya Mountains in his remark. "If the flesh of the sun's flesh is to be touched anywhere, it is here, among the incredible antiquity of these hills" (p. 132). Again, in Hindu legend the Vindhya Mountains, which separate the North Indian plain from the highlands of the Deccan, form the summit over which the sun rises to begin its daily transit of the firmament. Thus in his initial concept of the caves, Forster is recapitulating not only the physical configuration of India but also the great Aryo-Dravidian synthesis that had taken place as a result of this configuration.

These hills have, then, seen not only "the upheaval of the Himalayas from a sea" (p. 123) but also the rise of all formal religion and mythology, for they existed even before "the gods took their seats on them" (p. 123). They are "older than all spirit" because they represent matter, the primordial matrix of *Prakriti*. The expedition to these hills is symbolically a journey into the timeless past, an effort to fathom the mystery of the Primal Cause, a quest for Ultimate Reality, for a Timeless Absolute in relation to which our time-bound existence acquires meaning and significance.

Mrs Moore connects the Marabar caves with infinity, eternity, and vastness (pp. 149–50). "The Infinite," as Betty Heimann puts it "is boundless, but is still conceived under a vague notion of space."[5] The caves symbolize pure space cut out of solid rocks. Hence they suggest the Infinite. In all religio-philosophical systems of India, the Infinite is visualized under the symbol of *Sunya*, the Void, which, as Heimann says, mean "not a nothing, but a no-single thing".[6] This concept of emptiness, the void, vacuity, as Zimmer says, has been employed as "a convenient and effective pedagogical instrument to bring the mind beyond the sense of duality which infects all systems in which the absolute and the world of relativity are described in contrasting, or antagonistic terms".[7]

Since the Absolute is beyond any fixed notions of empirical knowledge and valuation, it can be expressed only in negative terms, *Na-iti, Na-iti* (not-this, not-this). The Absolute is also beyond the ethical concepts of good and evil, beyond any definition given by human reason. Forster is, therefore, right in saying that "if mankind grew curious and excavated, nothing, nothing would be added to the sum of good or evil" (p. 125).

Again, in the Indian concept of the Infinite, "matter and spirit, combined, form the transcendental and superempirical fullness. Spirit alone is considered not wide enough a concept to suffice to represent the Whole, the *purnatva*."[8] Jainism, the daughter religion of Hinduism, has emphatically stated that there is a living soul in stones also, as in the higher organized beings. No wonder if during the ascent to the Marabar caves, "the boulders said, 'I am alive', the small stones answered, 'I am almost alive.'" (p. 149) According to the Sankhya system, all unconscious matter (*prakriti*) is in a state of pure potentiality, and its evolution can take place only through the presence of the conscious spirit (*purusha*). Since in his comments on Fielding's reflections about the Marabar echo Forster implies that "a religious truth" must encompass "the complexities of matter and spirit", (p. 269), the Marabar caves enshrine "a religious truth" by incorporating both matter and spirit as suggested by the exquisite image of the flame in the cave.

The passage referred to suggests the mystery inherent in the development of life-monads (*purushas*) from unconscious matter (*prakriti*). The reflection of the match flame in the stone suggests that all matter is potentially infused with spirit but lacks consciousness. Hence the flame in the stone appears only when the flame in the air is lit.

From the Vedantic point of view, the match flame is the symbol of *Atman* (the *Katha Upanishad* compares *Atman* to a flame); the pure space of the cave represents Brahman (the *Chandogya Upanishad* makes frequent references to space as Brahman); the walls of granite suggest the phenomenal world; and the flame mirrored in the wall symbolizes the world of appearances created by Maya which displays universal consciousness as duality by separating the self from the true reality. So long as this illusion remains, there can be no merging of *Atman* and Brahman, for *Moksha* (liberation) comes by extinction, through enlightenment, of individual consciousness. Hence the world of appearances must be re-integrated into the Vast Immensity, that is, Brahman. According to Indian thought, there is no greater good than the joy of merging with Brahman, the eternal substratum of existence.

The cave's association with eternity is suggested by the recurrent image of the serpent and its coils. The Hindu and other ancient scriptures picture eternity under the old symbol of a snake swallowing its own tail. The circle thus formed represents eternity, without beginning and without end, in itself infinite, but enclosing a portion of finite space. The cycle of time continually revolves like the "eternally watchful" worm in the cave. The descending and ascending of the serpent has a special meaning in Jainism. According to the Jains, Zimmer tells us, "the present 'descending' (*avasarpini*) period was preceded and will be followed by an 'ascending' (*utasarpini*). *Sarpini* suggests the creeping movement of a 'serpent' (*sarpin*); *ava–* means 'down' and *ut–* means 'up'. The serpent-cycle of time will go on revolving through these alternating 'ascending' and 'descending' periods forever."9 In Hinduism, the circular coils of the snake also represent the wheel of *Samsara* (the endless round of transmigration of soul) from which the Indian mystic seeks release (*Moksha*), meditating on the divine symbol *OM*. As Lord Krishna says in the *Bhagavad-Gita*, "Aum is the one indestructible (sound), the Immensity. He who, his mind intent upon me, abandons his body and leaves the world uttering this syllable attains the supreme purpose of his destiny."10

It seems to me that Forster uses the composite image of the caves to suggest the various facets of the all-embracing Whole (*purnatva*), represented by the various non-Vedic and Vedic schools of Indian thought. The caves may then simultaneously represent the "impersonal cosmic principle" of the Ajivika sect, the total renunciation and isolationism of Jainism, the Nirvana or the Void of Buddhism, the irresoluble dichotomy of *purusha* (life-monad, always represented in the Sankhya system as an "imprisoned spirit") and *prakriti* (matter) represented by Sankhya and Yoga, and the undifferentiated oneness that lies at the root of the concept of Brahman in Advaita-Vedanta.

In one of the caves, Mrs Moore undergoes a tremendous spiritual experience which annihilates her inherited sense of Christian values and makes her ponder over the inadequacy of "poor little talkative Christianity" (p. 148). From the Indian standpoint, she has a vision of the Vast Immensity, the Hindu view of the Timeless Absolute, but from the Western standpoint her vision embodies a confrontation with Nothingness. She hears a "terrifying echo" (p.145) which proves to be nerve-shattering for her. Her reflections on the nature and significance of the echo suggest that it represents a particular aspect of Indian thought, and that it cannot be accounted for in Western religions and philosophies of life.

The echo in a Marabar cave is "entirely devoid of distinction," and "as far as the human alphabet can express it," its sound is "Boum" or "bou-oum", or "ou-boum" (p. 145). It is difficult to say, for certain, what Forster meant by this sound, but as Glen O. Allen and James McConkey have pointed out, it does have close phonetic resemblance with the Indian mystic symbol "*AUM*" or "*OM*", which stands for the inexpressible Absolute. Both these critics, however, associate the echo with evil, whereas *OM* is the most auspicious and spiritual symbol of the supreme One in Indian thought. It is, therefore, beyond good and evil. Only those who cannot understand the real meaning and significance of this mystic sound would associate it with evil. Mrs Moore certainly thinks, "Nothing evil had been in the cave, but she had not enjoyed herself" (p. 146).

The significance of the echo has been discussed in many *Upanishads*.[11] We are told that the sacred syllable *OM* consists of three and a half morae. The three morae are *A*, *U*, *M*, and the half mora is represented by the echo (*nada*). It is this half mora which bears the deepest meaning and leads to the supreme goal. *Dhayanabindu Upanishad* says:

Higher than the original syllable
Is the point, the echo higher than this;
The syllable vanishes with the sound,
The highest state is silent.

The highest state is that of *turiya*, supreme silence, corresponding to *samadhi*, representing Spirit in its undifferentiated unity. The supreme goal of every individual, according to Indian thought, is total reintegration—that is, return to fundamental unity underlying this cosmos.

The undifferentiated oneness suggested by the echo to Mrs Moore lies at the root of Advaita-Vedanta, and signifies the ultimate perception of the Hindu mystic. For Mrs Moore, however, such a concept is puzzling, for it cuts at the root of all her Western values. The echo points out to her that all is one: "Everything exists, nothing has value" (p.147). Even the categories of time are meaningless, for the idea of the beginning and the end of things suggested by "Let there be light" and "It is finished" does not hold good in view of eternity. The echo eliminates all distinctions. The concepts of Heaven, Hell, and Annihilation, which have sprung from the ethical importance attached to human actions, are all reduced to triviality, for action itself loses its significance because it perpetuates existence. Although soon after her arrival in India Mrs Moore had become aware of the inefficacy of her concept of God, as is evident from her spiritual awareness that "outside the arch there seemed always an arch, beyond the remotest echo a silence" (p. 51, 52), her vision in the cave terrifies her. She feels mystified and at the same time spiritually isolated. In her isolation even the elephant becomes "a nobody" (p. 147) for her. It is the isolation of spirit in spirit; abiding in one's own essence. It is soul's isolation from its own eternal and timeless essence, as Hinduism holds. She is later restless to know: "What had spoken to her in that scoured-out cavity of the granite? What dwelt in the first of the caves? Something very old and very small. Before time, it was before space also. Something snub-nosed, incapable of generosity—the undying worm itself. Since hearing its voice, she had not entertained one large thought...." (p. 203).

The *Katha Upanishad* says: "The wise who, by means of meditation on his Self, recognises the Ancient, who is difficult to be seen, who has entered into the dark, who is hidden in the cave, who dwells in the abyss, as God, he indeed leaves joy and sorrow far behind."[12] But Mrs Moore's concept of God is monotheistic and she cannot comprehend the metaphysical subtleties of the Advaita-Vedanta. Nevertheless, under the spell of her vision in the cave, she shrinks away from the forces of life and contemplates retiring into "a cave of (her) own" (p. 195). She loses interest in everything, in her children, in social responsibilities, in religion, even in God. She even mortifies her will-to-live by refusing to leave her bungalow when an attack was expected on the last night of Mohurrum (p. 195). She not only renounces all action but develops an attitude of apathy and inertia. She is no longer willing to continue her assigned role on the stage of life.

Judged by purely rational standards, she deteriorates into a state of psychic paralysis; but, from the Indian point of view, she is spiritually heading toward a state of supreme "isolation" (*Kaivalya*). Since the Absolute is beyond the confines of time and space, since it is before creation, it cannot be approached without turning one's back upon the phenomenal world. As a result of her experience in the cave, therefore, Mrs Moore not only turns inward, but also she lapses into a state of invincible noncooperation and detachment.... But that part of her which she has imbibed from personalized Christianity cannot easily be reconciled with her soul's newfound vision, for she is still imprisoned in her Ego.

Forster's description of her state as "the twilight of the double vision" in which "a spiritual muddledom is set up" remains deliberately ambiguous. In such a state, he says: "we can neither act nor refrain from action, we can neither ignore nor respect Infinity" (p. 203). In this state Mrs Moore lies suspended between the noumenal and the phenomenal world. Her experience in the cave has taught her that this world is empty and meaningless, and that all rational conceptions are inadequate to comprehend the mystery of the Infinite; but whether she attains that enlightened vision in which the soul is enwrapped in its own effulgence remains doubtful, for Forster gives no indication of her having come out of the state of "spiritual muddledom". Perhaps, as Ernest Beaumont has said, "the author's sincerity does not allow him to portray unambiguously an experience which was itself puzzling and unsatisfactory, an experience which cannot be clearly expressed, because it never was clear to the person undergoing it."[13] Or, perhaps she was destined to see only the "twilight" and not the irradiant light,[14] of the mystic vision.

Forster later called her experience a vision "with its back turned." The woman who had been life-affirming, who had a staunch faith in the world of personal relationships, and who wanted to be one with the universe is caught between fire and infinity and is utterly bewildered by the latter. The vision of the Vast Immensity—the Indian view of the Timeless Absolute—has strained all her nerves and tapped her spiritual resources. Now she seeks peace in quiet contemplation and longs for extinction in a state of purely negative isolation, as advocated by Jainism and Sankhya-Yoga. The Hindu *Upanishads* also recommend complete renunciation of the world as the only sensible way to attain the world of Pure Being.

Such a world-view may appear to be utterly pessimistic, unnatural, and incomprehensible to a Westerner because it seems to contradict the instinctive force within man, what Schweitzer calls, the "will-to-live"[15] but all the religiophilosophical systems of India, whether Vedic or non-Vedic, are agreed in regarding the attainment of final emancipation from *Samsara* (existence-in-flux) as the true status of the individual. To attain that status, they postulate that all the ties that ever fettered the life-monad must dissolve away and the soul be purified of all *karmic* matter. This demands not only renunciation and isolation, but also, as Schweitzer says, "the concentration of the spirit on the Supra-sensuous. The repetition of the sacred sound 'OM' plays a great part in such exercises of self-submergence."[16] Hence it is not without significance that for Mrs Moore "the echo began in some indescribable way to undermine her hold on life" (p. 147). Finally, she quit the stage of life as quietly as possible and met her death on the Indian Ocean. As she was departing from India, the thousands of coconut palms seemed to laugh: "So you thought an echo was India; you took the Marabar caves as final?" (p. 205)

Of course, to treat the Marabar caves as "final" is to pinpoint a particular facet of Indian thought to be "India". The Marabar caves represent only that aspect of Indian religious and philosophical thought which concentrates on the Impersonal Absolute and stresses the importance of complete renunciation, detachment, and isolation to achieve the trinity of transcendent reality (*sat*), awareness (*cit*), and freedom (*ananda*). As the "Caves" section comes to a close, Fielding remarks: "There is something in religion that may not be true, but has not yet been sung.... Something that the Hindus have perhaps found" (p. 270). This remark directly leads to the third section, "Temple", which, as Forster told Alan Wilde, "represents the same thing as the scene in the cave, "turned inside out". After her death on the Indian Ocean, Mrs Moore is spiritually reborn in the supreme moment of cosmic unity, symbolized by the Krishna Janamashtmi festival. Her vital presence in the mind of Professor Godbole at the Birth of Lord Krishna hints at the fulfilment of her supreme destiny, her absorption in the Absolute. In the *Bhagavad-Gita* Krishna is represented as the highest Godhead, the physical embodiment of the metaphysical Absolute, and, at the same time, the symbol of Cosmic Love and Unity. The Caves embodied *nirguna* (super-personal, without attributes) Brahman; the Temple represents *saguna* (personal, with attributes) Brahman—both being aspects of the same Lord.

NOTES

1. See specifically the following: Glen O. Allen, "Structure, Symbol and Theme in E. M. Forster's *A Passage to India, PMLA* 70 (December 1955) 934–54; James McConkey, *The Novels of E. M. Forster* (Ithaca. N.Y. 1957); Louise Dauner, "What Happened in the Cave? Reflections on *A Passage to India*," *MFS*, 9 (Autumn 1961), 258–70; Wilfred Stone, *The Cave and the Mountain: A Study of E. M. Forster* (Stanford, Calif., 1966); and George H. Thomson, *The Fiction of E. M. Forster* (Detroit, 1967).

2. See James Fergusson, *The Cave Temples of India* (London, 1880), pp. 37–38; and A. L. Basham, *The Wonder That Was India* (London, 1954), p. 352.

3. See Robert L. Harrison, The Manuscripts of *A Passage to India* (Ann Arbor: University Microfilms, 1965), pp. 235–36.

4. See Heinrich Zimmer, *Myths and Symbols in Indian Art and Civilization*, ed. Joseph Campbell (New York, 1946), pp. 113–14.

5. Betty Heimann, *Facets of Indian Thought* (New York, 1964), p. 122.

6. Heimann, p. 122.

7. Heinrich Zimmer, *Philosophies of India*, ed. Joseph Campbell (New York, 1953), p. 523.

8. Heimann, p 120.

9. Heinrich Zimmer, op. cit, pp. 224–25.

10 Alain Danielou, *Hindu Polytheism* (New York, 1964), p. 39.

11. See Paul Deussen, *The Philosophy of the Upanishads* (New York, 1966), pp. 391–92. For mystical sounds and their significance in attaining liberation, also see Mircea Eliade, *Yoga: Immortality and Freedom* (New York, 1958), pp. 390–91.

12. See F. Max Muller, ed., *The Sacred Books of the East*, XV (New York, 1962), 10.

13. Ernest Beaumont, "Mr. E. M. Forster's Strange Mystics", *The Dublin Review*, 225 (Autumn 1951), 46.

14. See Angus Wilson, "A Conversation with E. M. Forster," *Encounter*, 9 (November 1957), 54.

15. Albert Schweitzer, *Indian Thought and Its Development* (Boston, 1960) p. 3.

16. Schweitzer, op. cit. pp. 37–38.

WENDY MOFFAT

A Passage to India *and the Limits of Certainty*

In 1906, E. M. Forster addressed the Workingmen's College on the difference between life and art:

> In life we seek what is gracious and noble, even if it is transitory; in books we seek what is permanent even if it is sad. I uphold optimism in life. I do not at present uphold optimism in books. (Furbank, 148)

While this passage may seem to underscore the dichotomy between life and art, it actually asserts their mutual dependence: Forster's audience is balanced between life and art, living in both, looking to each for a moral lesson. Such dependence is at the heart of Forster's lifelong project to transfigure the world by individual action, to effect change through tolerance. It is not currently fashionable to assert art's moral force: hence Forster's reputation as a genial but rather naive writer and theorist.[1] Nevertheless, a close look at Forster's work reveals a writer bent on redefining simple and hackneyed ways of understanding. Just as tolerance (in the essay "On Tolerance") proves to be a tough resistant force in its application, so too Forster redefines "permanence" in this speech to working men. "Permanence" is the name Forster gives to the patterns in a text which reveal decisive meaning and

From *The Journal of Narrative Technique* 20, no. 3, (Fall 1990). © 1990 by Wendy Moffat.

interpretative wholeness, patterns which became increasingly unsatisfying for him. By the time he began to prepare for the series of lectures later published as *Aspects of the Novel*, Forster wrote admiringly of Sterne:

> How did he discover the art of leaving out what he did not want to say? And why was it lost until our own time? Can nothing liberate English fiction from conscientiousness? (*Commonplace*, 2–3)

For Forster, conscientiousness is the covering term for all the ways in which writing doggedly rehearses familiar conventions and rewards the expectations of a reader reluctant to be surprised. The manifestations of conscientiousness sound like deadly sins of fiction: an ironclad conception of genre; a carefully prepared closure; a narrow conception of the role of character; the burden of an explicit causality; the mechanical movement of plot in its temporal order.

Forster admires *Tristram Shandy* because it invites surprise by shedding conscientiousness while playing with conventions; he takes on the same challenge in *A Passage to India*. Intrigued by the "art of leaving out what [one does] not want to say," Forster systematically empties his final novel of elements of certainty. By omitting as well as telling, he requires the reader to participate in what he conceives to be the puzzle of the novel's world, a process which displaces the reader in interesting ways.

A novel of calculated ambiguities and deliberate omissions, *A Passage to India* paradoxically demands conscientiousness of its readers while it ridicules the same quality in its characters. To demonstrate Forster's method, I have chosen two of many aspects of the novel—the manuscript revisions of a crucial scene, and the genre implications of the inclusion of the final section, "Temple." My brief conclusion speculates on the motives behind Forster's ambiguities.

The Emptying of Plot

Forster took pains to widen and deepen the enigmatic character of his novel, to make it a puzzle insoluble within its own terms, or without. Early drafts of *A Passage to India* reveal a number of false starts. Forster repeatedly revised drafts of chapters thirteen through sixteen, which comprise the crux of the novel, the visit to the Marabar Caves (Levine, 81). When he began writing the novel, his intention was to make the cave scene central and significant, but he did not yet know how:

> When I began *A Passage to India*, I knew something important happened in the Malabar [sic] Caves, and that it would have a

central place in the novel—but I didn't know what it would be....
The Malabar Caves represented an area in which concentration
can take place.... They were to engender an event like an egg.
(*Paris Review*, 31)

The most radical turn from the manuscript to the finished version
occurs in Forster's conception of the attack on Adela Quested. In the
manuscript version, the "event engendered" by the caves is an act of human
violence:

> [Adela] stood for a moment in the cool, thinking about her plans
> and running a finger along the invisible wall. She thought what a
> pity it was ... that she was not in love [with] Ronny.... An extra
> darkness showed that someone was following her down the
> entrance tunnel. "Dr. Aziz—" she began, glad to continue the
> conversation.
>   At first she thought that he was taking her hand as before to
> help her, then she realised, and shrieked at the top of her voice.
> "Boum" shrieked the echo. She struck out and he got hold of her
> other hand and forced her against the wall, he got both her hands
> in one of his, and then felt at her breasts. "Mrs. Moore," she
> yelled. "Ronny—don't let him, save me." The strap of the Field
> Glasses, tugged suddenly, was drawn across her throat. She
> understood—it was to be passed once round her neck, she was to
> be throttled as far as necessary, and then.... [Forster's suspension
> points] Silent, though the echo still raged up and down she
> waited and when the breath was on her wrenched a hand free, got
> hold of the glasses and pushed them into her assailant's mouth.
> She could not push hard but it was still enough to hurt him. He
> let go, and with both hands on her weapon, she smashed at him
> again. She was strong and had horrible joy in revenge. "Not this
> time" she cried, and he answered—or the cave did. She gained
> the entrance of the tunnel, screamed like a maniac lest he pull her
> in when she stooped and regained the open air, her topi smashed,
> her fingers bleeding. (*Manuscripts*, 242–3)[2]

By contrast, in the published version, the only aspect of Adela's experience
which remains "solid and attractive" is her *doubt* about what happened in the
caves (*Passage*, 217). She tells Fielding after the trial that she may have been
alone, and confesses that she may have been suffering from a delusion of
being attacked—"the sort of thing—though in awful form—that makes some
women think they've had an offer of marriage when none was made" (228).

The episode in the early draft is organized around the watershed moment of the suspension points. Before the ellipsis Adela is passive, imagining the culmination of her attack in rape, calling out to her companions for help. Our sense of her helplessness is compounded by Forster's use of language here: the field glasses have more force of action than Adela (they are even capitalized), and the narration is cast in the passive voice. After the ellipsis, Adela rebuffs her attacker in a frenzy of revenge. There are two attempted rapes here, the first of Adela herself, the second Adela's figurative rape of her attacker. The violence on both sides of the ellipsis is figured in sexual terms: first Adela is forced against a wall and roughly molested; then "when the breath was upon her" she uses the field glasses as a "weapon" to push "into her assailant's mouth. She could not push hard but it was enough to hurt him.... She was strong ..." (243).

June Levine has remarked that Adela's rage here is uncharacteristic of her personality in the final version (92). Certainly Adela's motives are ambiguous. She seems to get joy from having a chance to victimize her attacker, but it is not the uncomplicated revenge of having the tables turned. Most curious of all is her retort "not this time." The attack incites a kind of passion in her; her diction implies that she desires sexual fulfillment in the form of a power struggle—not "not this way" but "not this time." The suggestion that Adela imagines Aziz as her rapist because she desires him, or because he desires sexual experience, which Levine dismisses, seems more plausible and interesting here than in the final version (91).

The moments before and after the ellipsis are revealed to us, but what happens *during* the suspended moment? The ellipsis marks the termination of Adela's rapid train of thought: it is her substitution for saying the word "raped," which she cannot articulate. "She understood—it was to be passed once round her neck, she was to be throttled as far as necessary, and then ..." (242). The ellipsis also marks the temporal lull between the aggressive fury against Adela and her furious defense. Most importantly, it exists as a suspended moment, unseen by the reader. As such it is a type for the entire scene, which is excised in the final draft, and for Forster's method in creating this scene in the final version.[3]

This draft raises several questions which it leaves unsolved. Even here we do not know for certain who Adela's attacker is, though it is quite clear she is attacked. We make the unquestioned connection between the pronoun "he" and Adela's assumption that Aziz is the "extra darkness" which follows her into the cave. But the narrator neither confirms nor denies our suspicions, and Forster breaks off this draft too quickly for us to sense his intentions. The enigmatic reply "not this time" muddies our sense of what

Adela fears and wants in this scene. She does not seem to be an entirely innocent victim; we might even (ungenerously) interpret these words to mean that she is asking to be raped at another time. At the least, Adela's statement shows she wants to fend off danger for the present; but the phrase reverberates in a weird way, and we cannot dismiss the sense that whatever the danger is, it remains both threatening and inviting.

But however troubling these questions, Forster rejects the early version because it solves too many tactical questions, and radically limits the interpretations of what happens to Adela in the cave. The draft offers the reader neither momentary nor permanent suspense. In contrast, the final version gives us both: the shift from Adela's point of view to Aziz's at this moment ("... thinking damn the English even at their best, he plunged into one [of the caves] ... to recover his balance" [144]) affords Forster the momentary suspense of Adela's return to Chandrapore without informing Aziz or Fielding, or for that matter the reader, of her accusations against Aziz. And it produces a more lasting suspension of understanding.

The final version creates a strategy which gives Aziz's arrest at the railroad station more dramatic force, while assuring the reader of his innocence; after all, we provide his alibi, being in the cave with him at the moment of supposed attack. But the more abstract outcome of the change in draft is that the central event remains "impermanent." Unseen by Fielding and Aziz, not directly reported by Adela (who is spirited away until the trial scene, when she repudiates her accusation against Aziz), the moment is left obscure. Though we know Aziz does not rape Adela, we never know with certainty what happened to her.

In abandoning the draft version of the attack, Forster empties his central scene of causality and point of view: what happens in the caves remains a cipher for all the characters. Our only witnesses are impaired—either close but not actually present (like Aziz), or incapable of articulation (like Adela). Thus Adela's experience in the cave in the final version, and its potential meaning, become a kind of metaphorical extension of Adela's strangled silence and the ellipsis in the earlier draft. It is open to us only through surmise, through Mrs. Moore's experience of the first cave (which may not be identical to Adela's) and Adela's strong but inexpressible sense of an "echo" or "living at half pressure" which persists in her mind. In the earlier draft Forster dubs his character Edith, a sensible if unglamorous Anglo-Saxon name. In the final version she has become Adela, from the Greek meaning unclear or "not manifest." The change reflects Forster's systematic recasting of the manuscript so as to increase the enigmatic texture of the novel, and so of his moral world.

The Ambiguous Genre

Because the subject of marriage is presented early in the novel as a central problem in Indian as well as Anglo-Indian life, we are lulled into a sense that *A Passage to India* will be a social comedy, a domestic novel of small entanglements.[4] The familiar resonance of the opening chapters, with their setting in the club and the parlor, encourage our impression that the world of India is essentially tame and knowable. The Indians cherish Victorian England and lament its decline, worry about proper matches for their friends and the social standing of their relations, gather together for the equivalent of a cigar at a men's club (the women being in purdah). We are drawn into the Moslem culture of Chandrapore, and despite its characteristic details, it seems no more exotic or alien than, say, the situations of the Bennet family in *Pride and Prejudice*.

From the outset, however, we are given evidence which belies our equation of India with the bright and narrow world of social comedy. The novel refuses to be bound. Just as Mrs. Moore is stifled and bored by the company at the Club and walks from the compound to the Mosque, so the focus of the novel moves restlessly away from the familial and the familiar. The settings shift from interior scenes to include the great arch of the sky, the river below, the distant hills, and the world of the novel moves from a neat circle of humans to a wilderness of mysterious creatures who live on, unseen or unidentified, in the dark. The scenes, comprised mainly of dialogue, celebrate human activity—conversation, wit, friendship. But they are set beside soliloquies of a distant and jaded narrator who sees Chandrapore as a world where the human is debased, unrecognizable, where the "inhabitants" are indistinguishable from "the excrescence of the soil" (2). Even the institution of marriage, which first served to shape our sense of the ready boundaries of the novel's genre, becomes a part of the unsettling of them. Forster's characters themselves undercut the celebratory connotations of the theme of marriage. In the face of this chaotic and mysterious world, they begin to see marriage as a mere ritual, a form applied like a cloak to cover our vast misunderstandings of ourselves. Well before her visit to the caves Mrs. Moore

> felt increasingly (vision or nightmare?) that, though people are important, the relations between them are not, and that in particular too much fuss has been made over marriage; centuries of carnal embracement, yet man is no nearer to understanding man. (127)

The uncertainty of the literary genre of *A Passage to India* is tied to our uncertainty about its moral world. Social comedy is too restrictive a literary label for what happens to Forster's characters: it excludes the wide world of India, much as the clergymen Mr. Sorley and Mr. Greysford's theology excludes Indian creatures from their heaven. Such work is impracticable but not entirely irrelevant, for unless we define boundaries we become lost in chaos. The "essential life" of this novel (to use Mrs. Moore's phrase) resides partly in the sense of security of its apparent genre. When Mrs. Moore is pressed into a reconsideration of the tone of her meeting with Aziz, she wants to find out "whose impression was correct," hers or her son's.

> Yes, it could be worked into quite an unpleasant scene.... Yes it was all true, but how false as a summary of the man; the essential life of him had been slain. (28)

Mrs. Moore chooses between alternatives, but we are not afforded such a clearcut choice. Mistaking the novel's genre, or not being able to grasp it, makes our task harder. If not social comedy, what? The genre of *A Passage to India* is disturbingly protean. Forster manipulates our expectations of genre in several ways, and if the novel were frozen at certain key scenes we would be convinced of its incontrovertible form as a melodrama, a detective story, a tale of the occult, a religious meditation, or a polemic against imperialism. The most primitive and shocking method of disrupting the reader's secure sense of the novel's world is to kill off a principal character unexpectedly. So the death of Gino's baby turns *Where Angels Fear to Tread* from a social comedy into a morality play; so Gerald's death moves *The Longest Journey* from the contemplative setting of the suite of rooms at Cambridge out into a riskier, less forgiving world. In *Howards End*, Margaret Schlegel steps into Mrs. Wilcox's place upon her death, not so much by marrying her widower as by accepting the spiritual responsibility which she feels is Mrs. Wilcox's intangible legacy. Each of the sudden deaths is shocking because it upsets our sense of the plot of the novel; sudden death in Forster's fiction seems divorced from causality, just as it does in life.[5] But more importantly, in the later novels, especially his last, Forster presents the news of death in so casual and so anticlimactic a tone as to leave us convinced of the indifference of nature and even of the narrator. Mrs. Moore withdraws from participation in the society of Chandrapore after the dissolution of her beliefs in the cave. The narrator describes her state flatly, in bureaucratic language, without the warmth which would give us a sense of his empathy or understanding:

> She had come to that state where the horror of the universe and its smallness are both visible at the same time—the twilight of the double vision in which so many elderly people are involved. (197)

Withdrawn from the action of the novel by her intense alienation, Mrs. Moore is absent from the trial. We learn of her death peripherally, through Fielding's reference about Ronny after the trial:

> Heaslop doesn't come out badly. Besides, Fate has treated him pretty roughly today. He has had a cable to the effect that his mother's dead, poor old soul. (234)

Distilled into the Hindu goddess Esmiss Esmoor, Mrs. Moore has become compressed into an image which other characters invoke to confirm their own sense of morality. The tragic resonance of her death is denied, both by her absence from the trial (when her name is introduced as a potential corroborative witness for Aziz, she is already dead) and by her greater irrelevance to the action of the story. Lionel Trilling has written that Forster is "always shocking us by removing the heroism of his heroes and heroines" (17); here he deflates our expectations of her special power by denying her death heroic significance.

The questions which have evoked the most interest among scholars are grounded in the novel's protean genre and the difficult and often contradictory expectations it places on the reader. The political divisiveness of India and the compelling depiction of the Anglo-Indian occupation have led more than one reader, especially Forster's contemporaries, to a reading of *A Passage to India* as a political treatise, and indictment of the Raj and of imperialism generally. As late as 1943, Lionel Trilling felt compelled to assert the novel's wider concerns: "Great as the problem of India is, Forster's book is not about India alone; it is about all of human life" (161). But the behavior of the British is a comparatively obvious target for satire, and the novel lacks the necessary didacticism to confirm this view. With the release of India from the British Empire, readings of *A Passage to India* as an attack on the British waned. More recent readings, and more compelling ones, center on the politics of the novel in the word's widest sense; Frederick Crews, for example, reads India as a figure for a greater incomprehensibility:

> The image of India as a whole is more important than any of the figures, English or Indian, who move across it. To understand India is to understand the rationale of the whole creation; but the characters do not understand it, and Forster's plot makes us ask

whether human faculties are capable of such understanding at all.
(144)

The third section, "Temple," raises particular questions of genre. Far shorter than the other two sections of the novel, set "some hundreds of miles westward" of the Marabar Hills and two years later in time than the preceding action, "Temple" seems to stand apart from the rest of the novel. Readers have tried to come to terms with it either as an integrated part of the action or as a coda.[6]

Perhaps the best way to see how the "Temple" section renews our uncertainty about genre is to ask what kind of novel *A Passage to India* would be if it ended after the "Caves" section. Like the completed novel, it would end with Aziz and Fielding parting on terms of mixed sympathy and understanding; for immediately after the trial Aziz suspects Fielding's motives in mediating against punitive damages from Adela.

But the "Caves" section ends with Fielding's rational view uppermost. We are instilled with a sense of proper Anglo-Indian proportion as we follow him in his journey toward a more familiar landscape:

> In the old undergraduate days he had wrapped himself up in the many-colored blanket of St. Mark's, but something more precious than marbles and mosaics was offered to him now: the harmony between the works of man and the earth that upholds them, the civilization that has escaped muddle, the spirit in a reasonable form, with flesh and blood subsisting. Writing picture-postcards to his Indian friends, he felt that all of them would miss the joys he experienced now, the joys of form, and that this constituted a serious barrier.... the Mediterranean is the human norm.[7]

As he retreats from India toward the more "harmonious" Venice, Fielding demonstrates a narrow ethnocentrism; he upholds a human norm which is Western in its orientation, and which is confused (perhaps shattered) by the alien and unrestrained ceremony of Gokul Ashtami in the "Temple" section.

Moreover, in this truncated version, the centerpiece of the novel would be Aziz's trial, with its elements of suspense, melodrama, and final resolution. After the trial, the novel contracts briefly. It seems to return to the world of the first chapters, where human institutions such as marriage and the law are capable of solving monstrous and untenable problems. Aziz's turning away from the experience of the trial, and his rejection of Western medicine, so essential to our sense of the untidiness of Forster's world, are introduced in the third section. Its inclusion denies us a "sense of proportion," which Fielding values and Aziz spurns; it also dwarfs Fielding's sense that "the Mediterranean is the human norm." Though to Western sensibilities justice prevails through Adela Quested's great personal courage and the staunch application of law in section two, the predictable resolution of melodrama evaporates in the final section.

What to make of Mrs. Moore's transcendent, almost occult knowledge of events she does not witness, which so irritated F. R. Leavis, among others, is also related to our unsettled sense of genre. The pattern of genre in *A Passage to India* is not presented as a dialectic—either comedy or tragedy, either fantastic or realistic, for example. Rather, we are turned back into a world which cannot be categorized, where intimations of interpretative wholeness are subverted once again.

Conclusion

I began with a passage which suggests a dialogue between art and life, a process which puts the reader, as interactor with the text and actor in the world, under particular pressures. Forster's calculated ambiguities in *A Passage to India* create a complex moral world for readers, by displacing them from a comfortable vantage point from which they might comprehend the novel. Like Emily Dickinson, Forster sees the promise of a completed, coherent experience as more gratifying than unity itself. He recognizes that to posit a monolithic "experience" is an act of narrative imperialism, a silencing of other sometimes chaotic ways of seeing. (Forster seems prophetic, since he arranges these other experiences along lines culturally divided, like gender, race, religion, and class.) Even as he addresses an audience of Western sensibilities, the echo of India's conflicting ways of seeing persists in the novel.

Forster is quick to undercut the reader's sense of becoming settled, and best at shaking us when we feel most complacent. Fielding's self-satisfied turn from India, his relief at seeing the Mediterranean, is revealed to us as a profound measure of his psychic limitation. To talk of the "norm," especially just before the mysterious and chaotic festival in "Temple," is especially shallow. How different a novel it would be if Fielding got the last word.

To assert multiple voices, different modes of experience, is not to deny or denigrate our natural yearning for unity. Rather, Forster's novel depends on the reader's persistent desire for "permanence." But it carefully balances our cultural bias against a world seen whole, in all its raggedness. After the incident in the caves, Godbole's mysticism is contrasted with both British empiricism, and Aziz and Fielding's exalted value of human relations. Godbole's philosophy, unlike the ridiculous categorization of Sorley and Greysford, draws no distinctions at all: it is a parody of Western premises about causality and responsibility,

> "I am informed that an evil action was performed in the Marabar Hills, and that a highly esteemed English lady is seriously ill in consequence. My answer is this: that the action was performed by Dr. Aziz." He stopped and sucked in his thin cheeks. "It was performed by the guide." He stopped again, "it was performed by you." Now he had an air of daring and of coyness. "It was performed by me." He looked shyly down the sleeve of his own coat. "And by my students. It was even performed by the lady herself. When evil occurs, it expresses the whole of the universe. Similarly when good occurs." (168–9)

Godbole's answer to Fielding is foreign to Westerners; it reminds us that both characters and readers, even perhaps Forster himself, are at a loss when human action is described in these terms. Godbole's analysis is disproportionate to our needs—the need of Fielding to know simply what Godbole thinks, the need to recognize Aziz's desperate situation, the need to believe in human justice. He defines the point at which our need for a sense of unity, of an encompassing interpretation of what happened in the cave, collides with our need for humanity. Even Forster professes his own feeling of bewilderment in an essay on "The Gods of India":

> Guidance there is [in Hinduism], but not toward a goal that has ever seemed important to a Westerner ... The Hindu is concerned not with conduct, but with vision. (220, 222)[8]

Ambiguity is a protective stance for Forster, not so much because he is afraid of certainty, it seems to me, but because he recognizes how much experience one person's certainty excludes. As a closeted homosexual, Forster existed in public guise as a King's College novelist and genial spokesman for tolerance, and in private as a man whose sexuality, unrepressed and undisguised, might land him in prison. Like many of his not overtly homosexual fictions, *A Passage to India* figures Forster's unity in essentially androcentric terms: the desperate embrace between Aziz and Fielding at the end demonstrates their most passionate, and most unattainable, love. That the reader's comfortable experience of centrality be continually displaced is the object of his fiction: the method of *A Passage to India* embodies its moral message.

NOTES

1. Feminist criticism, of course, is an exception to this rather crude rule. While there is little feminist criticism of Forster now published, feminism is a fruitful avenue to pursue in Forster's work. See Holly Stave's "Writing as Woman: *Howards End* and the Privileging of the Marginalized," unpublished paper.

I am grateful to Martin Price, who shepherded my writing with dedication and good humor, and to Daniel Schwarz, and my colleagues in the National Endowment for the Humanities 1988 Summer Seminar on "Critical Perspectives on the Early Modern British Novel" for their suggested revisions and advice.

2. Where the drafts of *A Passage to India* are especially rough—where, for example, Forster includes several alternative phrasings, or stricken words—I have smoothed the flow of the passage by using Forster's preferred phrase, rather than distracting the reader with manuscript clutter. I have not altered the sense of the draft.

3. In a letter to William Plomer (September 28, 1934) Forster describes his dissatisfaction with the ambiguity of the novel:

What seems to [be] not satisfactory in [*The Invaders*, Plomer's 1934 novel] is a thing which I find wrong in A Passage to India. [No underscoring] I tried to show that India is an unexplainable muddle by introducing an unexplained muddle—Miss Quested's experience in the cave. When asked what happened there, *I don't know.*

This letter confirms Forster's design of ambiguity, and refutes the critical assumption that he was being coy or evasive in his revisions. *Selected Letters*, Vol. 2, 125–126.

4. Forster used the phrase "Anglo-Indian" to describe the English who lived in India during the Raj; though it more commonly refers to persons of mixed English and Indian descent, I use Forster's meaning.

5. In *Aspects of the Novel*, Forster differentiates between narratives which have "an emphasis on causality" and those which do not.

Let us define a plot. We have defined a story as a narrative of events arranged in their time sequence. A plot is also a narrative of events, the emphasis falling on causality. "The king died and then the queen died" is a story. "The king died and then the queen died of grief" is a plot. (*Aspects*, 60)

We should notice that Forster does not arrange these narrative types hierarchically. The sudden deaths of characters in Forster's novels often give readers the sense of an indifferent narrator or an incompletely defined causality: they turn the genre (in Forster's terms) from a plot to a story.

6. See Crews and Allen for representative discussions.

7. For a valuable discussion of the narrator's ethnocentrism and other aspects of the character of the narrator, see Barbara Rosecrance.

8. Note how far Forster has come from his initial intentions in the early draft, when Aziz (presumably) did rape Adela. Godbole's diffuse sense of responsibility creates what Martin Price calls "the stupefying vision of unity ... The final anti-climax, the all but simpering gestures, the single-minded reductivism—all of these become near-farcical attributes of the proponent of unity," 619. For a quite different view of Godbole's role, see David Shusterman.

Works Cited

Allen, Glen O. "Structure, Symbol and Theme in *A Passage to India.*" *PMLA* 70 (1955): 934–54.

Crews, Frederick. *E. M. Forster: The Perils of Humanism.* Princeton: Princeton University Press, 1962.

Forster, E. M. *Aspects of the Novel.* Ed. Oliver Stallybrass. The Abinger Edition Series, Vol. 13. London: Edward Arnold, 1974.

———. *Commonplace Book,* Ed. Philip Gardner. Stanford: Stanford University Press, 1985.

———. "The Gods of India" (1914) in *Albergo Empedocle and Other Writings.* Ed. George H. Thomson. New York: Liveright, 1971.

———. *The Manuscripts of A Passage to India.* Ed. Oliver Stallybrass. The Abinger Edition Series, Vol. 6a. London: Edward Arnold, 1978.

———. "On Tolerance," in *Two Cheers for Democracy.* Ed. Oliver Stallybrass. The Abinger Edition Series, Vol. 7. London: Edward Arnold, 1972.

———. *A Passage to India.* Ed. Oliver Stallybrass. The Abinger Edition Series, Vol. 6. London: Edward Arnold, 1987.

Furbank, P. N. *E. M. Forster: A Life.* New York: Harcourt, Brace, Jovanovich, 1981.

———, and R. J. M. Haskell. "The Art of Fiction." *Paris Review* 1 (1953): 29–41.

Lago, Mary and P. N. Furbank, eds. *Selected Letters of E.M. Forster.* Cambridge: Belknap Press, 1985.

Leavis, F. R. "E. M. Forster" in *The Common Pursuit.* London: Chatto and Windus, 1962.

Levine, June Perry. *Creation and Criticism: A Passage to India.* University of Nebraska Press. 1971.

Price, Martin. "People of the Book: Character in Forster's *A Passage to India.*" *Critical Inquiry* 1:3 (1975): 605–622.

Rosecrance, Barbara. *Forster's Narrative Vision.* Ithaca: Cornell University Press, 1982.

Shusterman, David. "The Curious Case of Professor Godbole: *A Passage to India* Reexamined." *PMLA* 77 (1961): 426–435.

Stave, Holly. "Writing as Woman: *Howards End* and the Privileging of the Marginalized." NEH Summer Seminar. 1988.

Trilling, Lionel. *E. M. Forster.* New York: New Directions, 1943.

WILFRID R. KOPONEN

Krishna at the Garden Party:
Crises of Faith in A Passage to India

E. M. Forster undermines public school notions of friendship, love, and civility in *A Passage to India*. Romantic love, God's love, and friendship are exposed as futile. Adela Quested cannot love. Mrs. Moore's Clapham-style Christianity fails her. Aziz's belief in friendship shatters. Godbole's Hinduism remains intact, but only to debunk Christianity and Islam.[1]

The novel's key event is the outing to the imageless caves in the Marabar Hills, where Adela Quested, Aziz, and Mrs. Moore encounter the failure of what they most cherish. Words there turn into a booming echo, which unhinges Mrs. Moore "began ... to undermine her hold on life."[2] Mrs. Moore, who arrived in India confident of her beliefs, becomes frail and bitter, and never returns alive to England. The echo leads Adela Quested to nervous collapse. Briefly the object of British sympathy, she finds herself an outcast and her engagement broken. Aziz comes to despise the British, who victimize him.

The Marabar Caves, where the hysteria begins, are established in the opening and closing sentences of the first chapter. The landscape carries a weighty, enigmatic, symbolic content. Barbara Rosecrance notes it suggests a "bleak picture of human incapacity."[3] Sara Suleri says that Forster "constructs a symbolic geography that provides Western narrative with ... the figure of India as a hollow, or a cave."[4] G.K. Das sees the influence of Hindu

From *The International Fiction Review* 20, no. 1. © 1993 by the International Fiction Association.

mythology in the landscape "as living spirits having supernatural powers."[5] Benita Parry notes that "the concepts of the major Indian cosmologies are objectified in the landscape."[6]

The caves epitomize the great age of India and its invaders' inability to force it to conform to their beliefs: "even Buddha ... shunned a renunciation more complete than his own, and has left no legend of struggle or victory in the Marabar.... nothing attaches to [the caves], and their reputation... does not depend upon human speech" (*Passage* 124). Chaman L. Sahni observes that the Barabar caves, Forster's model for the Marabar caves, "were for centuries occupied by Brahmanical ascetics."[7] Forster admitted the Barabar caves were ornamented,[8] but for his purposes they would have to be empty and imageless. They undermine the meaning of forms, images, and words. The Marabar Hills are said to be "older than anything in the world," predating even "the arrival of the gods" (*Passage* 123, 125). The Barabar Hills do predate the Himalayas (Sahni 107). As the Creation Hymn of the *Rg Veda* says, "The gods themselves are later than creation."[9] The caves thus evoke the cosmic egg (Sahni 114), the "womb of the universe,"[10] or the primal chaos, when "The earth was without form and void, and darkness was upon the face of the deep" (Genesis 1:2).[11] The *Rg Veda* says, "At first there was only darkness wrapped in darkness."[12]

The Caves are indifferent to good and evil; if "excavated, nothing, nothing would be added to the sum of good or evil" (*Passage* 125). They seem morally neutral, but Forster likens them to the "Ancient Night" (*Passage* 76), evil itself. Mrs. Moore mirrors this ambivalence. At first, she thinks, "Nothing evil had been in the cave" (*Passage* 148), but later the echo gathers momentum, with "evil propagating in every direction" (*Passage* 187), hence the question: "What had spoken to her in that scoured-out cavity of the granite? ... the undying worm itself" (*Passage* 208), a name for Satan in Isaiah 66:24 and Mark 9:48. As a Christian, Mrs. Moore recoils from it, though in traditional Indian symbolism the snake represents reincarnation, its coils the web of *samsara*, and, if biting its tail, eternity (Sahni 126).

The outing to the caves becomes a muddle from the moment of the invitation, despite Aziz's assurances: "'I like mysteries, but I rather dislike muddles,' said Mrs. Moore.... [Fielding:] '... India's a muddle.' / 'India's—Oh what an alarming idea!' / 'There'll be no muddle when you come to see me,' said Aziz" (*Passage* 69). Aziz issues the invitation on impulse, knowing little about the caves. Professor Godbole tells Aziz, "'There are no sculptures at Marabar.' / 'They are immensely holy, no doubt,' said Aziz, to help on the narrative. / 'Oh no, oh no.' / 'Still, they are ornamented in some way.' / 'Oh, no.' / '... We all talk of the famous Marabar Caves. Perhaps that is our empty brag'" (*Passage* 75). Aziz, naming this an "empty brag," reveals words can be hollow; the supposed union between words and their referents may fail. His discomfort with the *Via Negativa* is shared by the Englishwomen, who are unprepared for the "spiritual silence" (*Passage* 140) they encounter en route to the caves. They hardly see the "pure space of the cave" as Brahman, as a Vedantist might (Sahni 120). They "wished the place could have turned into some Mohammedan object ... which their host would have appreciated and explained" (*Passage* 141). Aziz is at a loss for words.

The participants find the absence of what they wish to find. Instead of finding holiness, they confront evil; wishing for something picturesque, they find emptiness; rather than spaciousness, they are pressed against the crush of servants; they smell not incense but the stench of the unwashed. Instead of meaning, they find meaninglessness, not merely the absence of words, but an echo that undermines the meaning of all words. This is reflected in Forster's syntax. Gillian Beer notes, "Negative sentence structures, together with the words 'no,' 'not,' 'never' and in particular 'nothing' predominate."[13] Molly B. Tinsley observes that "Forster's sentences ... fight closure as consistently as they undermine climax."[14] All are unprepared: "They awaited the miracle. But at the supreme moment ... nothing occurred ... and a profound disappointment entered with the morning breeze. Why, when the chamber was prepared, did the bridegroom not enter ... as humanity expects?" (*Passage* 137). Here Forster alludes to the parable of the wise and foolish maidens who go "to meet the bridegroom," who is delayed, and thus hear the cry at an unexpected hour, after they have fallen asleep (Matthew 25:1–13, RSV). Mrs. Moore has learned "that life never gives us what we want at the moment that we consider appropriate. Adventures do occur, but not punctually" (*Passage* 25).

Aziz, the outing's host, expects triumph, but is humiliated. He treasures hospitality, and spares no expense to reveal "true courtesy—the civil deed that shows the good heart" (*Passage* 60), like Muslims he reveres. He claims, "This picnic has nothing to do with English or Indian; it is an expedition of friends" (*Passage* 161). Yet he wins no kudos for his hospitality. Aziz is arrested for accosting Miss Quested in a cave and thrown in jail. He becomes convinced that friendship is impossible with the English until they leave India.

Kindness and pleasantness are ideals held by Mrs. Moore and Aziz. Both see in the other a kindred soul. Mrs. Moore says, "Aziz is my real friend" (*Passage* 97) and Aziz tells Mrs. Moore's son Ralph, "Your mother was my best friend" (*Passage* 312). Aziz treasures Mrs. Moore as a friend, even though the Marabar, their final meeting, is only their third. For Aziz, "What did this eternal goodness of Mrs. Moore amount to? ... She had not borne witness in his favour, nor visited him in the prison, yet ... he always adored her" (*Passage* 312). Mrs. Moore, "As 'Esmiss Esmoor' becomes a Hindu goddess."[15] Even readers ascribe great qualities to her: Harold Bloom sees her as "the Alexandrian figure of Wisdom, the Sophia."[16]

Friendship is advanced more than marriage by Aziz and others. Mrs. Moore grows tired of love and marriage, as is evident in this narrated monologue: "The unspeakable attempt [of Aziz's supposed attack] presented itself to her as love: in a cave, in a church—Boum, it amount to the same" (*Passage* 208).Though jaded about marriage, Mrs. Moore regards Aziz as her friend. Aziz views friendship as sacred: "The Friend: a Persian expression for God" (*Passage* 277). Yet friendships in the novel are undermined by betrayal, often due to the disdain of members of the British Raj for Indians, widespread prior to World War I. Adela asks the Collector, Mr. Turton, to meet "those Indians whom you come across socially—as your friends," only to be told, "Well, we don't come across them socially" (*Passage* 28). Indians share these reservations. Aziz finds Hamidullah's guests discussing "whether or no it is possible to be friends with an Englishman" (*Passage* 10). Yet the most significant friendships in the novel are those between Mrs. Moore and Aziz and between Aziz and Fielding; that is, between an Indian and an Englishwoman, and between an Indian and an Englishman. Aziz waxes eloquent about friendship, yet after his trial he concludes that he and Fielding cannot be friends until the Indians have driven "every blasted Englishman into the sea" (*Passage* 322). Once Aziz feels "genuine hatred of the English" he thinks (in quoted monologue), "I am an Indian at last" (*Passage* 293), completing his own passage to India. He tells Fielding, "My heart is for my own people" (*Passage* 302). Yet as Rustom Bharucha comments, the separation between Aziz and Fielding "in the final moments of *A Passage to India* ... is so subtly juxtaposed with intimacy that one might say that Aziz and Fielding have acquired a mutual understanding."[17]

Most of the British long in India avoid friendships like Aziz and Mrs. Moore's, though Forster wrote, "What is good in people ... [is] their belief in friendship and loyalty for their own sakes."[18] Even Forster admitted, though, that "they are not enough" to withstand politics.[19] Most of the British sacrifice friendship with Indians to show unity when facing the natives collectively. They are scandalized when Fielding breaks ranks to side with Aziz. The British maintain unity to preserve their superiority, leaving behind Christian notions of loving-kindness to become as gods: "A community that bows the knee to a viceroy and believes that the divinity that hedges a king can be transplanted, must feel some reverence for any viceregal substitute. At Chandrapore, the Turtons were little gods" (*Passage* 28). Ronny Heaslop exemplifies this utilitarian religion his Mother detests; Mrs. Moore asserts, "Englishmen like posing as gods" (*Passage* 50). Ronny tells her, "we're not out here for the purpose of behaving pleasantly" (*Passage* 49). He upholds a nationalistic civil religion, as when the Anthem of the Army of Occupation is played at the Club: "The meagre tune, the curt series of demands on Jehovah, fused into a prayer unknown in England" (*Passage* 26). Mrs. Moore insists: "The English are out here to be pleasant.... God ... is ... love" (*Passage* 51). The words "God is love" reappear in the Hindu ceremony as "God si Love" (*Passage* 285, 289), enthusiastically if uncomprehendingly embraced by Hindus.

Hindus delight in the words "God si Love," but Heaslop is not amused. "Ronny approved of religion as long as it endorsed the National Anthem, but he objected when it attempted to influence his life" (*Passage* 52). Ronny views his mother as a harmless fool. But McBryde, the District Superintendent of Police, views Fielding as a traitor for aiding Aziz. McBryde tells Fielding that the Bengal Mutiny "should be your Bible in this country" (*Passage* 169).

Given the secularized religion of the British, Forster's allusions to the Bible and the *Book of Common Prayer* become ironic echoes. Judith Herz finds in the language in this novel "a sign system adrift from its signifieds."[20] Thus when Mrs. Moore first alludes to 1 Corinthians 13:1, "Though I speak with the tongues of men and angels, but have not love, I am a noisy gong or a clanging symbol" (*Passage* 52), a paean to love, she is confident that "the desire to behave pleasantly satisfies God" (*Passage* 52), though her son demurs. She fails to realize that "behaving pleasantly" is only a dim echo of "having love." She is like the "clanging cymbal" Paul belittles. Mrs. Moore's confidence rests upon an echo of St. Paul. When these words from Corinthians recur after Mrs. Moore's terror in the cave, her faith is gone. She "has moved closer and closer to Indian ways of feeling."[21] At "the edge of her mind, Religion appeared, poor little talkative Christianity, and she knew that all its divine words from 'Let there be light' to 'It is finished' only amounted to 'boum.' Then she was terrified" (*Passage* 150). "The novel ... discards Christianity ... firmly," Das insists.[22] Forster himself "lost his faith completely" at Cambridge and wrote, "I cannot believe that Christianity will ever cope with the present worldwide mess."[23]

Mrs. Moore's belief in pleasantness does not prepare her for India, where her faith collapses. She hears the echo as "boum," the sound of negation, not as "aum," the hum pervading the created universe. She grows feeble and dies. Her Christianity breaks down before the excursion. We learn that Mrs. Moore "found [God] increasingly difficult to avoid as she grew older ... though oddly he satisfied her less.... Outside the arch there seemed always another arch, beyond the remotest echo a silence" (*Passage* 52). Thus while asserting "God ... is ... love" (*Passage* 51), she hesitates, an equivocation Forster suggests via the ellipses. This collapse of her faith surfaces after she hears Godbole's song about "the desired spiritual union between Krishna and His *gopis*," suggesting "a religious devotee's complete self-surrender to God."[24] The song puzzles the English, particularly Mrs. Moore, to whom Godbole explains that his is "a religious song. I place myself in the position of a milkmaiden. I say to Sri Krishna, 'Come! Come to me only.' The god refuses to come.... This is repeated several times.... / 'But He comes in some other song, I hope?' said Mrs. Moore gently. / 'Oh no, he refuses to come,' repeated Godbole" (*Passage* 80). The milkmaiden's song foreshadows the disastrous outing and Adela and Ronny's failed love. It hints of the failure of Mrs. Moore's passage to India in order to see Heaslop joined to Miss Quested in marital union, a union that never occurs.

Mrs. Moore's Christian beliefs appear unassailable in her first encounter with Aziz, in the mosque. She asserts, "God is here" (*Passage* 20), a belief she cannot sustain in the Marabar caves, where she enters "a spiritual muddledom ... for which no high-sounding words can be found" (*Passage* 208). If one acknowledges that Aziz's belief in friendship is religious, then the religious beliefs of all who join in the outing are dashed by the Marabar. Only two fail to come in time to get on the train: Fielding, "a blank, frank atheist" (*Passage* 255) and Godbole, who does cope with the effects of the caves.

Godbole achieves an equivocal and subtle union with God. Forster suggests through Godbole that "Hinduism is more open to certain kinds of experience than is Christianity or Islam."[25] Forster "identifies himself wholly with Godbole," insists John Drew, who also finds that Godbole owes much to Forster's reading of the Neo-Platonic *Enneads* of Plotinus,[26] a view also advanced by Harold Bloom.[27] But Godbole's Hindu philosophy eludes his listeners. He clarifies: "Good and evil are different, as their names imply. But ... they are both of them aspects of my Lord. He is present in the one, absent in the other, and the difference between presence and absence is great.... Yet absence implies presence, absence is not non-existence, and we are therefore entitled to repeat, 'Come, come, come, come...'" (*Passage* 178). Frederick P.W. McDowell states that "Godbole's Hinduism takes us beyond good and evil to a cosmic force more often passive than positive and always unpredictable."[28] Is Godbole the incarnation of profound wisdom, or merely aloof and unfeeling? Godbole is at ease with absences. As Gillian Beer reminds us, this is "a book about gaps, fissures, absences, and exclusions."[29] In the ritual of the birth of Krishna, Godbole is said to be "in the presence of God" (*Passage* 283), although his understanding of this is paradoxical. Forster noted that "the Hindu festival represents the same thing as the scene in the cave 'turned inside out'" (Sahni 141), but he refused to state what happened in the cave. He claimed he did not know. Godbole refrains from expressing ultimate values directly in words. As one who has studied the

Upanishads, like the *Kena Upanishad* he might exhort: "That which cannot be expressed by speech, but by which speech is expressed—That alone know as Brahman."[30]

Godbole's facility for embracing paradox leaves him relatively unscathed by the Marabar. Rosecrance sees "the affirmation embodied in the Krishna ceremony" and its embracing of contingency as the opposite of "Mrs. Moore's nihilistic vision," but avers that Forster pulls back from Godbole by making his detachment unappealing.[31] Das contrarily implies that Godbole's participation in the Krishna ritual makes him appealing, for Das says that Forster sees the Krishna myth "as an embodiment of the Hindu vision of complete being."[32] Godbole himself, though detached, believes all is interconnected. Godbole says to Fielding, "'Nothing can be performed in isolation.... I am informed that an evil action was performed in the Marabar Hills ... [T]hat action was performed by Dr. Aziz.... It was performed by the guide .... It was performed by you.... It was performed by me.... It was even performed by the lady herself. When evil occurs, it expresses the whole of the universe. Similarly when good occurs'" (*Passage* 177–78). Godbole may grasp unity, but he is aloof from friendship and affection. Fielding talks about traveling light but befriends Aziz and marries Stella Moore. Godbole travels light and avoids all messy entanglements.

Aziz loves his connection with others, though the outing tests this. Aziz turns within and emerges a strong Muslim. Though he moves to a Hindu state, "he had no religious curiosity, and had never discovered the meaning of this annual antic" (*Passage* 291–92) of the celebration of Krishna's birth, a key Hindu festival. Likewise, his view of friendship contracts as he recognizes the pitfalls of associating with the English. Still valuing friendship, he expects less. Yet his dream of a unified, non-British India admits a fusion of Hindu and Muslim. Forster notes Muslim saints have been adopted by Hindus, and a Muslim poem absorbs "the call to Krishna." Aziz embraces the insights of Ghalib's poem, which he recited prior to the Marabar fiasco, a poem "less explicit than the call to Krishna," but which "voiced our loneliness nevertheless ... our need for the Friend who never comes yet is not entirely disproved" (*Passage* 106).

Union in friendship remains a chimera. Friends promise yet fail to come. Fielding promises Aziz, "We're coming to McBryde together," but "Aziz went on to prison alone" (*Passage* 162); later, after the trial, Aziz cries out: "Cyril, Cyril, don't leave me." Fielding promises, "I'm coming back" (*Passage* 232), but does not, causing Aziz to lament, "Cyril, again you desert" (*Passage* 235). Adela asks regarding her trial, "Can Mrs. Moore be with me?" Ronny says "Certainly" (*Passage* 195), but she does not come.

Adela is incapable of friendship. At the "bridge" party held in her honor, "friendly Indians were before her, and she tried to make them talk, but she failed" (*Passage* 43). The English are stirred by the violated feminine purity Adela represents, but fail to warm to her personally. Aziz finds coldness Adela's major shortcoming. Adela admits to Fielding that she tried to make "tenderness, respect and personal intercourse" take the place of love in her engagement (*Passage* 263). Fielding tells her, "'You have no real affection for Aziz, or Indians generally'" (*Passage* 259), to which Adela assents. Adela is Mrs. Moore's foil. Mahmoud Ali says, "Mrs. Moore ... was poor Indians' friend" (*Passage* 224). Indians warm to Mrs. Moore but are repelled by Adela's coldness; even her scrupulous honesty, which causes the British other than Fielding to abandon her, is rejected: "Her behaviour rested on cold justice and honesty; she had felt, while she recanted, no passion of love for those whom she had wronged. Truth is not truth in that exacting land unless there go with it kindness ... unless the Word that was with God also is God" (*Passage* 245). As we have seen, curious things happen to words under the influence of the Marabar. The above sentence alludes to the opening verse of the Gospel: "In the beginning was the Word, and the Word was with God, and the Word was God" (John 1:1, RSV), and possibly to heat and desire in the Creation Hymn of the *Rg Veda*: "That One which came to be, enclosed in nothing, / arose at last, born of the power of heat. / In the beginning desire descended on it."[33] Adela lacks such heat and desire.

Aziz is also a foil to Adela. He is as emotional and careless as she is rational and scrupulous. Anxious to get to know Cyril Fielding, he forgets his first invitation. Aziz is surprised by how literal-minded are the English regarding invitations. He is slow to adapt to this cultural difference. So are the new arrivals. Adela and Mrs. Moore fail to penetrate the "echoing walls of civility" (*Passage* 43) of the Bhattacharyas, who said their carriage would come that very morning, and await it, but it never comes. Despite this cue about invitations, they make the same mistake and take Aziz's invitation to the caves literally. The seasoned Heaslop, for once, is right: "The way those Bengalis let you down this morning annoyed me.... Aziz would make some similar muddle over the caves. He meant nothing by the invitation" (*Passage* 83).

Aziz distorts the truth to maintain the right feeling. He lies to Adela, saying he has a wife, feeling "it more artistic to have his wife alive for a moment" (*Passage* 152)! Yet Adela strains for factual clarity. Her coldness disorients her as she enters a cave in the Marabar, pondering love and realizing she does not love her fiancé. "Did she love him? This question was somehow dragged up with the Marabar.... Was she capable of loving anyone?" (*Passage* 212). Upon entering the cave, a symbol of the unconscious, the instinctual, and of motherhood and fertility, Adela becomes unhinged, suggesting a rejection of sexual union.[34] She breaks her engagement. She falls apart when her ascent to the caves with Aziz makes her anticipate the sexual act.

The frankly sexual desire for union suggested in the milkmaiden's song to Krishna is absent from Adela's engagement with Heaslop; Adela "regretted that neither she nor Ronny had physical charm" (*Passage* 153). Forster mostly holds ideal union in marriage to be unattainable in *A Passage to India*. Adela and Ronny's union, lacking love, never comes to pass; McBryde's unhappy marriage ends in divorce; later, Fielding marries, but is "not quite happy" (*Passage* 318); Aziz remarries, but his wife is never shown: she is in purdah, despite Aziz's poetry calling for the liberation of women, which, like many words, is a meaningless echo, without influence over events. Aziz merely wants someone to raise his children and to manage his household. In a narrated monologue, Aziz felt that "a friend would come nearer to [the place held by his late first wife] than another woman" (*Passage* 55). One reason Forster never wrote another novel after *A Passage to India* is that "being a homosexual, he grew bored with writing about marriage and the relations of men and women."[35]

The only happy marriages in the novel are those in which one spouse is already dead; Mrs. Moore's two husbands are dead, as is Aziz's first wife. But memory is unreliable. Aziz cannot even picture his late wife. Real union must be here and now, in time and space, and thus subject to change. In the ceremony of Krishna's birth, the author avers: "Not only from the unbeliever are mysteries hid, but the adept himself cannot retain them. He may think, if he chooses, that he has been with God, but as soon as he thinks it, it becomes history, and falls under the rules of time" (*Passage* 288). Godbole, though masterful at expressing subtleties in words, knows words cannot capture experience; they can only echo what once was present, and point to its absence.

Adela, who collapses when attempting to fathom her feelings and her fear of sex as she enters the cave, is terrified by her inchoate feelings, which blend in her mind with the echo. The echo leaves her only after she confesses at the trial that she was mistaken. With this release from the echo comes a newfound resignation to the limits of knowledge and words. Following the trial, Adela finds herself "at the end of her spiritual tether." She wonders, with Fielding: "Were there worlds beyond which they could never touch ...? They could not tell.... Perhaps life is a mystery, not a muddle; they could not tell. Perhaps the hundred Indias ... are one and the universe they mirror is one. They had not the apparatus for judging" (*Passage* 263).

Aziz desires a unified India and believes Muslims and Hindus can live in peace. Hatred of the British unites Muslim and Hindu after the trial.

Given the bloodshed after the British left India, Aziz's optimism seems naive. The ancient boom of the caves baffles foreigners and Indians. India "calls 'Come' through her hundred mouths, through objects ridiculous and august. But come to what? She has never defined. She is not a promise, only an appeal" (*Passage* 136).

NOTES

1. Frederick C. Crews, "A Passage to India," in *Critical Essays on E.M. Forster*, ed. Alan Wilde (Boston: G.K. Hall, 1985) 159.

2. E.M. Forster, *A Passage to India*, 1924 (New York: Harcourt Brace Jovanovich, 1984) 149. Subsequent citations provided parenthetically within the text after the abbreviation *Passage*.

3. Barbara Rosecrance, *Forster's Narrative Vision* (Ithaca, NY: Cornell University Press, 1982) 192.

4. Sara Suleri, "The Geography of *A Passage to India*," in *E.M. Forster*, ed. Harold Bloom (New York: Chelsea House, 1987) 171.

5. G.K. Das, "E.M. Forster and Hindu Mythology," in *E.M. Forster: Centenary Revaluations*, ed. Judith Scherer Herz and Robert K. Martin (Toronto: University of Toronto Press, 1982) 251.

6. Benita Parry, "The Politics of Representation in *A Passage to India*," in A Passage to India: *Essays in Interpretation*, ed. John Beer (London: Macmillan, 1985) 37.

7. Chaman L. Sahni, *Forster's* A Passage to India: *The Religious Dimension* (Atlantic Highland, NJ: Humanities Press, 1981) 103. Subsequent citations provided parenthetically within the text.

8. John Beer, "*A Passage to India*, the French New Novel and English Romanticism," in A Passage to India: *Essays in Interpretation* 115.

9. Qtd. in Eloise Knapp Hay, *T.S. Eliot's Negative Way* (Cambridge, MA: Harvard University Press, 1982) 160–61.

10. Wilfred Stone, "The Caves of *A Passage to India*," in A Passage to India: *Essays in Interpretation* 20.

11. Revised Standard Version Bible [RSV] (New York: William Collins Sons, 1973). Subsequent citations provided parenthetically within the text as RSV.

12. Qtd. in Hay 160–61.

13. Gillian Beer, "Negation in *A Passage to India*," in A Passage to India: *Essays in Interpretation* 45.

14. Molly B. Tinsley, "Muddle, Et Cetera: Syntax in *A Passage to India*," in *E.M. Forster: Centenary Revaluations* 259.

15. Lionel Trilling, "A Passage to India" in *E.M. Forster*, ed. Harold Bloom 25.

16. Harold Bloom, "Introduction" to *E.M. Forster* 5.

17. Rustom Bharucha, "Forster's Friends," in *E.M. Forster* 164.

18. E.M. Forster, "What I Believe," in *Two for Democracy*, ed. Oliver Stallybrass (1951; London: Edward Arnold, 1972) 69.

19. E.M. Forster, "Believe" 65.

20. Judith Scherer Herz, "Listening to Language," in A Passage to India: *Essays in Interpretation* 59.

21. Trilling 22–23.

22. Das 254.

23. P.N. Furbank, *E.M. Forster; A Life*, 2 vols. (New York: Harcourt Brace Jovanovich, 1978) 1:62; E.M. Forster, "Believe" 72.

24. Vasant A. Shahane, "Forster's Inner Passage to India" in *E.M. Forster: Centenary Revaluations* 269.

25. Stone 18.

26. John Drew, "The Spirit Behind the Frieze?" in A Passage to India: *Essays in Interpretation* 81, 84.

27. Bloom 6.

28. Frederick P.W. McDowell, "A Universe ... not ... Comprehensible to Our Minds," in *Critical Essays on E.M. Forster*, 132.

29. Beer 45.

30. Swami Nikilananda, ed., *The Upanishads* (New York: Harper and Row, 1963) 99.

31. Rosecrance 215, 224.

32. Das 254.

33. Qtd. in Hay 160–61.

34. Louise Dauner, "What Happened in the Cave? Reflections on *A Passage to India*," in *Critical Essays on E.M. Forster*, 152.

35. Furbank 2:132.

LELAND MONK

Apropos of Nothing: Chance and Narrative in Forster's A Passage to India

"Passage to more than India!
Are thy wings plumed indeed for such far flights?
O soul, voyagest thou indeed on voyages like these?
Disportest thou on waters such as these?
Soundest below the Sanskrit and the Vedas?
Then have thy bent unleash'd."
—Walt Whitman, "Passage to India"

India, without a doubt, made a profound impression on E. M. Forster. One of the things that most fascinated him about the country and its culture was the strange fusion of chaotic disorder and deep (if to him often baffling) spirituality he witnessed there. The Hindu Festival of Gokul Ashtami, for instance, which is recreated in the concluding section of *A Passage to India*, was one of the more memorable of Forster's Indian experiences. The eight-day celebration in honor of Krishna combined seemingly irrational activities with profound religious elements in a particularly wrought and intense way: "The frivolity, triviality goes on," he observed, "and every now and then it cracks ... and discloses depths." At one point in the ceremony he learned what the groups of worshippers were singing: "some praised God without attributes, others with attributes: the same mixture of fatuity and philosophy that ran through the whole festival."[1] When he came to write his Indian

From *Studies in the Novel* 26, no. 4. Copyright © 1994 by the University of North Texas.

novel, Forster tried to find a narrative equivalent for this "mixture of fatuity and philosophy"—the peculiar combination of absurdly meaningless and transcendentally meaningful actions and events—that he observed in India.

The three sections of Forster's *A Passage to India*, "Mosque," "Caves," and "Temple," each represent a different aspect of Indian religious and Cultural belief. Of course, more accurately, the three parts of the novel comprise different versions of an English writer's Western perspective on certain aspects of Indian culture. In this essay I want to characterize three different narrative modes Forster uses in relation to the three areas of Indian culture he considers in the novel, exploring the way he accommodates his subject matter and storytelling technique to the place, meaning, and philosophico-religious importance of Moslem mosque, pre-historic cave, and Hindu temple. In doing so, my emphasis will be not on India in its many aspects but instead on aspects of the novelist—that is, E. M. Forster's ideas about the sub-continent as they materialize in specific narrative practices. The storytelling techniques associated with the first two novelistic *topoi* are fairly conventional and exemplify a distinctively modernist narrative form; but as I hope to show, the "Temple" section of the novel is something else again, offering as it does an innovative version of the theory and practice of narrative in the British novel that strains the limits of modernist aesthetics. What distinguishes the narrative experiments of the third part of *A Passage to India* is its concern with the idea and importance of chance.

I.

The "Mosque" section of *A Passage to India* uses Moslem ideas of friendship and connection to thematize possible friendships and connections between the English and the Indians in the novel. The exceptional cross-racial intimacy of Dr. Aziz and Mrs. Moore, whose chance meeting in a moonlit mosque initiates the novel, as well as of Aziz and Cyril Fielding, are the signal instances of Part One's narrative method which proceeds, quite simply, by bringing characters together. Every chapter of this section stages a meeting or grouping of some kind, if not to dramatize the progress of Aziz's friendships then to make some comparison between East and West, usually at the expense of the Anglo-Indians. The so-called "Bridge Party" arranged for the new English visitors to India is the formal and institutional version of the "Mosque" section's effort to bring English and Indians together, and it is notable for its failure; genuine contact across racial and cultural barriers in Forster's novel takes place not in official convocations but in the informal and fragile tropisms of a cultivated friendship. Dr. Aziz voices the Moslem ideal of personal relations informing this part of the novel when he observes that "friend" is the Persian expression for God; but clearly the social ethic and narrative practice of the first section of the novel have as much to do with Forster's famous motto, in a very *English* novel, that we must "only connect" as it does with mosques or Mohammed.

It is difficult even to recognize the narrative method of the first part of the novel *as* a method because it is such a naturalized and conventional way to tell a story. The taken for granted nature of Part One only acquires a recognizable shape in dialectical relation to the second section, "Caves," which is a negation of everything affirmed in the opening chapters of the novel. If the social ethic and narrative practice of "Mosque" is "only connect;" the theme of "Caves" is "disconnection"—what the novel calls "the decomposition of the Marabar."[2] All the groupings and gatherings of the first section culminate in the disastrous expedition to the Marabar Caves the results of which fragment and level the camaraderie established in the earlier scenes. Not only are the relations between characters annihilated; as a result of her experience in the cave, Mrs. Moore comes to feel that she "didn't want to communicate with anyone, not even with God" (p. 144). The aspect of Indian culture associated with the Marabar Caves is the ancient atheist and ascetic tradition of the Jains which rejected the phenomenal world as the source of pain and suffering.[3] The Marabar Caves have a corrosive, nihilating effect on those who are susceptible to their power, and they become the central mystery of "mysterious India" in Forster's *Passage* thereto.

The "Caves" section of the novel is, quite literally, about nothing. Of the Marabar Caves, the novel observes: "Nothing is inside them, they were sealed up before the creation of pestilence or treasure; if mankind grew curious and excavated, nothing, nothing would be added to the sum of good or evil" (p. 119). The repetition underlines what is almost a pun: an excavated cave offers to the archaeologist, or the novelist, substantively—*nothing*. In her essay "Negation in *A Passage to India*," Gillian Beer analyzes the pervasive lexical and, eventually, thematic use of "nothing" in the novel. She remarks a peculiarity of the word, an ambiguity which is highlighted by its frequent reiteration:

> "Nothing" as a word has two natures. Set alone it expresses stasis, vacancy: Nothing. As soon as it becomes part of a sentence, though, it makes the whole organization of that sentence restless and unstable, expressive of contrary impulses.

Beer points out how the accumulated negations of the novel give density to this latter use of the word; "nothing" then comes to have a positive, not just a nihilating sense: "By the end of the book we are brought to see also that Nothing *has* value." That value for Beer resides in the way Forster's discourse of Nothingness "make[s] it possible for the text to register that which is not to be said, not to be written."[4] This sense of the ineffable conveyed by the novel's emphatic insistence on "nothing" accurately describes the thematic and narrative concerns of the "Caves" section of *A Passage to India*. But as I will show, Forster's deployment of nothingness in the third part of the novel makes possible a new way to tell his story—to say and to write "nothing"— that is not simply concerned with the unsayable.

It might seem frivolous, or else tautological, to talk of "nothing" as though it were a substantial something; but in fact, the subject has a long and distinguished literary and philosophical history. The idea of "nothing" has been matter for literary reflection at least since Lear's warning to the reticent Cordelia that "Nothing will come of nothing";[5] but Shakespeare's "nothing" is not Forster's. It is not a trans-historical term applicable in the same way to all forms of literary production. It is the specifically modernist inflections of the term that I want to examine in Forster's novel, a sense of nothingness at the core of the literary text the beginnings of which I would provisionally date with Henry James's 1898 story *The Turn of the Screw*.[6]

The idea of "nothing" has been a topic for extensive philosophical reflection, especially in this century. The dialectical relation of Parts I and II of *A Passage to India* represents a novelistic version of Being and nothingness; but Forster's interest in "nothing" is more closely aligned with Martin Heidegger's ontological project than with Sartre's existential analytics. Philosophically speaking, the "nothing" contained in the Marabar Caves is nothing less than what Heidegger calls non-Being, which constitutes the fundamental limit to all metaphysical inquiry organizing the ontological question, "Why is there something rather than nothing?" "In asking this question," Heidegger writes,

> we stand in a tradition. For philosophy has always, from time immemorial, asked about the ground of what is. With this question it began and with this question it will end, provided that it ends in greatness and not in all impotent decline, Ever since the question about the essent [an existent thing] began, the question about the nonessent, about nothing, has gone side by side with it. And not only outwardly, in the manner of a by-product. Rather, this question about nothing has been asked with the same breadth, depth, and originality as the question about the essent.[7]

I will return to the ontological question Heidegger tried to re-vivify with his thinking in order to consider what this most fundamental of questions, "Why is there something rather than nothing?", might mean in narratological terms.

As Gillian Beer observes, the narrative method informed by the nothingness inside the titular "Caves" is necessarily concerned with the ineffable. In another passage in *Passage* that reiterates and so substantializes the novel's sense of nothing, Forster writes: "There is something unspeakable in these outposts ... Nothing, nothing attaches to them, and their reputation—for they have one—does not depend upon human speech" (p. 118). The central section of *A Passage to India* is organized around a central mystery—what happened to Adela Quested in the cave? The narrative focuses on her up to the moment she enters the cave, then shifts (with a new chapter) to Dr. Aziz in another cave; he then a few minutes later sees Miss Quested in the distance departing in a car. The central, crucial, pivotal scene of the novel is not represented and, as the rhetoric attached to the caves suggests, it is strictly speaking unrepresentable. The answer to the question the rest of the novel asks but resolutely refuses to answer, "What happened to Miss Quested in the Marabar cave?," is "Nothing." But in this case, as the effects of the caves on Mrs. Moore, Adela Quested, and the novel's subsequent narrative experiments all illustrate, the "nothing" which happens in "Caves" takes on the status of an event—traumatic, disruptive, inexplicable and unassimilable. Of course a narrative organized around an unrepresented or even unrepresentable center has been a venerable novelistic practice at least since *Clarissa Harlowe*'s rape; but the idea of a mysterious and impenetrable blackness or blankness at the core of the literary work enjoyed an especially favored currency during the modern period, as that textbook case of modernism, Joseph Conrad's *Heart of Darkness*, both illustrates and names.

Most criticism of *A Passage to India* locates it firmly in the modernist tradition of texts which pull up short before and gesture obsessively at an unrepresentable and ineffable mystery at their center. Wilfred Stone, for instance, in terms that are representative of much of the criticism of Forster's novel, observes about the central importance of the Marabar Caves: "But most important are the hollowness and roundness of the caves, and all the mythological evocations of these forms. The novel is one great echo chamber, one great round."[8] It is easy to see how *A Passage to India* fits into this modernist niche, with the impenetrable mystery of the pre-historic caves at the structural center of the novel organizing its narrative progression. The Marabar Caves contain nothing, and nothing happens to Adela Quested in them. And one cannot after all represent "nothing." But in fact that is just what Forster, inspired by his understanding of the Hindu religion, attempts to do; in the last section of the novel, he tries to make something out of nothing.

II.

The narrative technique elaborated in the "Temple" section of *A Passage to India* takes a more interesting form than the conventional connections of "Mosque" or the modernist heart of darkness hollowing out the novel in "Caves." Professor Godbole is the spokesman for and representative of the Hindu philosophy as Aziz is for the Moslem religion (there is no character associated with the Marabar Caves because they are finally concerned with nothing human). As Godbole explains and exemplifies, the Hindu outlook incorporates a simultaneous awareness of Being and non-Being, but not at all in the form of a Hegelian sublation or synthesis. The Hindu God "is, was not, is not, was" (p. 277)—always and at the same time. The Hindu perspective is a double vision of Being and non-Being, past and present, presence and absence, existence and nothingness. As such, it entails a simultaneous affirmation and negation of the divinity it worships. The bland announcement with which the "Temple" section opens—"Professor Narayan Godbole stands in the presence of God"—is just as blandly denied as the passage continues: "God is not born yet—that will occur at midnight—but He has also been born centuries ago, nor can He ever be born, because He is the Lord of the Universe who transcends human processes" (p. 277). The Hindu festival described in Part Three of the novel celebrates and re-enacts the birth of Shri Krishna using various tokens that both do and do not represent Him ("The Napkin was God, not that it was" [p. 282]). After the ceremony, we are told,

> [n]o definite image survived; at the Birth it was questionable whether a silver doll or a mud village, or a silk napkin, or an intangible spirit, or a pious resolution, had been born. Perhaps all these things! Perhaps none! (p.284)

To the Western mind, this simultaneous affirmation and negation of divinity in Indian religious belief is confounding. Fielding the rational Englishman dismisses the phrase "There is no God but God" as "only a game with words, really, a religious pun, not a religious truth" (p. 269).[9] Similarly, after her experience in the cave, Adela Quested repeats to herself the phrase "[i]n space things touch, in time things part" and, in her rational mind, "she could not decide whether the phrase was a philosophy or a pun" (p. 187). For Fielding and Miss Quested, such phrases seem to dissolve the logical premises of their own assertions. They simply cannot comprehend this "mixture of fatuity and philosophy" that is India. The expression of a religious or philosophical truth (full of meaning) that can equally well be regarded as simply a pun (a merely accidental association of words with no meaning) is the linguistic model informing the narrative innovations of the "Temple" section of *A Passage to India*.

During the Hindu festival Dr. Godbole finds himself thinking of Mrs. Moore:

> Chance brought her into his mind while it was in this heated state, he did not select her, she happened to occur among the throng of soliciting images, a tiny splinter, and he impelled her by his spiritual force to that place where completeness can be found. Completeness, not reconstruction ... He was a Brahman, she Christian, but it made no difference, it made no difference whether she was a trick of his memory or a telepathic appeal. (pp. 280, 284)

Godbole's unsolicited awareness of Mrs. Moore articulates a narrative method according to which an event transpires in a transcendentally significant way (a "telepathic appeal") and at the same time takes place for totally insignificant reasons (the result of "chance," a mere "trick of his memory"). The linguistic model for the Hindu awareness of both Being and non-Being (a religious or philosophical truth which might just as easily be a pun) appears in the narrative operations of the novel in the form of an event that is the result of supernatural influence *and* the result of chance, both at the same time. We see this double perspective in the games played during the Hindu festival: "And the Lord bounds hither and thither through the aisles, chance, and the sport of chance, irradiating little mortals with his Immortality" (p. 283).

In every case, the narrative events which have this double valence of the supernatural and the aleatory are attached to Mrs. Moore. The other creature which comes without apparent provocation to Dr. Godbole's attention during the Hindu ceremony is a wasp he had seen somewhere— "He loved the wasp equally, he impelled it likewise, he was imitating God" (p. 280)—which occurs to him by chance, in a completely unconnected way; but it also further connects his receptive state of mind with Mrs. Moore, who had earlier, in her own way, blessed a wasp she found in her room: "'Pretty dear,' said Mrs. Moore to the wasp" (p. 28).

Mrs. Moore's association with narrative events that seem to happen by chance *and* according to some supernatural impetus first appears in relation to the strange experience Adela Quested and her fiance Ronny Heaslop have in the Nawab Bahadur's automobile. While driving on the Marabar Road, Adela and Ronny have an accident: a large creature, perhaps a hyena they think, collides with the car; but they can find no traces of the animal when they stop to investigate. When Mrs. Moore hears of the collision, she shivers and says "A ghost!" (p. 90). Though none of the English know it, the Nawab Bahadur also thinks the accident was a ghostly encounter: he ran over a man with his car years ago and, he believes, that man has been waiting for him ever since. Was the car crash an accident, a casual collision, or was it a supernatural phenomenon? The novel wants to have it and to see it both ways.

Such a double perspective is affirmed in relation to Mrs. Moore herself. In her first appearance in the novel, the chance encounter with Aziz in the Mosque at night, he thinks Mrs. Moore might be a ghost. And when Miss Quested and Fielding try to determine why and how Adela finally managed to tell the truth at the trial, Mrs. Moore and ghosts are again invoked. There is a moment of confusion between them when Fielding speculates that the examining Superintendent "exorcised" her. Fielding explains:

> "As soon as he asked you a straightforward question, you gave a straightforward answer, and broke down."
> "Exorcise in that sense. I thought you meant I'd seen a ghost."
> "I don't go to that length!"
> "People whom I respect very much believe in ghosts," she said rather sharply. "My friend Mrs. Moore does." (p. 234)

Miss Quested and Fielding finally acknowledge that their limited rational minds will never comprehend the truth of her experience in the cave; but Adela claims that Mrs. Moore *did* know the truth, perhaps by "[t]elepathy" (p. 256). About Mrs. Moore, the novel wants to have it and to see it both ways: she is an elderly English matron who suffers a breakdown, sails away from India, dies and is buried at sea; she is a Hindu goddess—"Esmiss Esmoor" the Indians chant during the trial—whose spirit impels Adela Quested to speak the truth on the witness stand and save her friend Dr. Aziz.

The novel's double perspective on a narrative event that is a chance encounter and, at the same time, a supernatural phenomenon is most pronounced in the climactic scene of the "Temple" section, the collision of Aziz's and Fielding's boats during the torchlight procession of the Hindu festival. The incident is merely another accident, two ships not passing but colliding in the night; at the same time, it is a reconciliation of Aziz and Fielding, presided over by the infinitely connective spirit of Mrs. Moore. I want to look at this scene in some detail because it is the place where the Western novelist's narrative methods most clearly intersect with his sense of the Hindu faith in all its fascination and perplexity. As the boat carrying Aziz and Ralph Moore (Mrs. Moore's son) approaches the procession ceremony, Aziz suddenly hears the Hindu chants sound "the syllables of salvation" (p. 307) he had heard during his trial, Mrs. Moore's name transposed to that of a Hindu goddess: "Esmiss Esmoor." They approach the Hindu celebrants gathered on shore who are there to praise God and, at the same time, "to throw God away" (p. 308). This ritual culminates in a beautiful naked young Indian man carrying into the water a tray on which is a replica of the village of Gokul made of clay with little dolls and carved figures. As the servitor pushes the tray out onto the waves, Aziz's boat collides with the boat carrying Cyril Fielding and his wife, Mrs. Moore's daughter Stella. The two boats, locked together, "drifted forward helplessly against the servitor. Who awaited them, his beautiful dark face expressionless, and as the last morsels melted on his tray, it struck them." They capsize, and "[t]he oars, the sacred tray, the letters of Ronny and Adela, broke loose and floated confusedly." The Hindu worshippers then break out in thunderous celebration and, we are told, "[t]hat was the climax, as far as India admits of one" (p. 309).

This scene is indeed the climax of Forster's Indian novel; and it is a moment of remarkable self-reflection. The little figures on the tray the servitor pushes before him on the water are described as "scapegoats, husks, emblems of passage" (p. 308). This scene itself provides an emblem of passage, of Forster's *A Passage to India*, as the author gathers together in a climactic moment all the little figures of his novel: Aziz and Fielding meet and renew their friendship; Dr. Godbole is watching from shore; Adela Quested and Ronny Heaslop are there in the form of their letters floating on the water; and Mrs. Moore is there as well, both in the form of her children Ralph and Stella (who are irresistibly drawn to Hinduism) and as the Hindu goddess Esmiss Esmoor. All characters present and accounted for. English, Moslem, and Hindu meet and mingle in this moment of aqueous fusion and confusion, Forster's fantasy of his fictional world coming together with the racial, cultural, and sexual Other that is India. This is as close as Forster's work gets to a narrative version of the Hindu religion's mutually *in*clusive sense of Being and non-Being as the Hindu and the novelistic emblems of Passage float and mingle on and in the dark water. This scene is at one and the same time a doubly accidental chance encounter—the collision of boat with boat, of boats with sacred tray—and a doubly blessed communion presided over by a transcendentally benevolent spirit—a Hindu goddess, and an English novelist.

The novel's concluding remarks on this scene indicate how Part Three of *A Passage to India* sketches, at least in outline, the contours of an aesthetic which moves out of and beyond the traditional modernist concern with an ineffable mystery at the core of the literary work. Such narratives construct their relatively stable meaning around an impenetrable void of non-meaning at their center, rather like the way rock candy crystallizes around a string. But the aesthetic at work in "Temple" is more nebulous and diffusive than the unrepresentable heart of darkness which defines the narrative form of the "Caves" section of the novel: "Looking back at the great blur of the last twenty-four hours," the novel observes after the Hindu festival has concluded, "no man could say where was the emotional centre of it, any more than he could locate the heart of a cloud" (p. 310).

III.

I want to conclude with some reflections about the status and use of ostensible chance events in *A Passage to India*. The novelists of the early twentieth century were very interested in chance phenomena, and that interest contributed in important ways to the development of modernist narrative forms. Of course Forster does not succeed in representing chance "itself" in his Indian novel. He is more interested in depicting accidental occurrences which open out on supernatural possibilities than he is in affirming the existential reality or ontological significance of chance *qua* chance. Such as it is, Forster's treatment of chance appears in the novel as a series of accidents, all having more or less to do with Mrs. Moore: Dr. Godbole becomes aware of her and, like her, of a wasp, simply by chance during the Hindu ceremony; she exclaims "A ghost!" about the mysterious car accident on the Marabar Road; and her spirit is invoked and seems to preside over the climactic collisions of character and culture in the boat accidents at the end of the novel. But in the words of literary criticism we frequently resort to in trying to articulate a story's meaning, "it is no accident that" these events converge in Mrs. Moore even if her character works as the place-holder for a narrative project, informed by Hindu principles, that strives for a simultaneous appreciation of the transcendental and the accidental.

I have argued elsewhere that chance marks and defines a fundamental structural limit to the operations of novelistic narrative.[10] According to Jacques Lacan's well-known formula, the Real is that which cannot be represented in language; similarly, and in a way that is not just an analogy, I maintain that chance is that which cannot be represented in narrative. The phrase "chance in narrative" then is really something of an oxymoron. It is not therefore very surprising that, when E. M. Forster tries to find a narrative equivalent for the Hindu religion's abstract regard for both Being and non-Being, he formulates events which are both supernaturally significant and, at the same time, simply aleatory. Forster's novelistic version of non-Being implicitly acknowledges the fact that if life, or a novel, really *is* nothing more than an endless series of accidents, casual collisions, and chance encounters, then there is simply no story to tell. The co-habitation of supernatural and accidental perspectives on the same event in Forster's "Temple" indicates the way chance marks and defines a fundamental limit to its narrative operations: chance is the "nothing" of narrative.

I do not mean to suggest that, in departing from modernist narrative forms, the last section of *A Passage to India* breaks through to what we would now call an aesthetics of the postmodern. Chance phenomena are indeed a matter of intense interest in postmodern fiction—think of the narrative permutations of Julio Cortázar's *Hopscotch*, William Burrough's cut-ups, or Chance the gardener in Jerzy Kosinski's *Being There*—but its treatment has more to do with the *immanence* of aleatory experience than with the transcendental possibilities it opens up. By insisting with his novelistic adaptation of Hindu thought that an event which seems to be a strictly random occurrence may also be understood as an effect of supernatural divinity, Forster seems to want it both ways. In fact, though, he is not very interested in admitting to the novel new and unaccountable forms of chance (a novelistic world truly governed by chance would be far too much of what Forster called a "muddle"). Rather, it seems to me that he is interested in renovating an old-fashioned and generally discredited way of ordering narrative experience which had come to seem irrelevant in his time and so could not be unequivocally affirmed. The narrative experiments of "Temple" indicate Forster's nostalgic longing for outmoded forms of storytelling that invoke the power of a providential force (be it deity or novelist) benignly guiding and watching over lives and events. The last section of *A Passage to India* departs from the standard practices of literary modernism, but it does so only to re-formulate under the guise of Hindu mysticism a regressive providentialism wherein a transcendental Being presides over narrative events and Nothing is left to chance.

When Martin Heidegger urges thinkers to re-think the question of Being, he says that one must begin by asking the question "Why is there something rather than nothing?"; and he insists on the importance of the second half of that question because this "nothing" provides a ground for, and a fundamental limit to, the ontological inquiry.[11] I would say that, in order to arrive at a clearer understanding of what narrative is and how it works, we could not do better than to ask: "What is chance?" The "Temple" section of *A Passage to India*, Forster's narrative correlative of Hindu thought, points beyond the dark heart of modernist aesthetics in its engagement with that question.

NOTES

1. E. M. Forster, *The Hill of Devi and Other Indian Writings* (New York: Holmes & Meier Publishers, 1953; repr. 1983), pp. 73, 67. In the first quotation, Forster is comparing the festival he witnessed to the tenth book of the *Bhagavad Purana*; the second quotation is from a 1921 letter Forster wrote describing the festival which is reprinted in this volume. This letter provided much of the material used in Forster's fictional depiction of Gokul Ashtami in *A Passage to India*.

2. E. M. Forster, *A Passage to India* (New York: Harcourt, Brace, Jovanovich, 1924; repr. 1984), p. 251. Page references to this edition will henceforth appear in parentheses after the quoted passage.

3. See Benita Parry, "The Politics of Representation in *A Passage to India*" in *"A Passage to India": Essays in Interpretation*, ed. John Beer (Totowa, NJ: Barnes and Noble, 1986), p. 39.

4. Gillian Beer, "Negation in *A Passage to India*" in *"A Passage to India": Essays in Interpretation*, pp. 50, 51, 58.

5. In *Signifying Nothing: The Semiotics of Zero* (Stanford, CA: Stanford Univ. Press, 1987), Brian Rotman analyzes the "nothing" of *King Lear* in the larger context of Renaissance financial and representational systems.

6. In James's story of ghost writing, it turns out that the Governess's revelatory letter to the Master purloined by Miles contained, to his dismay and her joy, a substantial nothing. When Miles admits that be stole and opened the letter, the Governess exclaims: "and you found nothing!"

> [Miles] gave the most mournful thoughtful little headshake. "Nothing."
>
> "Nothing, nothing!" [she] almost shouted in [her] joy.
>
> "Nothing, nothing," he sadly repeated.

Henry James, *The Aspern Papers and The Turn of the Screw* (Harmondsworth: Penguin Books, 1984), p. 258.

See Shoshana Felman's classic essay "Turning the Screw of Interpretation" in *Literature and Psychoanalysis: The Question of Reading Otherwise* (Baltimore: Johns Hopkins Univ. Press, 1980), pp. 94–207, for an insightful reading of this "nothing."

7. Martin Heidegger, *An Introduction to Metaphysics*, trans. Ralph Manheim (Anchor Books: Garden City, New York, 1961), p. 20.

8. Wilfred Stone, *The Cave and the Mountain: A Study of E. M. Forster* (Stanford, CA: Stanford Univ. Press, 1966), p. 307.

9. The phrase Fielding considers is of Moslem not Hindu origin, but it occurs to him within the general context of what eludes him about Indian belief systems.

10. Leland Monk, *Standard Deviations: Chance and the Modern British Novel* (Stanford, CA: Stanford Univ. Press, 1993).

11. In associating Forster's sense of "nothing" with Heidegger's, I do not mean simply to endorse their way of thinking on the subject. On the contrary, I think Forster's version of "nothing"ness—and the sense of Being which it subtends—is subject to the same critique that Adorno makes of Heidegger's ontological project. Adorno argues that Heidegger's concepts become reified and mystified in their attempt to express the inexpressible. Forster's similarly reified and mystified treatment of an aleatory "nothing" betrays his nostalgia for a regressive providential agency ordering narrative experience much as Heidegger's thinking about Nothing reveals his longing for a pre-technological order of Being. See Theodor W. Adorno, *Negative Dialectics*, trans. E. B. Ashton (New York: Continuum, 1983), pp. 97–131. For a discussion of the mystical, if not mystified and mystifying, aspects of Heidegger's sense of nothing, see John D. Caputo, *The Mystical Element in Heidegger's Thought* (Athens: Ohio Univ. Press, 1978), pp. 18–22.

YONATAN TOUVAL

Colonial Queer Something

Kindness, kindness, and more kindness—yes, that he might supply, but was that really all that the queer nation needed?
—*E.M. Forster*, A Passage to India

The Orient becomes a living tableau of queerness.
—*Edward Said*, Orientalism

The interstices of nationalisms and sexualities occupy a queer space—if we take "queer" to mean the mapping out, and in the process the demystification, of relations and identities that a hegemony of the normative would rather keep unexamined. In the climactic final chapter of *A Passage to India*, Aziz opens up just such a space, in a rhetorical performance that perceptively exposes the insidious collusion between colonial imperialism and Western sexuality. Addressing Fielding, but really addressing the British colonial regime in India at large, Aziz says:

> [It is the ol]d story of "We will rob every man and rape every woman from Peshawar to Calcutta," I suppose, which you get some nobody to repeat and then quote every week in the *Pioneer* in order to frighten us into retaining you! We know! (PI 312)

From *Queer Forster*, eds. R.K. Martin and G. Piggsford. © 1997 by The University of Chicago Press.

As a target of what ultimately proves to be a false accusation of attempted rape, Aziz is speaking, of course, from personal experience. For in the aftermath of the incident in the Marabar Caves and up until the termination of the trial, Aziz becomes the raison d'être of British colonial rule—of, more exactly, a tightening of that rule. In a discussion at the Club immediately following the incident, there is a plea among the members to "Call in the troops and clear the bazaars" (PI 178). "The crime was even worse than they had supposed—the unspeakable limit of cynicism, untouched since 1857" (PI 178). In collapsing sexual into nationalist (and military) violence, the reference to the Mutiny of 1857 also phobically abstracts the alleged sexual crime of one individual to the possibility of a nation-wide rampage. "It's the time for action," declares Major Callendar, echoing the sentiments of the Collector who "wanted to flog every native that he saw," but whose resistance to doing so hinges on one peculiar reason: "The dread of having to call in the troops was vivid to him; soldiers ... love to humiliate the civilian administration" (PI 178, 174).

There is doubtless something begging of (demanding?) humiliation in a colon(ial) muscle that's not flexed tightly enough ... at any rate, the allegations of rape, fear of insurgent nationalism, racial typologies and epistemologies, all collude in order to prevent the formation of any such (queer) space within the totality of the colonial—Oriental—project at large. Yet the queerness in Aziz's knowledge lies not only in a forceful understanding of how these different discursive regimes tighten ass, but also in the ability to destabilize the very coherence of the accusation—the accusation of the accusation—itself. "We will rob every man and rape every woman": what seems like an unproblematically straight pairing of two different kinds of violence (rob/man; rape/woman) immediately breaks down by the sheer insistence upon that unproblematicality, as "rape" and "rob" prove to be tongue twisters of a particularly dangerous kind. As labials differentiated in the English solely by whether they're voiced ("b") or voiceless ("p") plosives, "p" and "b" come close to performing a "punning" that—in Christopher Craft's words—"becomes homoerotic because homophonic" (Craft 38).[1] Or better still, that becomes queer because symphonic: for the binaric differential that breaks the plosives into two in English further breaks them into four in Urdu-Hindi, as each gets split into its aspirated and unaspirated variants. These labials which aren't—are no longer—two thus threaten to mismatch verb with object, rendering not only a woman robbed, but also, and far more problematically, a raped man.[2]

Even for the Westerner unschooled in the tricks of deconstruction, however, Indian sexuality would seem stunningly queer;[3] a single glance at the *Kama Sutra* should put *The Joy of Gay Sex* to shame. Still, to romanticize

Oriental sexuality would be to reify the worst kind of Western assumptions and ignorances—ignorances especially striking in light of a long history of (to adopt the idiom of the American) "abusive relations" among imperialism, nationalism, and Indian bodies. Much of the reading that follows will chart such relations as they map the scope of *A Passage to India*, but the extent to which these relations reach beyond the confines of the Marabar Caves is important to emphasize. In her recent essay, "Indian Nationalism, Gandhian 'Satyagraha,' and Representations of Female Sexuality," Ketu H. Katrak delineates Mahatma Gandhi's "uses of women's bodies" in the modeling of his crusade for passive resistance:

> Female sexuality was essentialized through Gandhi's appeals to the "female virtues": chastity, purity, self-sacrifice, suffering.... These "female" virtues were an "investment" in his nationalist, nonviolent strategy. "To me," Gandhi stated in 1921, "the female sex is not the weaker sex; it is the nobler of the two: for it is even today the embodiment of sacrifice, silent suffering, humility, faith and knowledge" (Katrak 396–98).

While Gandhi may have ultimately "essentialized" traditional stereotypes about womanhood—in a campaign, moreover, that was foremost concerned with national rather than women's liberation—it is important to note that within the parameters of gender politics qualities such as sacrifice and suffering are never so much essential as *relational*: to whatever extent womanhood "is" sacrifice or "is" suffering, womanhood is always sacrifice for another, or suffering in the interest of another, where "another" is presumed to be male. In calling upon men (as well as upon women) to embrace these supposed qualities of womanhood, therefore, Gandhi takes womanhood outside the domain of gender politics and, in so doing, neutralizes the political sphere within which womanhood is no longer "essentialized" so much as transformed into a platonic ideal: henceforth, all Indians are *like* women, all women are *like* Indians, all men are *like* women, and womanhood is *like* India just as India is *like* womanhood. Only during the years when Prime Minister Indira Gandhi had achieved the status of (nothing less than) an ego-ideal would the simile "like" be finally disposed of—in the famous line: "India is Indira and Indira is India."

If the Mahatma's vision of womanhood was therefore associated with passivity, it was a notion of passivity that—whether naively or brilliantly—was integral to an entire philosophy of resistance and, finally, independence; and by the time India felt comfortable assimilating its national identity to the figure of a woman, Indira had already established a reputation for being, at the very least, tough and dictatorial. In light of such touchstones in twentieth-century Indian history, it would be tempting to draw a narrative that would begin, say, with Gandhi's feminization of men and end with the masculinization of Indira. Katherine Mayo's famous *Mother India* (1927), which argued that Indian men's oppression of women had created a social psychology that had somehow made Indian society particularly susceptible to colonial rule, would fit neatly into the beginning of such a narrative, while Indira's sterilization program of the early 1970s would stand as that narrative's most spectacular conclusion.[4] And—why not?—into the middle of this narrative (say, into the months leading to Partition) we might as well interject a long-time Pakistani suspicion: that the British finally let India have Kashmir because the wife of the last viceroy (himself famously queer[5]) had Nehru. The value of such a sketch, of course, would lie chiefly in its formalism: as though the feminization of men would conversely precipitate a masculinization of women; as though, too, the Mahatma's wish to become "God's eunuch" would temporarily be answered by a hustling Nehru and finally be granted (*gratis*, we might add, plus a transistor radio!) by a castrating Indira.[6] But if history doesn't follow formalism, *A Passage to India* depicts a community—and I mean the Anglo-Indian one—that does. And the value of our imaginary narrative would lie precisely in the rhetorical force that, as Aziz would learn first-hand, sustains the very logic of the British Raj. Hence Ronny could theorize an India in which "the younger generation believe in a show of manly independence" (PI 27)—a remark that not only captures the uneasy paradox of a dual expectation that Indians at once put on a "show of manly independence" and still remain (in actuality?) in a position of womanly dependence, but also portends the epistemological quagmire that the specific incident in the Marabar Caves will inevitably posit: how can Aziz, simultaneously as it were, act the man and woman both?

This is ultimately what the trial is about, and the burden on the prosecution will be to resolve the apparent contradiction into a coherent formula that would neatly accommodate popular racism, evidential facts, political interests, and imperial misogyny. Something of the drift of that formula we begin to detect in the official charge against Aziz as outlined by the prosecution: "That he followed her into the caves and made insulting advances. She hit him with her field-glasses; he pulled at them and the strap broke, and that is how she got away. When we searched him just now, they were in his pocket" (PI 158–59). But it is Adela herself, who, though presumably lacking in the political shrewdness that makes for imperial sophistication, unwittingly stages the case for the prosecution's dazzling performance:

I went into the detestable cave ... and I remember scratching the wall with my finger-nail, to start the usual echo, and then, as I was saying, there was this shadow, or sort of shadow, down the entrance tunnel, bottling me up. It seemed liked an age, but I suppose the whole thing can't have lasted thirty seconds really. I hit at him with the glasses, he pulled me round the cave by the strap, I escaped, that's all. He never actually touched me once. It all seems such nonsense.... Naturally I'm upset, but I shall get over it. (PI 184–85)

For all the professed outrage over what allegedly happened in the Marabar Caves, at least part of the charge seems to derive—does it not?—from its own immateriality.[7] Not only, that is to say, was a woman assaulted, but—and here is the real violation—she was not assaulted enough. Yet let us be clear again about the context: popular racism *expects* Aziz to be a rapist; evidential facts show that, even if attempting to act on that racial stereotype, Aziz *failed* to rape; political interests demand that Aziz continue to emblematize a certain kind of threat; and imperial misogyny fuels this fantastical chain from the start with sincere wishes that Adela had been raped—or how else to read the aftermath of a trial in which everyone's greatest irritation seems to lie less in the fact that Aziz is vindicated than that Adela wasn't raped after all? Indeed, even Adela's physical recuperation upsets no other than the Civil Surgeon who—the novel makes explicit— "appeared to resent his patient's recovery" (PI 176). If Adela had only closed her eyes and thought of England, perhaps the British Raj would have found justification to maintain its grip for another hundred years. It is within precisely such an overdetermined colonial sphere, I'm arguing, that the prosecution goes on to reformulate the charge against Aziz, so that Aziz will now stand trial not for attempting to rape Adela *but for failing to rape her*.

Of course, if (as in most discursive regimes) the conditions most demanding of change are those which have already made it conceivable, the prosecution in Aziz's trial can likewise be said not to impose a formula so much as to draw it from the field of colonial discourse. Consider this exchange between Fielding and McBryde over the presence of Adela's field-glasses in Aziz's pocket:

Fielding: "It is impossible that, having attempted to assault her, he would put her glasses into his pocket."
McBryde: "Quite possible, I'm afraid; when an Indian goes bad, he goes not only very bad, but also very queer." (PI 160)

So fully rationalized is the evidence that, more than simply refuting any hopes of undermining it, McBryde gives it a spin that only tightens the claim to truthfulness. Meanwhile if we, like Fielding, "don't follow" (PI 160), let the cosmopolitan British Superintendent of Police remind us of our provincialism: "How could you? When you think of crime you think of English crime. The psychology here is different" (PI 166). The paradigm through which Aziz will now be newly imagined, it turns out, has always already existed.

Or let us go one step back: What is different? How is the "psychology" in India "different" from the "psychology" in England? Where does that difference lie, and how is it constituted? The distinguishing mark, of course, has already been offered by McBryde: the Indian can go "not only very bad" (like the English), "but very queer" (like no one else). *Things queer*: there is the "queer valley" by the Marabar Caves (PI 140), Godbole's "queer little song" (PI 125), and Fielding's "queer vague talk" with him later (PI 166). Aziz finds Fielding to be "a queer chap" (PI 113), there are "queer reports" circulating through Chandrapore in advance of the trial (PI 204), and the victory that emerges from it is registered as "a queer one" (PI 222). Adela Quested herself is referred to as "the queer cautious girl" (PI 19), and (after the trial) as "the queer honest girl" (PI 237). Mrs. Moore, too, becomes increasingly "disagreeable and queer" (PI 208), and her ghostly presence at the courtroom as "Esmiss Esmoor" provokes Adela to shudder, "Isn't it all queer?" (PI 215). Even, finally, at the end of the novel, when Fielding and Aziz seem for a moment to have become "friends again," they take their last ride together in a scenery described as "park-like as England, but"—perhaps foreshadowing their final rift—"it did not cease being queer" (PI 308).

The landscape, the talk, the trial, the echo, the reports, the song, the people: it's as though queerness is the stuff things Indian (or, like Fielding, Adela, and Mrs. Moore, things gone Indian) are made of, the very essence of Indianicity. Or if not India's essence, at least its identity. And like all forms of identity, India's will by definition be rather elusive. "But nothing in India is identifiable," the novel cautions, "the mere asking of a question causes it to disappear or to merge in something else" (PI 78). Queerness seems to spring everywhere and therefore also nowhere, although it usually (if not always) springs in order to qualify sonic relation (the relation?) between Englishness and Indianness. Set against a normative standard of what is expected from things English, queerness thus becomes constituted by its *difference* from the English. "The psychology here is different," says McBryde, as though by marking it as "different" he has sufficiently done the work of describing it. But of course the function of McBryde's statement is not to describe so much as to perform, for his statement intends to convey that no small share of his duties as Superintendent of Police is based on a superior epistemology that enables him, but not Fielding, to do what the police do (or are supposed to do) best: to know. And while queerness is never more explicitly defined than in the assertion that it lies somewhere in the difference between things Indian and English (but on the side of the Indian), McBryde's know-it-when-you-see-it brand of epistemology, as vague and arbitrary as it seems, is indicatively shared by the entire Anglo-Indian community. "I really do know the truth about Indians" (PI 21), declares one woman at the club in a statement that implies more than simple cosmopolitanism. In fact, if queerness is that difference in the Indian which the quality of being English enables (entitles?) one to know, that ability may well in fact also secretly constitute a correlative ability: the ability of the Anglo-Indians to imagine (or identify) themselves as a community.

Hence, Adela and Mrs. Moore are ultimately banished from Anglo India for refusing an identity politics that hinges on identifying Indians. Mrs. Moore, who from the start disassociates herself from the Anglo-Indian community, identifies with Indians rather than, transitively, identifies them, and so must be hastily shipped away at the crucial moment when she begins to shake Adela's confidence in, precisely, the *identity* of her assailant. Adela's confidence is lost altogether during the trial, and it bears repeating that it's that loss of confidence in identifying her Indian assailant that formally ends Adela's short tenure in Anglo India. "The prisoner followed you, didn't he?"—"I am not quite sure" (PI 217). Adela refuses to identify Aziz—even as the one who would have failed to rape her. But she does something even more dangerous than simply fail to identify by admitting to mistake an earlier identification: "I'm afraid I have made a mistake" (PI 218). Since in misidentifying the Indian, the Anglo-Indian calls into question her own self-identification, Adela's remark is greeted by calls to "stop these proceedings on medical grounds" (PI 223): Adela simply can't be herself. For the threat to the Anglo-Indian's constitution as an Anglo-Indian in the dramatic ending of the trial lies in the possibility that, if Adela was mistaken in the process of identification, the very politics of identity might have to be rethought. "But nothing in India is identifiable, the mere asking of a question causes it to disappear or to merge in something else." If queerness finally isn't identifiable (and hence, by implication, also containable) within things Indian, there's no telling with what and with whom queerness might choose to merge—especially when a hyphen persistently reminds us of the provisional bridge that no more separates than conjoins the "Anglo" and the "Indian."

The terror of the Indian—what incites an Anglo-Indian community to playing the police—lies to a significant degree in the impossibility of telling ahead of time the place and the medium through which queerness might strike, or creep. "They give me the creeps" (PI 22), Mrs. Callendar says about the Indians, coming close to admitting her inability to specify why. That specificity can never be fixed, of course, but for that reason alone it most demands to be theorized. In the Anglo-Indian community of Mrs. Callendar, vulnerability is answered by conviction, even if in the form of fiction; identity, after all, needn't be true, it simply mustn't be shown to be *un*true. Hence, perhaps, the great stakes in Aziz's trial, for in failing to rape Adela lies an implicit negation of at least two scientific theories dear to McBryde's heart (as well as, more generally, to Orientalism at large): first, McBryde's "theory of climatic zones," which, echoing something of Richard Burton's theory of the Sotadic Zone, states that "All unfortunate natives are criminals at heart, for the simple reason that they live south of latitude 30. They are not to blame, they have not a dog's chance—we should be like them if we settled here" (PI 158): and second, McBryde's "favorite theme" of "Oriental pathology," which claims that "the darker races are attracted by the fairer, but not vice versa— not a matter for bitterness this, not a matter for abuse, but just a fact which any scientific observer will confirm" (PI 208). What is interesting about these theories is the absence of gender (or sex) as a possible point of contamination, even when (sexual) attraction is raised to the fore. Since only race here charts the law of desire, the queerness of the Oriental extends precisely to the possibility that the Oriental might also be homosexual. And if Aziz had failed in his assault on Adela—or even if he had never launched one in the first place—the worse for him. For to refute one charge is invariably to produce another: if Aziz had merely *robbed* Adela of her field-glasses, there's no telling that he wouldn't *rape* the City Magistrate next.

McBryde's theories would prove flexible enough to accommodate the prosecution's reformulation of Aziz's crime as long as they aren't challenged head-on. But they are challenged—challenged when, for instance, someone in the courtroom suggests that it was Adela who was after Aziz rather than the other way around, since "the lady is so uglier than the gentleman" (PI 208); challenged, too, although somewhat less decisively, by Adela herself when she finally withdraws the charge. We might even say that, outside the courtroom, the narrative too seems eager to tear apart McBryde's theories, taking care to cite Aziz's dislike of Adela's looks—"Adela's angular body and the freckles on her face were terrible defects in his eyes, and he wondered how God could have been so unkind to any female form" (PI 61)—and Adela's (albeit tentative) attraction to Aziz:

> What a handsome little Oriental he was, and no doubt his wife and children were beautiful too.... She did not admire him with

> any personal warmth, for there was nothing of the vagrant in her
> blood, but she guessed he might attract women of his own race
> and rank, and she regretted that neither she nor Ronny had
> physical charm. It does make a difference in a relationship—
> beauty, thick hair, a fine skin. (PI 144)

Desire flows from fair to dark—against McBryde's theories, against (we
might generalize) a Northern racial aesthetic that, almost fifty years after
formally letting go, still shapes (doubtless by that invisible hand that adroitly
brushes the faces even of, as Bombay's film industry is known, Bollywood)
contemporary Indian ethic: for why else the furor, the scandal, and the
threats, over a kiss actress Shabana Azmi had placed on the cheek of Nelson
Mandela at a recent function? And why do bachelors advertising their
eligibility in the weekly matrimonials section of the *Times of India* so often
cite—next to their fortunes, Green Cards, and other worldly possessions—
their "fair" and "wheatish" complexions?

In *A Passage to India*, so threatening is darker skin that a predictable
defense mechanism habitually averts the Anglo-Indian's thoughts from dark
to fair. The novel itself performs such a shift when, during the trial, Aziz
disappears from the narrative almost altogether.[8] As for Adela, she is
paradoxically ignored by a community that prefers to abstract her particular
case to a general panic over "women and children":

> They had started speaking of 'women and children'—that phrase
> that exempts the male from sanity when it has been repeated a
> few times. Each felt that all he loved best in the world was at
> stake, demanded revenge, and was filled with a not unpleasing
> glow, in which the chilly and half-known features of Miss
> Quested vanished, and were replaced by all that is sweetest and
> warmest in the private life. (PI 174)

If part of the rhetorical force of this abstraction lies in the muddling of the
specific charge of assault, that strategy, however, must ultimately fail. For
whatever unspecifiable queerness is said to endanger English family values,
such values turn out to be as unspecifiable as that against which they are so
religiously shored up: we are left wondering what an Anglo-Indian exempted
from sanity might actually *do* ...

| | |

A QUEER EXCURSUS

If only we knew what the unspecifiable was: on the one hand, the queerness that threatens—on the other—the "sweetest and warmest." Let our hunch guide us through between the enchanting and the dangerous of a double bind that can't quite speak its name. Or let us, rather, attempt something infinitely more liberating: recognize that, for all the paranoia invoked, no double bind need actually exist; that the dangerous and enchanting aren't two walls that threaten to close in on us, shut us for good, but a modern mirage of competing aesthetics. Let us, in other words, for one precious moment, enjoy homosocial bonding without suffering from homosexual panic. Let us, I propose, jump into Aziz's bed.[9]

We won't be alone (what would be the point?) or, more snugly, alone *with* Aziz (let us postpone that to our wilder fantasies). Aziz is sick but entertaining guests ("One, two, three, four bumps, as people sat down upon his bed" [PI 94]), and we, too, if there's any room left—though particularly if there isn't—are invited to join in. And I mean, of course, not as some kind of fifth column, but as faithful participants in all that will be going on—in all, it bears repeating, without a tinge of paranoia. If we must be late (by playing the Indian, or, what at least in this novel amounts to the same, adhering to queer chic), then fine. Just as long as we don't miss a word beyond the first few exchanges (whose topic on the ill health of Hindus isn't part of our lesson here anyway), and plunge into the scene right in time for Aziz's recitation of a poem by Ghalib. "it had," happily enough, "no connection with anything that had gone before, but it came from his heart and spoke to theirs" (PI 96):

> They were overwhelmed by its pathos; pathos, they agreed, was the highest quality in art, a poem should touch the hearer with a sense of his own weakness, and should institute some comparison between mankind and flowers. The squalid bedroom grew quiet; the silly intrigues, the gossip, the shallow discontent were stilled, while words accepted as immortal filled the indifferent air.... Of the company, only Hamidullah had any comprehension of poetry. The minds of others were inferior and rough. Yet they listened with pleasure, because literature had not been divorced from their civilization. The police inspector, for instance, did not feel that Aziz had degraded himself by reciting, nor break into the cheery guffaw with which an Englishman averts the infection of beauty.... The poem had done no "good" to anyone but ... it voiced our loneliness nevertheless, our isolation, our need for the Friend who never comes yet is not entirely disproved. (PI 96–7)

So intimate a scene, and all in bed—pathos, weakness, flowers, the pleasures of literature, the beauty of recitation: all emblematic of a certain (why not quote the text?) "fundamental gaiety," the kind that Aziz "reached when he was with those whom he trusted" (PI 48). If we still haven't got it, Ghalib's Urdu verse belongs to an ephebophilic tradition, as does the motif of the "Friend who never comes."[10]

| | |

While Aziz's masculinity may strike an Englishman like McBryde as rather "queer," the quest for the "Friend who never comes" is much more than simply permissible for the presumptively heterosexual Indian male, but is rather expected as part of the institution of Indian maleness. To read this institution from an Anglo-European perspective, however, may still prove revealing, if not exactly of Aziz's sexuality, then of Anglo-Indian homophobia. Thus, for instance, we may note that Aziz's "queer effect" is drawn as much from an apparent absence as from a conspicuous excess of masculine self-consciousness. On the one hand, by cultivating the figure of the Mughal Emperor Babur, Aziz reveals a capacity for the kind of self-fashioning typical of the European veneration of St. Sebastian; on the other hand, Aziz exhibits a kind of natural abandon that emblematizes a different (but no less recognizable) kind of personage—the one whose maleness is reckoned all too lightly under guard. This type would be read into an Aziz who cries out, "Fielding! Oh, I have so wanted you!" (PI 146), or later, "Cyril, Cyril, don't leave me" (PI 221). Yet to the extent that the queerness of Aziz is, by definition, Anglo-European, it ultimately attaches itself most profitably to the Anglo-Indians themselves. To ask, therefore, who Aziz's friends are (or better: who among these friends isn't an Indian male? Or simpler yet: if not Indian, can he still be male?) betrays an interesting pattern, not least because Fielding stands out as its odd exception: if Indian, then the friend is necessarily male; if not Indian, which is to say English, then the friend is either Mrs. Moore, to a lesser extent Adela, or Fielding. In other words, the basic temperament required for friendship with Aziz is either that of an Indian male (or, in British terms, "queer") or that of an English woman (although that must be qualified by her being exceptionally nice and particularly unattractive). So that while Mrs. Moore and Adela can become Aziz's friends by being affined to the category of Indian men—"Aziz found the English ladies easy to talk to, he treated them like men" (PI 61)—Fielding is left to choose between two categories whose algebra *ugly English woman* = *queer Indian man*, even for so liberal a guy, must be hard to take. If only he hadn't been English, Fielding's masculinity might just have been spared.

As an Englishman, however, Fielding can't fool anyone, not least the astute Anglo-Indian women whose stake in identifying Fielding's kind is understandably the highest. "They disliked him. He took no notice of them, and this, which would have passed without comment in feminist England, did him harm in a community where the male is expected to be lively and helpful" (PI 56). A bachelor who isn't merely disinterested in looking for a wife but is clearly hateful of the wives of others, Fielding and his preferences must be deemed suspicious. That, moreover, even after having "discovered that it is possible to keep in with Indians and Englishmen, but that he who would also keep in with Englishwomen must drop the Indians" (PI 56), Fielding should sacrifice the company of the Englishwomen for that of the Indians', bespeaks more than a simple break of convention. The novel, in fact, presses the point: "Most Englishmen preferred their own kinswomen," but Fielding "had found it convenient and pleasant to associate with Indians and he must pay the price" (PI 57). Where proper male decorum dictates dropping the company of either Englishwomen or Indian men, still "to keep with" Indian men is—for whatever racial, racist, sexist, British standards of behavior—necessarily reducible to, and can only be explained by, a desire for Indian men, a desire strong enough, at any rate, to be entirely consistent with "dropping" the women. (A note on my own "keeping with" several Pakistani friends: the very plurality of my having more than one friend from Pakistan has given occasion among my white, liberal friends to jokes—jokes certainly unhomophobic but less certainly unracist—that I'm into "Pakistani boys." Now what salacious logic has transformed the category "Pakistani *friends*" into "Pakistani *boyfriends*," or, more simply, into "Pakistani *boys*"—period? And how, I dare not wonder, would Sadia Abbas respond to being thus unsexed? As though to have more than one "such" friend violates, on the one hand, the bigoted sensibility of having even one, and, on the other, the politically correct sensibility of daring to have more than one. Less a predisposition on my part than, to diffuse any gay sentimentality, "a stroke of good luck," I've become, nevertheless, a curry queen.) Similarly, in *A Passage to India*, chumming with the Indians isn't merely socially queer (although it is), but must also be explainable by a queer predisposition.[11]

Not, however, that once he categorically drops the women Fielding is free of homosexual panic. A bachelor, who at least until the end of the novel seems intent on remaining one, Fielding may have rehearsed a retort for the pertinent question—*Q*: "Why are you not married?" *A*: "Because I have more or less come through without it" (PI 110)—but can't finally contain his panic at the slightest provocation:

"Why don't you marry Miss Quested?"

"Good God! why, the girl's a prig.... Of course, I don't know her, but she struck me as one of the more pathetic products of Western education. She depresses me." (PI 110)

"Any suggestion that he should marry always does produce overstatements on the part of the bachelor" (PI 111). What begins as a little ritual of male bonding—by Aziz's "great compliment" to Fielding of showing him the photo of his late wife (PI 109); by Fielding confiding in Aziz "a little about myself" (PI 110)—soon develops into a moment of remarkable divisiveness, where the priorities and desires of an Indian male are revealed to be wholly different from those of an Englishman. At the very least, Aziz can, and often does, express his feelings (as when he talks about his late wife), while Fielding only "wished that he too could be carried away on waves of emotion" (PI 109). But Aziz is also quite lustful for women, whereas on this count too Fielding can't but remain somehow dumb. Thus even as Fielding dismisses Adela for being what he calls a "prig," Aziz (who tellingly doesn't even know the word) sees her fault—her *only* fault?—in having "practically no breasts" (PI 111), thereby throwing the label "prig" onto the embarrassed Fielding himself. "There is always trouble when two people do not think of sex at the same moment" (PI 263).

Unlike Aziz, whose desire for women is continuously invoked in lecherous fantasies of taking a trip to the brothels of Calcutta, Fielding's idea of sex remains circumscribed within the institution of marriage. True, the novel seems careful to intimate that it had not always been so with Fielding, but it relegates any such suggestions to mere innuendos. "His career," we read of Fielding, "though scholastic, was varied, and had included going to the bad and repenting thereafter" (PI 55). And when McBryde later calls Fielding's attention to a letter Aziz wrote a friend "who apparently keeps a brothel" in Calcutta as proof that Aziz "was fixing up to see women," Fielding momentarily suspends his usual discretion: "I dare say you have the right to throw stones at a young man for doing that, but I haven't. I did the same at his age" (PI 161). Significantly, it is upon the occasion of Fielding's visit to Aziz that the narrative allows for this singular revelation:

He looked back at his own life. What a poor crop of secrets it had produced! There were things in it that he had shown to no one, but they were so uninteresting, it wasn't worth while lifting a purdah on their account. He'd been in love, engaged to be

married, lady broke it off, memories of her and thoughts about
her had kept him from other women for a time; then indulgence,
followed by repentance and equilibrium. (PI 109)

But it is a revelation more homosocial than heterosexual, for it emerges from
Fielding's desire to reciprocate Aziz's gesture of showing Fielding the
photograph. "What had he done to deserve this outburst of confidence,"
wonders the half-panicked Fielding; "and what hostage could he give in
exchange?" (PI 109).

If marriage continues to trouble Fielding up until, as well as after, his
own at the end of the novel, it does so only in relation to, and the extent to
which, his bachelorhood affects his relationship with Aziz. "It is on my mind
that you think me a prude about women," Fielding writes to Aziz just before
heading to England. "I had rather you thought anything else of me. If I live
impeccably now, it is only because I am well on in the forties—a period of
revision" (PI 268). And although he ultimately marries, Fielding's view of
marriage is sinister at least:

Marriage is too absurd in any case. It begins and continues for
such very slight reasons. The social business props it up on one
side, and the theological business on the other, but neither of
them are marriage, are they? I've friends who can't remember
why they married, no more can their wives. I suspect that it
mostly happens haphazard, though afterwards various noble
reasons are invented. About marriage I am cynical. (PI 250–51)

Still, even after his marriage to Stella, Fielding's heterosexuality continues to
be challenged, at once by Aziz's blunt question—"Is Stella not faithful to you,
Cyril?" (PI 308)—and by the reality of that marriage itself: "He was not quite
happy about his marriage. He was passionate physically again—the final
flare-up before the clinkers of middle-age—and he knew that his wife did not
love him as much as he loved her, and he was ashamed of pestering her" (PI
308). Ironically, if at first Fielding is to some degree separated from Aziz for
lacking a desire for women, Fielding is now forever to remain separated from
Aziz for finding such desire: "Fielding has thrown his lot with Anglo-India
by marrying a countrywoman" (PI 309).[12]

One reason why Fielding's friendship with Aziz fails to improve even
after Fielding's marriage is that, once *too* interesting as a bachelor, Fielding is
now less than interesting as a married man. "I was thinking of telling you a
little about myself some day if I can make it interesting enough," he confides
to Aziz before his marriage (PI 110). Yet if whichever way Fielding goes he

finds himself unable (as people of his kind often try so hard) to "get it right," it is because Fielding never will. For the sad fate is that precisely when he is most sure of having reached "it," Fielding is destined for that dramatic slip (or is it, incurred by its own internal slippage, *lisp*?) that will keep him outside the mode of normality by the sheer self-consciousness that has overdetermined, not to say curiously *mis*pronounced, what is at best a highly delicate code. When it comes to marriage, Fielding completely misreads that code, failing to recognize that the state clearly privileged in *A Passage to India* is neither to get married nor not to get married, but rather to have been married. Such, certainly, is the example of both Aziz (who marries once) and Mrs. Moore (who marries twice), whose close friendship with each other serves as one clear indicator of the many benefits the novel wishes to advertise about the status of widowhood.[13] The other benefit, just as important, is that widowhood wields the needed authority for legitimating the rebuke of marriage, a rebuke that makes itself a project in all of Forster's novels with the exception of *A Room with a View*.

| | | |

To end, but with this queer paradox: at a certain section of Bombay, a section known as Dongri, just steps from a local mosque, a modest door leads to an ancient establishment. Whether one is tempted to call it a bathhouse, or (as the sign over the door declares in Urdu) an "Irani hammam," its function and tradition remain the same. It has been there for over a hundred and fifty years, catering to a bustling male clientele. They flock there in the hundreds, especially on Fridays before prayers—men who, for ten rupees, procure a treatment of exquisite pleasures. In a large hall, just before the inner sauna, they unbutton their shirts and undress. Some then lounge in discreet alcoves, while others wrap around their waists the lungis provided for them to wear in the baths. As they enter the main bathing area, they are met by professional masseurs who, for time unspecified, rub and scrub their bodies in the thick mist. Signs on the stone walls warn: "Those suffering from V.D. or heart disease are strictly not permitted." Some distance away, not far from the Taj Mahal Intercontinental Hotel, in the touristy section of Bombay's waterfront, one of the city's increasingly open gay bars is packed. In its air-conditioned room, men, some dressed in fashionable jeans, but all aptly dressed, spend an evening with friends. They drink beer, listen to music, chat, make plans for the following day. Perhaps a lucky few will later have sex.

The queerness of "East meets West": not merely in the sense that both of these institutions exist side by side, but also that the ancient one, the bathhouse (the bathhouse that, once part of medieval Europe and closed by the Church in its efforts to curtail male prostitution, later became part of gay liberation only to be shut down by the State in its attempt, equally zealous, to curtail gay sex) seems so much sleazier than its modern counterpart, the gay bar. For while in the first, naked men rub naked men, in the second, although ("Kama Sutra") rubbers might be on hand, any actual rubbing is postponed for another location. And while the Irani hammam becomes the simulacrum of hybridity itself, offering ancient luxuries (the cleansing ritual) in the face of modern realities ("heart disease," "V.D."), the gay bar exemplifies the paradox of a clientele more frank about what it seeks but also less likely to find it there. Still more, the Irani hammam, whose most regular bathers are precisely those most likely to deny the very thing they are there to enjoy, represents a culture (if not a religion) with relatively few injunctions against homosexuality; the gay bar, meanwhile, the prototype of a specifically Western emergence of a distinct gay culture (where *khush*, for happy or gay, is the new code word), represents the historical reason for its own precarious existence: gay sex is illegal in India only as a holdover from the British colonial statutes.

NOTES

An early version of this essay was presented at the First Quebec Lesbian and Gay Studies Conference in November 1992 as part of a panel on "Sex, Nation and Metaphor." I'd like to thank the chair of that panel, Judith Scherer Herz, as well as the respondent, Jody Berland, for exceedingly helpful suggestions. I'm also grateful to Robert K. Martin for taking an interest in my own interest in E. M. Forster, and for doing so even before I dreamed my thoughts were interesting enough to make public. Additional helpful advice came from Jean McClure, Samina Najmi, Sadia Abbas, Sarah McKibben, Amir Najmi, Eleanor Kaufman, and L. Ramakrishnan.

    1. "Aurally enacting a drive toward the same, the pun's sound cunningly erases, or momentarily suspends, the semantic differences by which the hetero is both made to appear and made to appear natural, lucid, self-evident" (Craft, "Alias" 38).

    2. Similar confusion has extended itself in Forster criticism to the sexual significance of the Marabar Caves with at least two competing interpretations. Frances L. Restuccia, for one, in an essay otherwise devoted to indeterminacy in *A Passage to India*, confidently proceeds to determine the gender of the caves: "The Caves are not only female morphologically but perhaps linguistically as well" (Restuccia 122); and Sara Suleri, in an alternative reading, suggests that "the category 'Marabar Cave' roughly translates into the anus of imperialism" (Suleri 132).

    3. I say would "seem" queer, since we should remain wary of the *un*queer (because misogynist) drift in numerous Hindu traditions—including that, of course, of *sati*. As Ketu H. Katrak points out, "The notion of female suffering in the Hindu tradition is dangerously glorified through such use of mythological models" (Katrak 398). Still, some

of these mythological models encompass countless different forms of sexual dualism (as, for instance, the half-male, half-female Siva), triadic structures (as in the notion of yoni, of female twins conjoining a third point representing earth), and diverse kinds of polymorphism (as in the Tantric philosophy of the six *chakras*, or nerve centers, whose basal one lies in the region of the rectum). Perhaps because of its monotheistic origins, Islamic culture has been unable to compete with the sexual diversity of the Hindu tradition; but it, too, especially in the literature that has emerged from the Mughal era, provides complex histories of sexual behavior. For a unique collection of essays on South Asian traditions and sexualities, see Rakesh Ratti; for the more academic stuff, see also the essays by R. Radhakrishnan and Gayatri Chakravorty Spivak in Andrew Parker et al.

4. Katrak rightly points out that "Mayo's orientalizing approach focused solely on the most dramatically visible forms of abuse—heaped upon Indian women by Indian men. She did not discuss at all the colonizer's role in women's oppression" (Katrak 403).

5. There is no "proof" that the last British viceroy to India was queer, but the flamboyance of Lord Mountbatten of Burma has earned him a place in Roland Barthes's journal in an entry that rustles with its own Barthesian queerness: "—En rentrant, à la radio, j'ai appris l'attentat de l'IRA contre Lord Mountbatten. Tout le monde est indigné, mais personne ne parle de la mort de son petit-fils, gosse de quinze-ans" (—Returning home, on the radio, I learned of the assassination of Lord Mountbatten by the IRA. Everyone is indignant, but no one mentions the death of his grandson, a fifteen-year-old) (Barthes 88).

6. Ignored by such a narrative would be the precarious position of women in India especially in times—as in today—of "Hindutva," or Hindu fundamentalist resurgence. For an excellent overview of contemporary legal debates in India, see Ratna Kapur and Brenda Cossman 35–44.

7. In her subtle reading of the novel, Restuccia argues that it's "Eastern indeterminacy in *A Passage to India*, which keeps alive the theoretical possibility of an attempted rape whose vagueness precludes the act from being prosecutable" (Restuccia, 111). I wish to carry her reading onto a different trajectory and suggest that Eastern indeterminacy more than simply "keeps alive the theoretical possibility of art attempted rape," but in effect *constitutes* it.

8. For this, as for a whole host of invaluable insights into the novel's narrative, style, history, and criticism, see Herz, *Passage*.

9. On "homosexual panic," consult Sedgwick, *Epistemology*, especially the chapter on "The Beast in the Jungle," 181–212; see also her *Between Men*.

10. See Tariq Rahman, "Significance" and "Homosexual."

11. For a consideration of personal relationships within a cross-cultural framework and biographical analogies between Aziz's friendship with Fielding and Forster's with Ross Masood, see Rustom Bharucha.

12. We might speculate that if Fielding had run his school in England rather than India, his bachelorhood would have provoked considerable anxiety from quite another direction. Compare his fate to that of Herbert Pembroke in *The Longest Journey* (1907) whose status as a single man prompts the parents of his charges to "demand that the house-master should have a wife" (LJ 63).

13. The novel creates the possibility that Aziz in fact remarries at the end of the novel, but the elusive suggestion seems to raise more questions than answers, including whether the new attachment is not a bride so much as a mistress:

Life passed pleasantly, the climate was healthy so that the children
could be with him all the year round, and he had married again—not
exactly a marriage, but he liked to regard it as one—and he read his
Persian, wrote his poetry, had his horse, and sometimes got some
shikar while the good Hindus looked the other way. (284)

Restuccia rightly notes: "We may wonder if this nonchalance is a matter of Aziz's lack of
interest in his mate or if the narrative complies with Aziz's desire to protect his treasured
mate from aliens" (Restuccia 121).

DEBRAH RASCHKE

Forster's Passage to India: *Re-Envisioning Plato's Cave*

Literary Modernism, as much interpretative commentary continues to reveal, oscillates between a desire for an impossible certainty (all that Western philosophy promised in various renditions until the close of the nineteenth century) and a reciprocal terror that ultimately nothing can be known. The cryptic images associated with this uncertainty are familiar: an ambiguous line drawn down the center of a painting in Woolf's *To the Lighthouse*; Stephen Dedalus's enigmatic forging in Joyce's *Portrait of the Artist as a Young Man*; the culminating toothbrush hanging on the wall in Eliot's "Rhapsody on a Windy Night." Intractable and persistent, interpretations of Modernism still pursue collapsing centers, elusive origins, and vanishing falcons.[1] Epistemology (even if a failed epistemology), for obvious reasons, remains key.

In this spirit of uncertainty, the Platonic, which depends on fixity and the stability of boundaries, may initially seem incongruent.[2] Yet the attempts within Modernism to flee from the constraints of time and narrative so fervently critiqued by Georg Lukács and Fredric Jameson do at least ambivalently recall the Platonic vision (although not necessarily the commensurate reactionary, political implications). Socrates tells us in the *Phaedo* that the philosopher comes closest to truth when he is closest to death, when the material world is the furthest away: "The true votary of

From *The Comparatist* XXI. © 1997 by Debrah Raschke.

philosophy is likely to be misunderstood by other men; they do not perceive that he is always pursuing death and dying" (*Dialogues: A Selection* 56). Likewise, aestheticism functioning as a kind of substitute Platonics also takes us out of this world, enacting yet another ruse that points the reader's eyes toward the symbol (and toward the heavens) away from bodies, away from sexuality.[3] Aestheticism underlies the tension in Yeats in which at least one of his personas yearns to be gathered into "the artifice of eternity" or to merge into the "breathless starlit air" where "all thought is done." It underlies Eliot's urge toward unity in *The Waste Land* and the culmination of that desired unity in *The Four Quartets*, in which weighty imagery and a consistency of meter propels the reader simultaneously toward death and a higher metaphysical vision.

This disjuncture within Modernism between Platonic underpinnings and a ubiquitous uncertainty, however, is less strange than its evasion of gender, particularly given poststructuralist critiques of metaphysics as insidiously steeped in desire. If knowing is inseparable from desire, then Modernism's epistemological crisis (still primarily regarded as gender-neutral) cannot be separated from a crisis in sexuality. E. M. Forster, although less stylistically experimental than many of his counterparts, is remarkably radical in his vision on this account, for he sees in the Modernist metaphysical collapse, not an abyss, but an opportunity. Most specifically, Western metaphysics for Forster clearly informs desire. When Western metaphysics collapses, it offers not only a liberating new way of seeing the world, but also a revitalized vision of sexuality—since bodies and materiality (most frequently associated with the feminine) become pariahs to the visionary quest.

That Forster was interested in issues of sexuality goes without saying. That he was interested in metaphysics also nearly goes without saying. *Maurice* contains explicit allusions to Plato's *Symposium* and *Phaedrus*. *Howards End*, in its injunction to "only connect," challenges the binary structure inherent to Western metaphysics, and *The Longest Journey* begins with a discussion of the reality of a cow:

> It was philosophy. They were discussing the existence of objects. Do they exist only when there is someone to look at them? Or have they a real existence of their own? It is all very interesting, but at the same time difficult. Hence the cow. She seemed to make things easier. She was so familiar, so solid, that surely the truths that she illustrated would in time become familiar and solid also. Is the cow there or not? (1–2)

One of the most poignant critiques of philosophy occurs in *Passage to India*, which reveals Plato's "Allegory of the Cave" to be an insidious epistemology. For Forster, this collapse (representative of the collapse of certainty, in general) is not ominous, but salvific. Interweaving Platonic allusions into the descriptions of the Marabar Caves and then subverting them, *Passage* refuses Platonic flight, which soars into the philosophical skies and forgets the material world below. In doing so, Forster's text collapses an epistemological and a sexual order in which pure masculine reason dominates, writes off, or buries what has been labeled, at least archetypally, as feminine; and, in doing so, it also challenges traditional conceptions of romance, which depend on metaphysical substructures for its survival.[4]

In Plato's "Allegory of the Cave," an unidentifiable number of prisoners are chained by the neck and groin in a womb-like cave, composed of the dark earthiness of the material world. Behind and above the prisoners are firelight and a parapet, which projects a continual dumb show captivating its viewers with shadows and unsubstantial images. Possessing a long, uterine-like passage that functions only as an exit, Plato's cave is supposedly responsible for all kinds of distorted (but pleasurable) fantasies from which one must flee in favor of a purer philosophical truth. Its dwellers do not see well. They live in a dream-world where projected fire is mistaken for the sun, and shadows are mistaken for reality. Misunderstandings prevail, and truth is indecipherable.

Since the prisoners, chained as they are, can know only the part of the cave which is in front of them, they can offer only their own private, limited version of this mesmeric dumb show. They are imprisoned both literally and metaphorically. Imprisoned literally by chains, the cave dwellers have no opportunity for physical communion, and verbal communication, if it exists at all, is muffled and distorted. Imprisoned metaphorically, each cave dweller is locked into his own version of the show. Thus Plato's underground cave imprisons with pleasurable deceptions, representations its captors think are real, but which are only a product of their chained vision.

A path of "steep and rugged ascent" leads to the exit of this prison, a one-way passage out. A metaphor for the journey of the soul, for the ascent into truth, this is the journey up and out that only the mind severed from the murky obsessions of the body will attain. Under the tutelage of the philosopher, the liberated prisoner discovers the definition of "truth" to be fixed, unequivocal, and separate from the body (or cave). As part of the bargain, he must forget the sensory pleasures of his first dwelling and, by extension, the pleasures of being connected to the feminine. As Luce Irigaray notes, the prospective philosopher must "disengage himself from his human double, his female understudy, launching himself into the sky into a philosophical flight" and must never lose his "wing feathers" if his vision is to remain untainted (*Speculum* 322). Bodies and materiality, in other words, get in the way.

So Platonic philosophy becomes a means not only of seeking truth, but also of rejecting one form of desire (feminine) for another. By cutting off this early experience and by setting up the position of the sun/father as the only truth, Plato in one move legitimizes a hierarchy that privileges the masculine as the only truth, solidifies binary oppositions that require a fixed definition of truth and sexual construction, and, through those definitions, relegates the feminine (associated with subterranean dreams and amorphous pleasures) to contained structures—such as caves, houses, or beautiful worlds of their own. For truth to be seen in Plato, the corporeal must be distanced and eventually forgotten; in Forster, the corporeal leads to mistakes.

Recalling the epistemological frame of Plato's Cave, Marabar invokes its central metaphors: a speculative search for knowledge and truth, the impediments of imprisonment and fancy, and a severing of the sensory cave experience from the supposed liberation into pure speculative truth. "Older than all spirit" and recalling the "primal" India and its myths of origin, Marabar Caves are no ordinary caves (*Passage* 124). They are, in fact, a speculative space that haunts many of its visitors, and as *Passage*'s structural center, this section functions as a catalyst for both an epistemological and a sexual crisis. A place of many unresolved riddles, the Marabar Caves provoke (like Plato's cave) a litany of questions that are hardly the usual fare for inquiries into caves: why is there an "inlaid mirror" that "divides and reflects"?; what is the echo or "aboum" that haunts Mrs. Moore?; was Adela sexually assaulted?; why, as in Plato's cave, is there a forced entry?

Secondly, Marabar, at least ostensibly, is hardly a place to be trusted. Like Plato's dumb-show, it offers a show of illusions where what seems to be may not be at all, and where one cannot trust what one hears, sees, or touches. One cannot know what produces sliminess, aboum, or images of seduction. The caves play tricks. The interpretation of what one sees and hears is clearly limited by one's preoccupations or angle of vision (a bit like being chained by the head and groin): when Adela enters the cave, she is thinking of the lack of passion in her relationship with Ronny; just before Mrs. Moore enters the cave, Aziz reminds her of their encounter in the mosque. After the cave experience, Adela obsesses about seduction and Mrs. Moore about religion.

If, however, Marabar recalls some of the physical and metaphorical details of Plato's cave, it revises considerably Plato's meaning. Marabar may be the site of illusions and trickery, but it fosters insight as well, which means that the dream-world of the cave, as producing truths of its own, cannot be denied. Its memory enables Adela to tell her story in court with clarity and prompts her to realize the deficiency of her relationship with Ronny. Although Marabar may invoke illusion and trickery, so does the "*new hocus-pocus, of reason*" that purports to leave the experiences of the cave behind forever. As Irigaray notes, the philosopher who lifts the cave's veil and reveals the little "statues" as its sole cause of misunderstanding conceals his own motives of desire—the giddy effects of "swinging from the chandelier-Idea," the "fixture-fixation," which in recalling the chaining of the head and groin, has its origins in the cave (*Speculum* 271). Forster's Marabar, presaging Irigaray, critiques any movement toward truth that abstracts itself from the body and desire. The movement toward truth in *Passage to India* is not simply up and out.

Marabar, unlike Plato's cave, will not go away, will not recede into an abandoned consciousness that the liberated prisoner must forget once he comes under the tutelage of the philosopher. Haunted by their experience in the caves, neither Mrs. Moore nor Adela can sever their cave-experience from their conscious lives. Mrs. Moore, in repudiating any meaningful interactions with others, enacts the despair she experiences in the caves, while Adela mentally traverses the scene of the supposed crime. More generally, the caves intrude on the experience of everyday life, interrupting the seamless landscape. The sky, which gains its strength from the sun, "settles everything" at the end of the first chapter—everything but the Caves, where to the south of the horizon, "fists and fingers are thrust up through the soil" (9). Things connected with material existence and with sexuality continually interrupt the plot. They rise up out of the night and out of the bowels of the earth, like the undefined stricken animal that suddenly emerges out of the hills on Marabar Road. The interruptions emerging from the night and the omnipresent caves suggest that the earth cannot be split from the sky, body cannot be split from spirit, that the process of "knowing" must incorporate both. Such too is the message conveyed by the humorous legend in "Temple" of the young Mohammedan of Mau, who, ignoring the absence of his head (which had been chopped off by the police), went about his business of freeing prisoners, so that his body fell in one place and his head in another.

Things rise out of the earth in *Passage*, and they rise out of the body. When Adela cannot speak after Marabar, her body speaks for her. The body becomes a theater of physical symptoms without any identifiable organic cause. The body demands attention.[5] Hysteria, she calls it, not madness. Lying in bed, Adela mentally re-enters the cave and sees Aziz as innocent and eventually will see the fraudulence that marks her romance with Ronny. In

Adela's case, the cave and the body become associated with a truth that will not be ignored. If it is ignored, the body takes revenge, feeding upon itself unhealthily (193).

In direct contrast to Adela's ruminations is Ronny's intransigent linear thinking, which severs mind from body. In attempting to silence Adela's "hysteria" by persuading her that her bodily vision is false, Ronny assures her that she has a right (and obligation) to prosecute, that there is no room for her questionings, that the machinery once started cannot be stopped. "Truth's empire," as Irigaray notes, "permits no hint of indecision," no admission of fantasy (*Speculum* 270). Functioning as a kind of metaphysical metaphor, Ronny's insistence that Adela abandon her Marabar musings recalls the philosopher's demand that the liberated prisoner see his previous existence as a den of misguided perception that must be forgotten and suppressed at all costs. Once liberated from the cave, he must persevere in a straight line toward truth, without hesitation. Adela, likewise, if she is to be considered sane by her British friends, must turn her back on her memory of the caves and the vision they elicit. Relinquishing the dream-world of the cave for the pleasure of truth as a singular vision that shuts out alternative "false" visions, however, simply does not work in *Passage*. The caves, in one way or another, always come back, as does the multiplicity they reflect.

Conversely, for Plato, fixed meanings exemplified by the Forms are the highest possible truth, and although forever postponed, this knowledge is still the ultimate goal. Plato, throughout his dialogues, resists relativity. In the *Phaedo*, for example, Socrates argues the infallibility of binary opposites, positing that "essential opposites exclude one another" and can never become their opposite either in the abstract or in the concrete (*Dialogues: A Selection* 104). In the *Theaetetus*, the attempt to define pure knowledge (episteme) begins with an opening conversation that works "to fix the (ideal) historical accuracy of the report" (Friedländer 3:145) and then establishes the need to define the nature of knowledge in the most precise terms. Dismissing other attempts to define knowledge such as the Heraclitean relatively (the world as flux) and Protagoras' subjectivity (that man is the measure of all things), Socrates asserts that knowledge is not merely perception subject to random forces of the universe (247), and not merely "right opinion" (318). Nor is it proficiency in craft or even mathematics, which is a concrete manifestation of knowledge. Moreover, firmly establishing what knowledge is not, the *Theaetetus*, as well as the *Sophist*, *Timaeus*, *Parmenides*, and *Phaedo*, postpone an ultimate solution, not because a solution does not exist, but because reducing its terms to language makes the eternal (Forms) subject to the temporal and changeable world. For Plato, "Form, or Idea," as Friedländer notes, is "something absolute" (3:207).

In *Passage*, however, the desire for fixing meaning is misguided, eliciting a false certainty tantamount to epistemological error, what Irigaray characterizes as "life in philosophy": a dangerous, narcissistic stasis in which everything is always the same—a morphology displaying only self-replication in which there is no change, no "ups and downs" (*Speculum* 303), a sunset remaining forever posed as a rosy flame in the Western sky, Aziz imposing on the architecture of the mosque a landscape of his own desires. This essentially Platonic episteme is the (supposedly) "ideal morphology," which, in excluding all change, limits "truth" to one meaning (*Speculum* 320). In this system, there is no quibbling with the Ideal, which must be made a standard Form. Intolerant of deviation, this vision exiles all that is different or Other (most specifically the feminine) into negation.[6] Mrs. Moore's despair after her experience at Marabar is less related to Marabar itself (which is undefinable) than it is to a confining fixity. Interpreting the history of Christianity from "Let there be Light" to "It is finished" as amounting only to "boum" (150), she limits her experience in the caves to a single meaning—some inherent nihilism—which may indeed be one meaning, but certainly not the only one. Not until she realizes that "boum" is only one of many visions does her despair lift. Upon approaching the "soupy dawn of Bombay," she concludes that the echo was not final, not the only India (210). Her last vision is "soupy," flexible, giving way to a multiplicity of meanings. Similarly, when Adela recounts what she sees as Aziz's innocence to the courts, she has a similar realization: "Her vision was of several caves" (228). Nor is this fluid truth just some feminine delusion, for it is Godbole's vision as well: Godbole summons a God who is mother, father, and everybody. There are many Indias in *Passage*, many caves, no single truth. In offering a polyphonic view of the world, Adela, Mrs. Moore, and Godbole thus thwart the epistemological assumption that truth is ultimately situated in a fixed, Platonic Absolute.

Ronny and Aziz, in contrast, are obsessed with certainty (with fixing truth), what Irigaray defines as the "fixture-fixation"—the dynamic for the pupil–teacher relationship in Plato (*Speculum* 271). Ronny, unable to cope with multiple meanings, will see only one truth about India and one truth about Adela's supposed seduction. He insists, moreover, that Adela and his mother provide him an idyllic unity of mind by mirroring back his views. In "Mosque," before the ordeal of the caves, Ronny orders his mother not to speak to Adela about Aziz because he is Indian and, in Ronny's view, a possibly corrupting influence who might cause Adela to question Ronny's imperialistic stand on India. Mrs. Moore agrees to do as Ronny wishes, but her acquiescence is not enough. Ronny still wants more: her agreement or her mind as mirror/speculum: "There you go again, mother" (34), Ronny complains when she questions his judgment. Noting the "anxiety in his voice," Mrs. Moore comments on how Ronny is still much "the little boy, who must have what he liked," who, in other words, becomes anxious when his mother does not mirror his own thoughts. In refusing to remain the only "fixed point in a world gone mad" (Hultberg 251), Mrs. Moore defies the definition of femininity in which the woman reflects for the man his own image.[7] Her failure to mirror instills panic in Ronny, paralleling the terrors of Marabar. There is nothing of man in the Marabar caves. As for the mirror "inlaid with lovely colors," given the darkness of the caves, it would seem that this lovely mirror would reflect back nothing, certainly not any coherent image of self.

Ronny's frustration with his mother (and perhaps some critics' frustrations with her as well) stem from the fact that she will not mirror (will not provide a space for Ronny's autospecularization) and will not remain fixed. She takes on several different personas—mother, friend, mystic, recluse and cynic, and, finally, Hindu goddess Esmiss Esmoor. In her death, Mrs. Moore becomes testimony to this multiplicity. Several legends materialize surrounding her demise and, "at one period, two distinct tombs containing Esmiss Esmoor's remains were reported" (257). It seems that Mrs. Moore cannot be contained. Exasperated at this uncontainability, Ronny insists on burying her fluidity. In response to legends that metamorphosed her into an undefinable Hindu goddess and to the actual watery tomb where his mother lies, Ronny confines her memory to a respectable image. He plans to erect an enclosed structure: a tablet in Northamptonshire Church where she worshipped, bearing her name and the record of her birth and death. By inscribing her memory in stone in a church where she is not, Ronny attempts to fix his mother's memory, to refute the fluid oral tales surrounding her death that refuse not only closure, but also fixed truth. Ronny's inscription encloses her story, editing out the "revolting" ruptures such as her transfiguration into a Hindu goddess. As the narrator indicates, it was "revolting [for him] to hear his mother travestied into Esmiss Esmoor" (225).

Adela poses an equal threat to Ronny's sensibilities. In her desire for movement, she resists both physical and mental confinement. Her wish to explore is viewed by Ronny and her British friends as a rather unladylike activity both literally and metaphorically. She will not be cloistered by what Bonnie Finkelstein (122) calls the "veil of ladylikeness."[8] Moreover, after she accuses Aziz of seduction, she still resists the British wives' attempt to refashion her as the "darling girl" and wants no one's company except Mrs. Moore's (180). In other words, she refuses a fixed definition. Finally, she refuses to construct the proper sexual ending to her story. She violates the genre of the romance, whereby she would passively wait as the court defends her purity by inscribing its version of her story and punishing the dark offender. Instead, she decides she does not like the script and tells her own story. Her version of the Aziz story in court is a refusal of the romance as much as it is a refusal to lie, a refusal to become the passively inscribed woman who is rescued by and defined by the storming, chivalric hero.

Ronny's persistent demands on his mother and Adela to believe as he believes, his intransigent insistence on Aziz's conviction, and his arrogance toward the Indians all reflect a resistance against multiplicity and uncontained sexuality that threaten his ordering of the world. His sense of himself as an autonomous, knowing subject who enters the court as the rescuer of truth/chastity (they become synonymous in this case[9]) is dependent upon his securing a way of knowing that is severed from dreams, from the body and from Adela's hysteria, all of which threaten his vision of the world. Notably, after the trial, Ronny virtually disappears from the text except for planning the monument he intends to erect for his mother. It is as if the collapse of his version of the Aziz story simultaneously collapses his identity as romantic hero and patriarchal guardian. As his epistemological vision ceases to exist, he, too, literally ceases to exist.

For Ronny, and likewise for Aziz, the act of fixing is, as with Plato, inextricably connected with issues of sexuality—that which is to be both escaped and controlled. If the feminine matrix of Plato's cave is to be escaped, its propensity for multiple and alternative misreproductions, its supposedly spawning "misbegotten freaks and abortive products" (*Speculum* 255)—what Adela, Mrs. Moore and Godbole further—must be controlled. In addition to Plato's coerced forgetting of the cave experience, the cave itself, as "outside the scope of philosophical vision" and never fully represented (Larisch 151) is a means of controlling representation. It is a space that remains elsewhere, a blank onto which philosophical judgments are later transposed and a medium through which alternative ideas are exorcised. The winnowing machine of Plato's *Timaeus* (a later version of *The Republic*'s allegorical cave), is an even more incisive control of the feminine. This reproductive site receives "all forms" (correct ideas) but, the feminine that houses this process has "no form" of its own (*Dialogues* 737), what Butler terms "formless femininity" (53).[10] Having no distinct form of its own, the function of this mute space is to receive and reproduce the ideas with which it is germinated, a process that becomes metonymic for failed sexual interchange in *Passage*.

Aziz, like Ronny, intertwines his epistemological desire for fixity with his sexual fantasies. As a victim of British imperialism and of Ronny's caustic dismissal, he certainly occupies a different and more complicated cultural space than does Ronny and is thus a far richer character. Nevertheless, the still-dominant readings of *Passage* that place Aziz and variations of the Anglo-Indian problem as center continue to elide Aziz's conceptions of women, which function only when real woman are absent (and thus contained). When Aziz looks at the photograph of his wife, his initial response is unhappiness (a natural response—since she is dead), but as he continues to look, he becomes taken with delight. Her image, fixed in that photograph and detached from the material world, gives him pleasure, precisely because the image is fixed and the actual woman is absent. Similarly, in "Temple," Aziz's poetry fixes on one subject—the distant and idealized conception of Oriental womanhood.

When Aziz contemplates "meaning" at the mosque, he likewise attempts to fix its definition and thereby projects his epistemological vision onto the landscape. Functioning as an Edenic garden, the mosque contains and isolates. A low wall surrounds the courtyard where the mosque is located, a gate (now ruined) is the only entry. The frieze that contains the 99 names of God (suggesting that the meaning of the universe can be contained within 99 definitions) polarizes light and dark: the engraved black names on the white marble, the white marble against the black sky. Aziz enjoys the dualism. "The contest between this dualism and the contention of the shadows within pleased Aziz, and he tried to symbolize the *whole* into some truth of religion or love" (19; emphasis mine). Truth for Aziz is polarized and contained, devoid of messiness and contradiction. There is no slippage of the sign that mixes dark and light, masculine and feminine, no opposite metamorphosing into its opposed other, no excess, only a duality that ultimately mirrors one way of thinking—his. For Aziz, the "mosque alone signified," and the signification (at least as Aziz understands it) walls out the "complex appeal of the night" (and sexuality). Still, Aziz's epistemological construct is suspect. As the narrator notes, Aziz decked the mosque "with meanings the builder had never intended" (19).

It is Mrs. Moore, however, who really shakes the epistemological frame. Her entrance interrupts Aziz's homoerotic affair with his own mind, in which he produces a union between the architectural structure of the mosque and his own projected desires for polarity and sexual absence. With increased agitation, Aziz watches, as one by one, three pillars of the mosque quiver, the third quiver signalling Mrs. Moore's entrance into the mosque. This disruption prompts him to retort angrily: "Madam! Madam! Madam! ... Madam, this is a mosque; you have no right here at all; you should have taken off your shoes" (20). The shoes (which Mrs. Moore has already removed) hardly seem relevant. It's the "you have no right here" that stands out. This quivering, which has sexual connotations to begin with, becomes even more relevant when we realize Aziz first suspects that Mrs. Moore is a young woman:

"Mrs. ___." Advancing, he found that she was old. A fabric bigger
than the mosque fell to pieces, and he did not know whether he
was glad or sorry. She was older than Hamidullah Begum, with a
red face and white hair. Her voice had deceived him. (20)

Aziz, in his earlier meditative state, has exorcised excess, sexual excess
included, out of his vision of the world until it comes quivering back in. In
Lacanian fashion, Aziz gets love and religion, God, and woman all mixed
up.[11] Aziz's garden meditation, where he is momentarily at peace, is an act
of what Irigaray defines as "autospecularization"—the philosopher's
relegating to unreality any ideas that do not conform to his Idea of truth
and the transformation of his own vision into universalized truth (*Speculum*
296). As Irigaray notes, the source of the philosopher's vision begins as a
mirror:

> The enlightenment of the Idea makes flames just like a mirror
> that has concentrated the light. Of the Sun, of the Good. And, in
> a different way, of the eye, of the soul, of the eye (of the) soul.
> Since these are also specula. This speculogamy blinds all the
> more effectively because it amounts to a *specular auto-gamy*.
> (*Speculum* 294)

This seems to explain why Aziz is so badly shaken when Mrs. Moore enters
the mosque: she shatters his mirror.

Vexed, Aziz in three different moves attempts to secure some control
over the unruly Mrs. Moore, and inadvertently over his previous
epistemological frame. First, he engages her in chatter, as if mere words
would make the sexual quivering go away. Secondly, he calls attention to her
position as mother by taking delight in the names of her children and by
putting her in the position of listener and sympathizer as he breaks into a
tirade over the wrongs done to him by the Club women. Mrs. Moore (like a
good mother here) patiently listens. Thirdly, he attempts to transpose
chivalric roles onto their meeting, insisting that she not walk alone and that
he be her protector. After all, there are bad characters (such as snakes)
lurking in the night. His position finally affirmed as she becomes his
sympathizer and his object of gallantry, Aziz once more becomes happy; he
looks at the mosque and feels all is well. The two actions are inextricably tied.
He has restored the polarized order of the mosque and contained the
disruptive Mrs. Moore, placing her under his control. For within their brief
conversation, she becomes for him mother, blank page, and weaker vessel.
That Mrs. Moore remains acquiescent to patriarchal structures, that truth

lies in a neatly packaged dualism, and that all is well with the world, however, remains Aziz's fantasy.

Ronny and Aziz infuse the women they encounter with an imaginary blankness onto which they project their own epistemological and sexual certainty; both fail miserably in their attempts. Their attempt to recreate an imaginary oneness (with themselves) is, in Lacanian terms, a fusing of the Symbolic with the lost desires of the Imaginary. If entry into language or signification can be interpreted, as Lacan suggests, by a loss of a previous imaginary Oneness in which the child thinks he is united with his entire ambiance, representation is, in part, an attempt to recuperate that loss, an attempt to recuperate through language the experience of an imaginary wholeness or completeness. Language, culture, philosophy—all of which constitute the Symbolic—thus become fused with desire and with vestiges of the Imaginary, in which an uncomplicated Oneness is re-enacted. Witness, for example, the movement of the *Symposium*, in which the ascent toward "absolute beauty" reveals in its radiance not only beauty, but Truth. As Diotima instructs: "He who has been instructed thus far in the things of love, and who has learned to see the beautiful in due order and succession, when he comes toward the end will suddenly perceive a nature of wondrous beauty," which in conjoining truth and beauty, produces a vision that is "everlasting, not growing and decaying, or waxing and waning" (*Dialogues: A Selection* 230–31). Thus, the Platonic quest, in its unconsummated desire for oneness, becomes a substitute romance. Because this desire-surfeited fusion occurs, however, through language (through a metaphysical system) there is the illusion of control in which an imagined truth (the metaphysical system) becomes the mirror of the philosopher's mind. It is a fusion (a romance) without risk. The process of fixing representation, by recalling the unitary experience of the imaginary state, then becomes both a paradisiac space and an illusory means for assuring control.[12] Making one's own obsession a reality (as Ronny and Aziz do) is thus "an act of autospecularization" that guarantees the illusion of sameness—a becoming one with the world or God and a masking of desire that denies its connections with the Imaginary (to amorphous and dream-like pleasures of the Cave). This is what underlies Aziz's transposition of his own mental landscape onto the mosque, his walling out the excesses of the night.

Passage refuses not only this substitute romance, in which the fusion of an autospecularization becomes a point of ecstasy, but the tenets on which this ostensibly higher philosophical flight is based. Both Aziz's and Ronny's attempts to limit vision fail miserably. Multiple meanings, shifting identities and shifting landscapes keep erupting in the text, and the image of woman as fixed and passive simply will not hold. Mrs. Moore and Adela simply will not stay in their allotted spaces. Ronny may desire to fix her as pious old churchwoman, but that is not the image we have of her as she bids the hills good-bye. Aziz may want to turn Adela into a hag and Ronny may want to make her a distressed maiden, but that is not the image we have of her at the trial.

Passage thus restages Plato's cave by subverting key Platonic foundations (fixity of meaning, the severing of mind and body). Such a recasting simultaneously demands both a different way of seeing the world and a different way of constructing erotic relations. Transposing a failed Platonic epistemology onto erotic relations (as Ronny and Aziz both attempt to do by fixing a right definition of womanhood and by evading physicality) functions as an illusory haven, which, if not ill-fated, is simply senseless. Aziz thinks he must protect Mrs. Moore from leopards, snakes, and other bad characters of the night in their short walk back from the mosque, and he believes that his chivalric actions (simultaneous with his glancing back at the mosque) have contained Mrs. Moore and restored a fixed epistemological order, but that is fantasy. Ronny thinks he is Adela's romantic rescuer as he ostentatiously enters the courtroom expecting a verdict of guilty that will exonerate both female respectability and the patriarchal authority to which he is guardian, but he gets something else. Adela refuses to be the rescued, passive victim, refuses even innocence, and in her refusal breaks the prototype that maintains that if a woman is not wholly pure, she undoubtedly must be a whore. Such a possibility disrupts the order of sexual exchange in which the woman as elevated object of the man's desire becomes severed from her own physicality and from any desire of her own. Refusing this blankness through which Ronny receives back his own mirrored image, she claims her own desires. As a desiring subject, she ruminates on love, inquires about the details of Aziz's love life, whether he is married, how many wives he has (perhaps how many times he has had sex). As Aziz tells his story, he becomes the object of her gaze. She does what no woman supposedly should do: she asks about sex and then gazes back. So too, the romantic ending explodes as Adela journeys toward the cave. In contrast to Plato's liberated prisoner who moves away from the cave (the earth, the body, and sexuality) in order to find truth, Adela, in order to find the truth about Aziz, journeys back to the cave and thinks about sexuality. The revelatory journey is toward the cave, not, as in Plato's story, away from it. Adela thinks about Ronny's limitations, about love, and then about where she had had these thoughts before, remembering finally that they emerged as the car hit the animal on Marabar Road, an incident described as a phantom rising out of the earth. As she mentally travels back to the cave, she sees that her romance with Ronny is a lie: "Not to love the man one's going to marry! Not to find out until this moment! Not even to have asked the question until now! Something else to think out" (152).

Staring at the "sparkling rock" in the dusk, she asks herself whether she should break the engagement. Her speculative question, which encompasses the conventions of romance with all its trappings (hierarchical relationships, grand passion, and closure), becomes intertwined with the construction of truth. But instead of a Platonic vision that moves upward toward the sun, her vision emerges as she gazes at the rock, which presumably, in its "sparkling," emits flashes of light. Her epiphany is the Platonic vision inverted. The movement is toward the cave. The light (traditionally associated with the sun and with the spirit) is reflected from a rock (from the physical world). What that light emits is a vision of many caves, a movement away from fixity and a movement away from romance, which defines woman as exalted Other, emptied vessel, and passive mirror to someone else's desire. Romance with Ronny, as Adela discovers, is really rather sexless. As long as Adela accepts the fiction of her romance with Ronny, she accepts, at least in part, his bifurcated and false vision of the world: Aziz's guilt, fixity of truth, herself as icon, a kind of pale, marbled body indifferent to desire. It is no wonder then that as Adela looks at the sparkling rock and ponders her own desires, she simultaneously rejects Ronny, sees many caves, and subsequently begins *to see* differently.

NOTES

1. For recent discussions of Modernism as an epistemological crisis, see Beja, Jackson, London, Levenson, Meisel, Menand, Schwartz.

2. See also Menand and Meisel, who also recognize an ambivalent resuscitation of Platonism in Modernism.

3. See Felski's discussion in *The Gender of Modernity* of how aestheticism shifts notions of femininity from an expression of opposition to appropriation; in the process, however, women become associated with the superficiality and vulgarity that the aesthete most abhors.

4. For other commentary on the links between Marabar and Plato's cave in Book 7 of *The Republic*, see Dauner. For commentary addressing epistemological concerns in general, see Beer, Das, Dowling, Drew, Hultberg, Martin, Nierenberg, and Pintchman.

5. Irigaray reads the *hystera* as the "unrepresentable," as well as the ultimate. See *Speculum* (244, 254),

6. See Irigaray (*Speculum* 320) and her commentary in "Woman's Exile," in which she discusses Western discourse as enacting a "certain isomorphism with the masculine sex": the privilege of unity and form, of what is visible and specularisable. Constructions of sexuality thus become intertwined with notions of truth in Western metaphysics, Lacan notwithstanding. Quoting Lacan's plea to women, "I beg them on my knees to tell me what they want and they tell me nothing," Irigaray notes that Lacan "cannot bear that someone else speaks anything but *his truth* as he describes it," which "ensures the foundations of the symbolic order"; if a "woman tries to express her pleasure—which

obviously challenges the male point of view—he excludes her, because she upsets his system" ("Woman's Exile" 71). Irigaray's contention that systems of discourse, exchange, and epistemological positioning cannot be separated from the male fantasies which dominate the sexual scene has been key to this analysis.

7. Hultberg's condemnation of the later Mrs. Moore for being a failed mother, for becoming "mean, unfair, selfish and even malicious" is best understood in the context of his assessment of the early Mrs. Moore as the only "fixed point in a world gone mad" (251). He sees her later deviation (or liberation?) from this fixed point as deception and betrayal. Nierenberg makes a similar argument.

8. Finkelstein compares the "veil of ladylikeness" to the purdah.

9. Showalter makes a similar point.

10. Note Butler's extension of Irigaray's critique of Plato: "The problem is not that the feminine is made to stand for matter or for universality; rather, the feminine is cast outside the form/matter and universal/particular binarisms. She will be neither the one nor the other, but the permanent and unchangeable condition of both—what can be construed as nonthematizable materiality. She will be entered, and will give forth a further instance of what enters her, but she will never resemble either the formative principle or that which it creates" (42).

11. See Lacan's discussion of how Woman as fantasy, as object of courtly fealty, parallels the Oneness characteristic of the "Good old God" and how jouissance parallels mysticism in "God and the *Jouissance* of ~~The~~ Woman."

12. According to Lacan, entry into the Symbolic (into signification or language) regulates how we line up as gendered beings, distinctly male or female. But as Lacan indicates, naming is impossible. The categories of male and female constantly slip, miss the meaning, and the representation which seems fixed belies a fluid complexity. See "The Function and Field of Speech and Language" in *Écrits*.

WORKS CITED

Armstrong, Paul B. "Reading India: E. M. Forster and the Politics of Interpretation." *Twentieth Century Literature* 38 (1992): 365–85.

Beer, Gillian. "Negation in *Passage to India*." *Essays in Criticism* 30 (1980): 151–66.

Beja, Morris. *Epiphany in the Modern Novel*. Seattle: U of Washington P, 1971.

Benjamin, Jessica. *The Bonds of Love: Psychoanalysis, Feminism, and The Problem of Domination*. New York: Pantheon, 1988.

Burke, Carolyn, Naomi Schor, and Margaret Whitford, eds. *Engaging With Irigaray: Feminist Philosophy and Modern European Thought*. New York: Columbia UP, 1994.

Butler, Judith. *Bodies That Matter*. New York and London: Routledge, 1993.

Das, G. K. "*A Passage to India*: A Socio-Historical Study." A Passage to India: *Essays in Interpretation*. Totowa: Barnes & Noble. 1–15.

Dauner, Louise. "What Happened in the Cave? Reflections on *A Passage to India*." *Modern Fiction Studies* 7 (1961): 258–70.

Dowling, David. "A Passage to India through 'The Spaces of the Words.'" *Journal of Narrative Technique* 15 (1985): 256–66.

Drew, John. "The Spirit behind the Frieze?" A Passage to India: *Essays in Interpretation*. London: Macmillan, 1985. 81–103.

Felski, Rita. *The Gender of Modernity*. Cambridge: Harvard UP, 1995.

Finkelstein, Bonnie B. *Forster's Women: Eternal Differences*. New York: Columbia UP, 1975.

Flax, Jane. "Mother–Daughter Relationships: Psychodynamics, Politics, and Philosophy." *The Future of Difference*. Eds. Hester Eisenstein and Alice Jardine. 1980. New Brunswick: Rutgers, 1987.

———. *Thinking Fragments: Psychoanalysis, Feminism, and Postmodernism in the Contemporary West*. Berkeley: U of California P, 1990.

Forster, E. M. *Howards End*. New York: Vintage, 1921.

———. *The Longest Journey*. 1922. New York: Vintage, 1962.

———. *Passage to India*. New York: Harcourt Brace, 1924.

———. *Maurice*. 1971. New York: Norton, 1987.

Friedländer, Paul. *Plato: The Dialogues, Second and Third Periods*. Vol. 3. Trans. Hans Meyerhoff. Princeton: Princeton UP, 1969.

Harding, Sandra. "Is Gender a Variable in Conceptions of Rationality?: A Survey of Issues." *Discovering Reality: Feminist Perspectives on Epistemology, Metaphysics, Methodology, and Philosophy of Science*. Eds. Sandra Harding and Merrill B. Hintikka. Dordrecht: Reidel, 1983. 43–63.

Hultberg, Peer. "The Faithless Mother: An Aspect of the Novels of E. M. Forster." *Narcissism and the Text: Studies in Literature and Psychology of the Self*. Eds. Lynne Layton and Barbara Ann Schapiro. New York: New York UP, 1986.

Irigaray, Luce. *Speculum of the Other Woman*. Trans. Gillian C. Gill. Ithaca: Cornell UP, 1974.

———. "Woman's Exile." Interview. Trans. Couze Venn. *Ideology and Consciousness* 1 (1977): 62–76.

Jackson, Tony E. *The Subject of Modernism: Narrative Alterations in the Fiction of Eliot, Conrad, Woolf and Joyce*. Ann Arbor: U of Michigan P, 1994.

Jardine, Alice. *Configurations of Woman and Modernity*. Ithaca: Cornell UP, 1985.

Lacan, Jacques. *Écrits, A Selection*. Trans. Alan Sheridan. NY: Norton, 1977.

———. "God and the Jouissance of The Woman." *Feminine Sexuality: Jacques Lacan and the École Freudienne*. Eds. Juliet Mitchell and Jacqueline Rose. Trans. Jacqueline Rose. New York: Norton, 1985.

Larisch, Sharon. "Old Women, Orphan Girls, and Allegories of the Cave." *Comparative Literature* 40 (1988): 150–71.

Levenson, Michael H. *A Genealogy of Modernism: A Study of English Literary Doctrine 1908–1922*. Cambridge: Cambridge UP, 1984.

———. *Modernism and the Fate of Individuality: Character and Novelistic Form from Conrad to Woolf*. Cambridge: Cambridge UP, 1991.

London, Bette. *The Appropriated Voice. Narrative Authority in Conrad, Forster and Woolf*. Ann Arbor: U of Michigan P, 1990.

Martin, John S. "Mrs. Moore and the Marabar Caves: A Mythological Reading." *Modern Fiction Studies* 11 (1966): 429–33.

Meisel, Perry. *The Myth of the Modern: A Study in British Literature and Criticism after 1850*. New Haven: Yale UP, 1987.

Menand, Louis. *Discovering Modernism: T. S. Eliot and His Context*. New York: Oxford UP, 1987.

Moi, Toril. "Representation of Patriarchy: Sexuality and Epistemology in Freud's Dora." *In Dora's Case: Freud-Hysteria-Feminism*. Eds. Carolyn G. Heilbrun and Nancy K. Miller. New York: Columbia UP, 1985.

Nierenberg, Edwin. "The Withered Priestess: Mrs. Moore's Incomplete Passage to India." *Modern Language Quarterly* 25 198–204.

Pintchman, Tracy. "Snakes in the Cave: Religion and the Echo in E. M. Forster's *A Passage to India*." *Soundings* 75 (1992): 61–78.

Plato. *The Dialogues*. Trans. Benjamin Jowett. Vol. 3. Oxford: Oxford, UP, 1968.

———. *The Dialogues of Plato: A Selection*. Trans. Benjamin Jowett. New York: Liveright, 1927.

———. *The Republic*. Trans. Benjamin Jowett. New York: Heritage, 1944.

Schwartz, Sanford. *The Matrix of Modernism: Pound, Eliot, and Early Twentieth Century Thought*. Princeton: Princeton UP, 1985.

Showalter, Elaine. "*A Passage to India* as 'Marriage Fiction': Forster's Sexual Politics." *Women and Literature* 5 (1977): 3–16.

BENITA PARRY

Materiality and Mystification
in A Passage to India

Discussion on the imperial project in British literary consciousness has customarily been confined to the colonial novel, a category of convenience covering a range of genres and qualities. More recently work disclosing the material and psychic dissemination of empire in the metropolis has included detecting its symbolic, reconfigured or displaced presence in canonical and popular writing.[1] The preferred procedure of critics is to trace how colonial tropes and rhetorics were brought by nineteenth- and early twentieth-century writers to their dramatizations of dominant gender and class conditions within the imperial homeland. Such work which draws attention to the larger if blurred horizons of the English novel has also introduced into the discussion the problems associated with the use of analogical strategies in criticism: by reiterating the fiction's unsecured metaphoric linkages as constituting social knowledge about the ideological coalescence of gender, race and class, these critics conflate the sites and temporalities of different oppressions.[2] In this way, such criticism collapses the distinctiveness of the discourses and topoi that represent those oppressions.[3]

Theorists of the novel, however, who address the transcoding between historical processes and textual practices, and perceive the effects of empire in literature as mutable, locate these signs in form rather than figurative recastings. Edward Said, who discerns the assertion of narrative authority as

From *Novel*, Spring (1998), © 1998 by Benita Parry.

characterizing the British novel during the age of imperial consolidation
connects the emergence of literary modernism with changes in metropolitan
apprehensions of empire. For Said the turn from "the triumphalist
experience of imperialism ... into the extremes of self-consciousness,
discontinuity, self-referentiality and corrosive irony ... which we have tended
to derive from purely internal dynamics in Western society and culture,
includes a response to the external pressures on culture from the *imperium*"
(*Culture* 227). In a different argument which all the same intersects with
Said's understanding of the correspondence, Fredric Jameson maintains that
the modernist crisis in the novel was intensified by imperialism, the stylistic
ingenuity of Conrad's novels providing "key articulations of the increased
fragmentation of individual consciousness in an age of growing
commodification and brutal colonization" (*Political* 17).[4]

The relationships of historical moment to novelistic practice observed
by Said and Jameson suggest that if we are to decipher the always fluctuating
and historically inflected marks of empire on the body of British literature,
then colonial fictions should be regarded as a subset of the English novel, and
inscriptions of empire's overt and cryptic presence in this literature should be
in turn studied as constituting the same area of enquiry. Jameson, who is
singular in defining imperialism as the dynamic of capitalism proper and
therefore in recognizing imperialism as coextensive with the globalism of late
colonialism, has proposed that the "traces of imperialism" in modernist
writing, must not be sought "in obvious places, in content, or in
representation." Rather they are to be found in the invention of "forms that
inscribe a new sense of the absent global colonial system on the very syntax
of poetic language itself" (*Modernism* 18). Thus when enlarging on the
aesthetic response to a universal imperial order, in which "internal national
or metropolitan daily life is absolutely sundered from this other world
henceforth in thrall to it," he chooses a domestic novel, *Howards End*, in
order to show how the representation of "inner or metropolitan space itself,"
becomes a substitute for "an unrepresentable totality" (*Modernism* 17, 18).

A schema which restricts imperialism's signs in literature to "the
stylistic or linguistic peculiarities" particular to modernism and asserts that
the specific literature of imperialism is not modernist in any formal sense
(*Modernism* 5), by definition excludes those modernist novels like *Heart of
Darkness* and *Nostromo* which do negotiate "the representational dilemma" of
the imperialist order and refuse to map an itinerary of empire's ordered
progress.[5] How then should we place a proto-modernist fiction in which
another and distant world is manifestly present and the disjoined spheres are
brought into uneasy proximity, but which also, *pace* Said, undermines
imperial grandiloquence and offers a disenchanted perspective on empire,

registers a dispersed consciousness, and by reflecting ironically and critically on its own project, manifests a waning of narrative power?

The reputation of *A Passage to India* as conventional in form, language, and attested value has inhibited discussion on an emergent modernism that is inseparable from the novel's failure to reach the destination intimated in its title.[6] Said has remarked that for him the most interesting thing about the book is the use of India "to represent material that according to the canons of the novel form cannot in fact be represented—vastness, incomprehensible creeds, secret motions, histories and social forms" (*Culture* 214). This judicious comment recognizes that Forster's innovations were induced by an attempt to render India legible within western fictional modes. It could be extended to observe that in the process, *A Passage to India* construes the sub-continent's material world, cultural forms, and systems of thought as resistant to discursive appropriation by its conquerors: "How can the mind take hold of such a country? Generations of invaders have tried, but they remain in exile" (*Passage* 148). This meditation serves to alienate the Raj's belligerent claim to discursive power over the sub-continent, and it discloses the inevitable frustration of the novel's own narrative ambition.

Neither stylistically nor syntactically does *A Passage to India* display that "constitutive sense of creation through rupture and crisis" which has been described as the vocation of an aesthetic modernism (Calinescu 92). All the same, a fiction which moves between the mundane and the arcane, gives voice to the contingency of the material world, and is haunted by the transcendent, exists at the limits of realist writing, the affinities with modernism evident in the prominence of its anti-referential registers. On the one hand, as an architecturally composed text exhibiting that "vital harmony" Forster believed essential to works of art—described by him as "the only objects in the material universe to possess internal order" (*Two* 93)—the book augurs both the pleasures afforded by an elegant design and the reassurance of lucidity. On the other, the perplexity with which the novel reconfigures the distant, alien complex of cultures that is its ostensible subject, signals an anxiety about the impasse of representation. Thus the aesthetic closure, once hailed by critics as instigated by a rage for order that issued in a coherent and integrated text, can be seen as a formal resolution to the historical conflicts, cultural chasms, social dissension, cognitive uncertainties, and experiential enigmas elaborated by a structurally, intellectually, and discursively fractured fiction.

By the time Forster wrote his novel, the romantic India of the eighteenth-century western imagination was dead and gone, buried under a library of subsequent books itemizing the defects of a chaotic and degenerate sub-continent mired in irrational beliefs and incapable of self-determination (see Parry, *Delusions*). Recent studies have emphasized the contradictions and tensions within British Indian texts (see Suleri, Moore-Gilbert). But while such discursive instabilities are apparent to contemporary critics, the writings were delivered in a declarative mode to the literate colonized as a preemptive reply to dissent, and received in their own time by a metropolitan audience as a warrant for British rule. If this literature included mythologizing a land of secret delights, hidden truths, statically organic village communities, and intrepid "martial races," it also construed a degraded population ruled by despots and given to thuggee, sati, child marriage, zenanas, idolatry, temple prostitution, male debauchery and effeminacy, female concupiscence, insensate violence, and pathetic contentment. At stake was the creation and ordering of India's difference as deviations from western norms of historical development, aesthetics, civil society, and sexuality (see Metcalf).

Despite its emergence from within a literary tradition already sated with prior configurations, Forster's fiction eschews both "the Scented East of tradition" and the corrupt land of a febrile British imagination (233). Such a proposition does not advance truth claims for an invention which remains wedded to the sensibilities of the Mediterranean, never abandons its moorings in western structures of feeling, and reiterates rumors of a recondite "India." Indeed the use of India as an icon of the metaphysical derives from what has been described as a "scholarship ... replete with preferences for the speculative, religious-minded, idealist and/or Orientalist kind" (Ahmad 277). Hence alongside its many material and sentient Indias, which act to estrange the time-honored topos of a mysterious land, the novel also construes an obfuscated realm where the secular is scanted, and in which India's long traditions of mathematics, science and technology, history, linguistics, and jurisprudence have no place.

Since its publication in 1924, *A Passage to India* has been variously received in the west as an existential meditation and a liberal criticism of politics and life in British India. Its crafted thematic composition and polysemous symbolic resonances once prompted critics preoccupied with literature's animations of the timeless to explain the book as mythopoeic and wholly detached from history; while its performance of a temporally-situated social drama was cherished as a humanist affirmation of the sanctity of human relationships egregiously violated by colonialism. If the first construct is indifferent to the specificity of the novel's moment, the other overestimates its grasp of colonialism's charged interactions during that moment. More recently the fiction's place in the rhetoric of empire has been examined, and the novel read as yet another exercise in Orientalism. Consequently praise for *A Passage to India* as a poised and sympathetic account of the sub-continent's landscape, history, and culture which Indian critics of older generations had offered, has since been repudiated by their descendants as "emanating from a colonized consciousness" (Pathak et al. 198, 199).

Prominent amongst new glosses is a particular interest in demonstrating that the book's sexual and gender representations are implicated in colonialist discourses, and are determinant in the novel's version of a colonial relationship.[7] I will be offering my own understanding of how gender and the erotic are disposed within a larger cultural, geopolitical, and epistemological canvas—and one on which, contra Joseph Bristow and unlike Forster's private memoir, sexual desire is uncolored by fantasies of imperial domination.[8] Meanwhile, I want to remark that ingenious commentaries preoccupied with the sexualizing of race and the racializing of sexuality contract an orchestration of dissonant themes to a single strain, by this overlooking that amongst the novel's many Indias is one whose topography evades colonialism's physical invasion, and whose cognitive modes elude incorporation within normative western explanatory systems. Were a case for the novel's radicalism to be made, this would need to rest on the recalcitrance of this "India," and not on its manifestly inadequate critique of a colonial encounter.

I.

The novel's cosmic reach and non-realist registers are inspired by an imagined India whose infinite embrace offers vistas of a sphere more comprehensive than the time–space world and intimates an ecumenical ethic admitting all animal, vegetable, and mineral forms to its prospect. Such allusions to an atemporal, ahistorical universe are underwritten by non-linear narrative movements which interrupt the sequential recitation of quotidian events. Not only is the fiction's itinerary spatial—from Mosque to Caves to Temple—but images recur in unrelated situations: a wasp, flies, a stone, a pattern traced in the dust of Chandrapore and repeated on the footholds of a distantly located rock in the Marabars; marginal characters who make aleatory appearances at critical moments—Miss Derek's providential arrivals, the presence of a young army officer on the maidan and in the Club; and phrases which are echoed in unlike circumstances—the reiteration of Godbole's petition to Krishna, his demurral of "Oh no," and the reprise of invitations, both earthly and divine.

But as Forster noted elsewhere and with regret, a novel tells a story, and in this aspect *A Passage to India* uses the language of realism to chronicle a tragicomedy of cultural discord and political conflict, observing shifts within the fabric of Indian societies and the power relationships of British

India. Youths are seen "training" (75); with Aziz's arrest, the sweepers stop work in protest, and Muslim women, perceived by the Anglo-Indians as invisible, go on hunger strike, inducing in the European community the fear that a "new spirit seemed abroad, a rearrangement, which no one in the stern little band of whites could explain" (218); a Hindu–Muslim entente is forged, and in the association between Aziz, the descendent of the Moghuls who had fought the British invaders, and Godbole, whose Mahratta ancestors had defended an independent Deccan against the foreign onslaught, the novel alludes to the growth of an Indian nationalism attracting protagonists who share different memories of armed struggles against the British conquest.

A Passage to India, then, remains of interest for its evocations of a phase in the Raj, registering the growing disaffection of a population increasingly disinclined to collude in its own domination, and commenting on the demeaning effects which complicity with their rulers had on India's hegemonized elite. But although the indirections of its aversion to empire separate Forster's book from the self-justifying contemporaneous "problem" novels which set out to account for Indian discontent while reinstalling the British ideal of disinterested service, as a novel of manners performed in a colonial context, *A Passage to India* now appears circumscribed.[9] The alternately gentle and irascible reprimands of Indian unreliability, obsequiousness, and evasiveness, as well as the mimicry of Anglo-India's ignorant beliefs and foolish self-regard, are dependent on sardonic reiterations and parodies of the stereotypes and clichés that were the stuff of British writing about India. Nor is the version of a colonial relationship played out in a low key between British officials and members of an Indian middle class adequate to the fraught transactions of an encounter which initially met with military resistance, subsequently generated widespread and continuous insurgency from peasants and laborers, and earned the militant opposition of both the educated and the illiterate.[10]

To observe the limits on the novel's heterodox version of life and politics in the closing decades of the Raj is not to ignore that the novel also sabotages recurrent themes in Anglo-Indian and British writings about India. These subversive reworkings, which include ruining the notion of empire's functionaries as ethical and altruistic Stoics, focus on Adela Quested's misprision of rape. In this event where an Englishwoman already disquieted by India is infected by a nervous community's fantasies of cultures charged with erotic intensities and dangers, there still persists a heterosexual model of the colonial relationship which is elsewhere displaced.[11] To the Anglo-Indians, Miss Quested is the victim of the infamous lust of Indian men; and in the story of her derangement, the Indian landscape figures as a violent male principle—the rocks of the Marabar Hills appearing to rise "abruptly, insanely," and her body pierced by the spines of cactuses growing on the hillside (137). Much that is important to the understanding of the novel has been written about the articulations of sexualities in an imperial situation, and I will be returning to the many meanings adhering to the circulation of homoerotic affect in the text. What concerns me at present is another aspect of the fiction's sexual and gender politics as this intersects with an ingrained political liberalism and deflects from an overt censure of the Raj.

Kenneth Burke has suggested that the social and political relationships which the novel draws into its texture are expressible in terms of personal associations dramatized either as sexual and filial bonds, or as friendships. Of these the only one to be consummated across the colonial divide, and that ceremonially, is between Aziz and Mrs. Moore. This nexus traverses generations and comes to imitate the never-existing but idealized union of benign imperial motherland with grateful colonial dependency fabricated by empire's ideologues. The figure of this imagined parent–child symbiosis was Queen Victoria, Empress of India, of whom Hamidullah and Mahmoud Ali speak affectionately when lamenting the impossibility of friendship with the chilly Anglo-Indians. Such an exemplary imperial matriarch is incarnate in the elderly Mrs. Moore. Mrs. Moore has many avatars in the novel: she is a tolerant but commonplace middle-class Englishwoman well-disposed to the National Anthem and a banal West End play performed at the Club; a sibyl and seer, and a spokesperson for an idea of empire which unlike a Raj that rests on fear, would be based on "good will" (71). It is her displeasure at the uncivil conduct of Anglo-Indians which is the occasion for the fatuous narrative comment, "[o]ne touch of regret—not the canny substitute but the true regret from the heart—would have made him [Ronny Heaslop] a different man, and the British Empire a different institution" (70). Furthermore, a sentiment absurdly inappropriate to a colonial situation is, without benefit of irony, ascribed to Aziz before he turns his back on British India and ceases to conduct himself as a toady: "Mr. Fielding, no one can ever realize how much kindness we Indians need.... Kindness, more kindness, and even after that more kindness. I assure you it is the only hope" (128).

Mrs. Moore enters India through *Mosque*, passes into accidie in *Caves*; she is redeemed by the enactment of universal salvation in *Temple*, buried in the Indian Ocean, transmigrates into a demi-goddess, and bequeaths her benign powers to her children, Stella and Ralph, whose presence moves the now disaffected Aziz to "want to do kind actions all round and wipe out the wretched business of the Marabar for ever" (312). Thus does a mother-figure of "good empire" permit the staging of an act of formal reconciliation within the unreconciled and irreconcilable conflicts of an imperial relationship. Perhaps a symbolic accord which simulates the skeptically narrated ritual of universal harmony performed during the Hindu Gokal Ashtami Festival is similarly calculated to invite disbelief, since it is countermanded by the parting of Aziz and Fielding, for whom "no meeting-place" exists in British India. Yet the gesture to a rapprochement effected within the conflictual conditions of the Raj undermines an already attenuated criticism of empire, its admonition of colonialism addressing the cruelties large and small inflicted by Anglo-Indians, but omitting to summon either the western impulses to colonialist dispossession or the ideology of imperial domination, for explication and demystification. In this aspect, the silences in *A Passage to India* rehearse the lacunae of British Indian texts, from which all traces of base interests—India as a source of raw materials, cheap labor, markets and investment opportunities, and India as a linchpin of Britain's wider imperial ambitions—were erased.

II.

The novel's dissident place within British writing about India does not reside in its meager critique of a colonial situation, however, but in configuring India's natural terrain and cognitive traditions as inimical to the British presence. When discussing Georges Bataille's text on "the language of flowers," Pierre Macherey explains that it served as

> *a starting point for his reflections on the natural logic of existence, which he terms "the obscure intelligence of things." The principle behind this logic is a fundamental clash of values governed by a polarity of above and below which testifies to "an obscure decision on the part of the plant world." The decision is expressed in a sort of pre-linguistic language: the language of "aspect," which exists prior to the language of words, introduces "values that decide things."* (118)

The notion of evaluations which are "the judgments of reality itself as it asserts, primitively and immediately, its basic tendencies," is suggestive for reading the semiotically saturated physical landscape of Forster's India as "a direct expression" of "the truth of things" which exists "prior to symbolization" (Macherey 118). The eloquent stones, boulders, rocks, and caves of an awesome and ancient geological formation, the animate fields and ambulant hills, the inhospitable soil, the importunities of a prominent inarticulate world, the creaturely power of the sun, these speak a defiant *material* presence which is both a scandal to the invaders' epistemological categories, and a threat to their boast of possessing India: "The triumphant machine of civilization may suddenly hitch and be immobilized into a car of stone, and at such moments the destiny of the English seems to resemble their predecessors', who also entered the country with intent to refashion it, but were in the end worked into its pattern and covered with its dust" (215).

As a novel which orbits around a space which is unrepresentable within its perceptual boundaries, *A Passage to India* is impelled to obfuscate that of which it *cannot* speak, a self-declared incomprehension that issues in fabrications of contradictory Indias. Hence the evocation of India's pre-linguistic language of obduracy towards the conquerors spoken by its physical structures must compete with intimations of India as a civilization hospitable to the unseen; while its fluency in the meta-linguistic could signify either an intelligence of things obscure, or that which the novel is unable to render intelligible. In response to a question about what had happened in the Caves, Forster indicated that India had enabled his venture into the realms of the unfathomable:

> *My writing mind is ... a blur here—i.e. I will it to remain a blur, and to be uncertain, as I am of many facts of daily life. This isn't a philosophy of aesthetics. It's a particular trick I felt justified in trying because my theme was India. It sprang straight from my subject matter. I wouldn't have attempted it in other countries, which though they contain mysteries or muddles, manage to draw rings round them. Without this trick I doubt whether I could have got the spiritual reverberation going. I call it "trick": but "voluntary surrender to infection" better expresses my state.*
> (Letter to G. Lowes Dickinson, qtd. in Stallybrass 26)

It is therefore not accidental that disquiet about the limits of syntactic language are explored on a fabricated *Indian* space that is simultaneously rendered as palpable and emblematic. On approaching the Marabar Hills, "a new quality occurred, a spiritual silence which invaded more senses than the ear ... sounds did not echo or thoughts develop.... Everything seemed cut off at its root, and therefore infected with illusion" (152). This sensory and intellectual detachment from the empirical world is translated into the severing of words from their referent:

> *What were these mounds—graves, breasts of the goddess Parvati? The villagers ... gave both replies. Again, there was a confusion about a snake, which was never cleared up. Miss Quested saw a thin, dark object ... and said, "A snake!" The villagers agreed, and Aziz explained: yes, a black cobra.... But when she looked*

though Ronny's field-glasses she found it wasn't a snake, but the
withered and twisted stump of a toddy-palm. So she said, "It isn't
a snake." The villagers contradicted her. She had put the word
into their minds, and they refused to abandon it.... Nothing was
explained. (152–53)

On arriving at Caves, the narrative encounters meanings, sensations,
and events that escape exegesis in its available language. Their reputation
"does not depend upon human speech" (138), and their echo—"'Boum' is
the sound as far as the human alphabet can express it" (159)—is not the
resound of any utterance the fiction can identify. This untranslatable
murmur deprives Mrs. Moore, accustomed to "poor little talkative
Christianity" (161), of a trust in language: "'Say, say, say.... As if anything can
be said.' ... in the twilight of the double vision a spiritual muddledom is set
up for which no high-sounding words can be found" (205, 212). Thus a novel
which cherishes the names of the marvelous places "that had sometimes
shone through men's speech," and which discerns in "the bilingual rock of
Girnar" the transformation through language of a physical object into a
cultural artifact, also contemplates things both benign and ominous which
cannot be spoken, or of which it cannot speak (214). When trying to
communicate the attraction Hinduism holds for Stella and Ralph Moore, the
rationalist Fielding confesses, "I can't explain, because it isn't in words at all"
(313). In attempting to render comprehensible the unexplained or
inexplicable significance of the imitations, impersonations, symbols, and
images invoked during the all-embracing Hindu festival of Gokal Ashtami,
the narrative admits its inability to transcribe an event which cannot "be
expressed in anything but itself" (285).

Such allusions to the aphonic must be distinguished from the book's
many hints of the supernatural, which reiterate a predilection for mysteries
also evident in Forster's other novels.[12] Perhaps we are invited to understand
experiences of the meta-linguistic as emanating from "the part of the mind
that seldom speaks" (111), and therefore as an existential condition: on
undertaking to describe the caves, Godbole retreats into silence, just as Aziz's
mind had sometimes been silenced by "a power he couldn't control" (92). On
the other hand, the many and diverse inscriptions of the unspoken and the
inexpressible can also be read as echoes of the "spiritual reverberation"
induced by an India whose religious pursuits and eloquent landscapes
provoke intellectual doubt and promote noumenal anxieties in the novel's
western protagonists: Fielding, who is a "blank, frank atheist" (254), muses
that "Where is something in religion that may not be true, but that has not
yet been sung.... Something that the Hindus have perhaps found" (274),

while the Indian scene troubles both him and the logical Adela Quested with rumors of things they did not know, and a universe they had "missed or rejected" (272).

Forster's title is borrowed from Walt Whitman's visionary poem, "Passage to India" (1871), and the contemplation of an esoteric India may have been further influenced by his friend Edward Carpenter, who had known Whitman and shared the poet's conviction in India's spiritual vocation.[13] But although Forster does juxtapose a mystified to a material and historical India, he did not follow the utopian writers in affirming India as the Wisdom-land of Carpenter's expectations, or in designating it as that farthest destination "where mariner has not yet dared to go" (Whitman 328). For when the novel invokes the quest after transcendence, this is for its psychological truthfulness, rather than its arrival at Truth, for the passion of its aspiration, and not its always deferred achievement: the calls to Krishna or the Friend who never Comes; the longing for "the eternal promise, the never-withdrawn suggestion that haunts our consciousness" (127); the faith that confers grace on the believer during "the moment of its indwelling" (282); the substitutions, imitations, scapegoats, and husks of the Gokal Ashtami Festival, which are signs of "a passage not easy, not now, not here, not to be apprehended except when it is unattainable" (309); the hope that will persist "despite fulfillment" (299). If the novel transfigures the religious sensibility as desire born of discontent, what it does not validate is the victory of "the human spirit" in "ravish[ing] the unknown":

> *Books written afterwards say "Yes." But how, if there is such an event, can it be remembered afterwards? How can it be expressed in anything but itself? Not only from the unbeliever are mysteries hid, but the adept himself cannot retain them. He may think, if he chooses, that he has been with God, but, as soon as he thinks it, it becomes history, and falls under the rules of time.* (285)

Such skepticism about India's access to gnosis registers an agnosticism that abates the novel's modulated and questioning iterations of an Orientalism spellbound by the fabled East.

III.

Amongst the many resonances of the title is a reference to cartography, and consequently to the colonial topos of a voyage into unknown territory. About the book's map of India's geography, we can ask: does *A Passage to India* reproduce what John Barrell has described as the East's entry into the western European imagination "as an unknown, empty space empty of everything ... except its appropriable resources, imaginative as well as material," its objects "covered with decoration and imagery not understood and not thought worth understanding discerned as "blank screens on which could be projected whatever it was that the inhabitants of Europe, individually or collectively, wanted to displace, and to represent as other to themselves"? (7–8). Is the major source of friction in the novel, as Bristow argues, "the enduring contradiction between the thematics of 'friendship' ... and the sexual violence that we find at its centre, a form of violence that does everything it can to sever East from West"? ("Passage" 147). Can Forster's India be received as yet another textual act inflected by imperial and/or sexual aggression, and reiterating as Said has written of Orientalism, the will "to control, manipulate, even to incorporate what is manifestly a different (or alternative and novel) world"? (*Orientalism* 12). Said was subsequently to ask "how one can study other cultures and people from a libertarian, or a non-repressive and non-manipulative perspective ... how knowledge that is non-dominative and non-coercive ... [can] be produced in a setting that is deeply inscribed with the politics, the considerations, the positions and the strategies of power" ("Orientalism" 15).

Despite misgivings about Forster's reified India, I want to suggest that the novel approaches Indian forms of knowledge with uncertainty, without asserting the authority of its representations, and unaccented by a will to enforce an ontological schism.[14] The book's triadic structure has been variously glossed as corresponding to the Indian seasonal cycle (Cold Weather, Hot Weather, and Monsoon), the movements of a musical score, the Hegelian dialectic of thesis–antithesis–synthesis, the recurrent process of birth, destruction, and re-birth recited in Hindu mythology, and as metonyms of Muslim India, Anglo-India, and Hindu India. In the reading I am proposing Mosque, Caves, and Temple are perceived as figures of three Indian philosophical-religious systems. The association of Mosque with Islam in India, and Temple with a particular performance of Hindu devotions (*bhakti*), presents fewer problems than the polysemous connotations of Caves. When the magistrate Mr. Das points out that "[a]ll the Marabar caves are Jain" (225),[15] he is disputing their official identification as Buddhist, his disagreement having earlier been confirmed in the narrative commentary which dissociates Caves from this tradition: "even Buddha, who must have passed this way down to the Bo Tree of Gaya, shunned a renunciation more complete than his own, and has left no legend of struggle or victory in the Marabar" (138). If we take Das's designation seriously, then Caves, although rejected by Buddhists, can be understood as inhabited by and signifying the world-rejecting precepts of the Jain's non-deistic cosmology, its uncompromising atheism and asceticism surpassing the austerities of Buddhism, a related system also rooted in ancient India (Parry, *Delusions*).

Since the route of the novel's attempted journey becomes more arduous as it moves from Islam through India's more speculative traditions, a puzzled version of Hinduism's ecstatic spiritual observances is invoked, and the tenets of the Jain's quietist stance are obliquely enunciated. If aligned with ontological goals that are respectively daring and awesome, the monotheistic system of Islam necessarily appears as limited: "'There is no God but God' doesn't carry us far through the complexities of matter and spirit; it is only a game with words, really, a religious pun, not a religious truth" (272). Instead Islam, by way of an elite segment of the Muslim community, is manifest as a culture rather than a profound creed. When its religious temperament does feature, it is in a mode transformed through long residence in India, where its misshapen shrines appear as "a strange outcome of the protests of Arabia" (293), its "symmetrical injunction melts in the mild air," and mystical Sufi tendencies are privileged over theological severities: just as the ragas of the Hindu Godbole invite a Krishna who always fails to arrive, so do the adherents of Islam voice "our need for the Friend who never comes yet is not entirely disproved" (119).[16]

Without asserting that the ontologies and theisms enunciated by the novel should be read as authoritative expositions of Indian knowledge, I am suggesting that the fiction, far from rendering India as epistemologically vacant, reconfigures the sub-continent as a geographical space and social realm abundantly occupied by diverse intellectual modes, cultural forms, and sensibilities. This perception is not shared by critics who find that Forster's India is an empty space and the symptom of an amorphous state of mind, its principal landmarks Mosque, Caves, and Temple functioning primarily as cavities to contain western perceptions of that which is missing from the East, its symbolic terrain a hollow site which the narrative, parodying an act of rape, violently penetrates (Suleri, "Geography"). Nor does it conform with the inference of Francesca Kazan's rhetorical question: does not Forster in his ambitious task of representing the Orient, also seek to control it by fixing it and rendering it mute?

When Forster is charged with representing India as null and void, Caves are invariably offered in evidence. For Suleri the novel should be read "as an allegory in which the category of 'Marabar Cave' roughly translates into the anus of imperialism"—an infelicitous choice of imagery when conducting a discussion of the novel's "engagement with and denial of a colonial homoerotic imperative" (*Rhetoric* 132, 147). In Kazan's view Caves are a figure of absence and silence which replicates the inscrutability of the East within the western structure of the surrounding text; while Zakia

Pathak, Saswata Sengupta, and Sharmila Purkayastha, who contend that caves are described as without a history, jointly undertake to disperse their "primordial miasma":

> *What we read into the representation of the caves is not the absence of history but the* suppression *of history which marks the paranoid response of the Orientalists to processes which they could not understand, since ... this knowledge was withheld from them by the natives.* "Primal," "dark," "fists and fingers," "unspeakable," *fearsomely advancing to the town with the sunset—these phrases signal the fear and insecurity the imperialists experienced, confronted with what they could not master; to reduce it to stasis was to contain that fear and hold that threat at bay.* (200)

That Caves are a symptom of what the novel is unable to comprehend intellectually, accommodate within its preferred sensibility, or possess in its available language, is abundantly inscribed in a fiction which adumbrates both the nonverbal expression of a physical space and the doctrines of an exorbitantly transcendental philosophy, circuitously, elliptically, and with perplexity. But as the site of a cosmology incommensurable with positivism, humanism, or theism, and as the most potent figure of an India which challenges the west with its irreducible and insubordinate difference, the representation of Caves is neither circumscribed by dread of a maleficent essence ("Nothing evil had been in the cave" 159), nor is their "history" suppressed.

   To accept Mrs. Moore's reception of Caves as a primordial miasma and the dissolution of ethical meaning is to be deaf to the valences of the "Nothing" emanating from Caves. Elsewhere the reiteration of negatives— no, not yet, never, without, meager, mean, abased, ineffective, indifferent, renunciation, relinquish, refuse—invokes a diversity of connotations reverberating themes elaborated by the novel. In configurations of the Indian landscape, negatives mark a deviation from English and Mediterranean scenes, and with this a disturbance of western perceptions; when brought to events that do not happen, invitations that are neglected, omissions which are social solecisms ("[I]t's nothing I've said ... I never even spoke to him" is Ronny Heaslop's obtuse reassurance to a Fielding concerned about Aziz's evident discomfiture in the company of his English guests [94]) they register the poverty of colonial relationships. But with Caves, negatives take on affirmative resonances whose import is anticipated by the circumlocutions of the opening paragraph: "Except for the Marabar Caves ... the city of

Chandrapore presents nothing extraordinary.... There are no bathing steps on the river front, as the Ganges happens not to be holy here; indeed there is no river front ... In the bazaars there is no painting and scarcely any carving" (31). Thus to learn that there are neither sculptures in the Marabar Caves nor ornamentation (92), that they are not large and contain no stalactites, and that the Brahmin Godbole necessarily refrains from describing the site of another belief-system as "immensely holy" (92), is to be alerted to the possibility that negation has alternative significations: "Nothing, nothing attaches to them.... Nothing is inside them ... if mankind grew curious and excavated, nothing, nothing would be added to the sum of good or evil" (138, 139).

In Burke's reading, the use of negatives in the novel is a "partly secular variant of what we encounter in 'negative theology'" where God is described as "*in*comprehensible, *un*bounded, *un*ending, etc." (224). This understanding conforms with the tenets embraced by Godbole for whom good and evil "are different, as their names imply. But ... they are both of them aspects of my Lord. He is present in the one, absent in the other.... Yet absence implies presence, absence is not non-existence" (186). But it is the Jain tradition, which unlike Islam and Hinduism has no sentient protagonists in the book, that has written its antique Indian philosophy of renunciation over a material space already in possession of a language without syntax and expressive of abnegation. As the incarnation of Nothing doubly charged with semantic content, Caves engender the epigram "Everything exists, nothing has value" (160), a gnomic phrase compressing the Jain recognition of the physical world as abundantly corporeal and verifiable and its assignment of merit to detachment from all things secular—a construction in which nothing *has* value. This paradox is condensed in the mismatch between the adamantine concreteness of the stone, rock, granite, boulder, and bald precipice of a looming and grotesque land mass and the "internal perfection" of a cave's sublime emptiness.[17]

Neither Godbole's nuanced understanding of negatives, nor the Jain version of negation as a deliberated abrogation of the all too solid and degraded empirical universe, is available to Mrs. Moore. After (mis)recognizing the voice of Cave as speaking of nullity and (mis)translating the echo which she hears as "entirely devoid of distinction" into a proclamation effacing discriminations, she subsides into moral and psychic torpor: "Pathos, piety, courage they exist, but are identical, and so is filth. Everything exists, nothing has value" (158–60). To an Englishwoman familiar with the landscape of "dearest Grasmere" everywhere domesticated by human labor, a geological stratum that is "older than anything in the world ... without the proportion that is kept by the wildest hills elsewhere ...

bear[ing] no relation to anything dreamt or seen" intensifies her dislocation within an epistemologically inscribed physical environment that infringes on her expectations and escapes her comprehension (137).

Since Fielding, the only other English person present, is "unimpressed" by Caves, the phantasmagoric experience known by Adela Quested and Mrs. Moore appears as a gendered vulnerability to India's difference, manifest to them in different registers as an assailant. A related but different event is restaged in *Picnic at Hanging Rock*, Peter Weir's film of a novel by Joan Lindsay set in late nineteenth-century Australia, where four European women—three of them virginal school-girls, and one, a teacher possessed of a "masculine mind"—are mesmerized into offering themselves up to the phallic rock of a land in which they are colonizers and strangers. As with their disappearance, the catastrophic entry of Mrs. Moore and Adela Quested into an untranslatable sphere is inseparable from the cultural constraints on their capacity to confront the otherness of meanings both immanent in and attached to India's material spaces and forms. That these same restrictions are also apparent in a rhetoric at once convoluted, ambiguous and opaque, is testimony to the novel's admission of its own incapacity to bring this alien realm into representation.

IV.

In referring to those studies concerned with recuperating the novel's hitherto hidden "sexual politics," I suggested that representations of gender and the erotic should be understood as written across the multiply inscribed script of Forster's India. This proviso is not unmindful of the extent to which homoeroticism circulates within the text, inverting the contempt for an androgynous and pederastic India prominent in British Indian writing (Sinha, Drucker, and Parry, *Delusions*). The novel's overt homophilia is apparent in the presence of three superb and marginal Indian male figures: the naked gatherer of water-chestnuts who, as he listens to Godbole's song, parts his lips with delight, "disclosing his scarlet tongue" (95); the splendidly-formed, physically perfect punkah-wallah, viewed as a "beautiful naked god" (233); and the broad-shouldered, thin-waisted, naked servitor officiating at the Gokal Ashtami Festival, exhibited as an icon of "the Indian body again triumphant" (309).[18] All who are of "low-birth" and, unlike the loquacious elite Indians, have no lines to speak are offered as sources of a voyeuristic excitation to be surveyed as captive objects of desire without the expectation of a gaze returned. But although their muteness *does* signify the exercise of a homoeroticized cultural power by the narrative's seeing eye, the novel's language registers not violence but affect, and the silence ascribed the figures has resonances other than the scopophiliac—to which I will return.

Because the libidinal is woven into an intricate narrative web, a discourse in the tradition of homosexual Orientalism is inseparable from the fiction's meditations on friendships within colonial conditions. In what Suleri calls "the most notoriously oblique homoerotic exchange in the literature of English India," a multivalent transaction within a relationship overdetermined by colonialism is staged when Aziz inserts his stud into Fielding's collar (*Rhetoric* 138).[19] If, as Suleri maintains, this scene belongs with a discourse where "colonial sexuality" is reconfigured into "a homoeroticization of race" (135), then it also meets with other stagings of homosociality which impinge on both the novel's performance of cross-cultural interactions, and its contemplation of other cultural modes. It is noticeable that in a memoir published after his death, Forster recorded his reluctance to use the sexual services available from Muslims in the princely state where he was employed, because of their "general air of dirt and degradation" (*Hill* 311). But fiction does not imitate life, and the Muslims in the novel are gracious figures whose cultivated sociality is suffused by the homoerotic. The accounts of easeful male associations to which Fielding is admitted, resonate the courtly same-sex eroticism of the Arab–Persian–Islamic literary tradition and fulfill a fantasy of unconcealed homosexual associations still forced into secrecy in Britain (Drucker 81–82). At such gatherings, where guests recite the poetry of the Muslim-Indian Ghalib alluding to intimacy amongst men, the homosocial shades into the homoerotic. As certainly, intonations of homophilia pervade Forster's wistful glances at his Muslim protagonists who accomplish "something beautiful" when they stretch out their hands for food, or applaud a song. (250–51) But in celebrating a society which accommodates homoerotic love, the novel, which also observes the refined deportment of Aziz's wife and the Begum Hamidullah, registers a romanticized appreciation of a cultural sensibility:

> *The banquet, though riotous, had been agreeable, and now the blessings of leisure—unknown to the West, which either works or idles—descended on the motley company. Civilization strays about like a ghost here, revisiting the ruins of empire, and is to be found not in great works of art or mighty deeds, but in the gestures well-bred Indians make when they sit or lie down.... This restfulness of gesture—it is the Peace that passeth Understanding, after all, it is the social equivalent of Yoga. When the whirling of action ceases, it becomes visible, and reveals a civilization which the West can disturb but will never acquire.* (250–51)

A similarly coded display of sensual desire situated in the context of a stranger's bemused esteem for Indian cultural forms also marks the representation of the Gokal Ashtami Festival. Although described as "[n]ot an orgy of the body," the ceremonies are invoked in a scarcely veiled vocabulary soliciting the presence of a homoerotic content (285). Amongst the celebrations of Krishna's birth, which also include enactments of the merry and polymorphous God sporting with milk-maidens, are "Performances of great beauty in the private apartments of the Rajah ... [who] owned a consecrated troupe of men and boys, whose duty it was to dance various actions and meditations of his faith before him.... The Rajah and his guests would then forget that this was a dramatic performance, and would worship the actors" (299). But this yearning to discover an untroubled absorption of homosexual love into religious devotions does not exhaust a narration which, albeit from a distance of disbelief, also animates a hunger for the sacred.

Hence I suggest that the evocations of the homoerotic, as well as the heterosexual disturbance assailing an Englishwoman, should be read as scenes within the fiction's larger drama. This returns me to the further significance of the naked and voiceless figures who, although the objects of western libidinal surveillance, elude its narrative grasp. To the authors of a radical critique of the book's complicity with Orientalist discourse, it is Godbole's silence when asked about the caves which registers a refusal on the part of the colonized to impart knowledge to their rulers, thereby constituting an instance of resistance (Pathak et al.). As it turns out, this provocative contention is not sustainable, since on other occasions a garrulous Godbole readily provides his European audience with a detailed explanation of a song summoning Krishna's presence and presses an exegesis about Hindu notions of good and evil on a distracted Fielding (96). Whatever can be inferred from Godbole's withholding information about the site of beliefs remote from his own, I would suggest that the import of silence within the novel resides rather in the lowly Indians, whose aphonia alludes to their habitation of a realm beyond the ken and the control of western knowledge, and who join India's material being and cognitive traditions in resisting incorporation into a western script.

V.

For Said, the novel's ending is "a paralyzed gesture of aesthetic powerlessness" where "Forster notes and confirms the history behind a political conflict between Dr. Aziz and Fielding—Britain's subjugation of India—and yet can neither recommend decolonization nor continued colonization. 'No, not yet, not here' [sic] is all Forster can muster by way of resolution" ("Representing" 223). As I read the open-ended closing act, all the novel's reflections on social and perceptual failure are rehearsed, but now there are gestures to a still deferred post-imperial condition which temporally the novel has not the means to articulate "No, not yet"—and which in the space the fiction occupies, cannot be realized—"No, not there" (316). For with the "Not yet" first spoken by Ralph Moore in response to Aziz's lament that "the two nations cannot be friends" (306), and repeated in the last lines of the book, the negatives pervading the novel's rhetoric come to intimate not only a philosophical category and the prevailing constraints on both inter-cultural associations and displays of consummated same-sex intimacy, but a time when the existential discontents, social divisions, cultural chasms, and perceptual restraints which the novel configures will be superseded.[20]

This postponement is itself a utopian greeting to an always unrepresentable future, and is positioned within a rhetoric of the gulf between illimitable desire and the circumscriptions of existence: "[t]he revelation was over, but its effect lasted, and its effect was to make men feel that the revelation had not yet come. Hope existed despite fulfillment" (299); "a passage not easy, not now, not here, not to be apprehended except when it is unattainable" (309). The reconciliations and separations of the closing pages happen during the monsoon, named by Aziz as "the time when all things are happy, young and old," and which the novel bathes in a magical aura (306–07). At Aziz's meeting with Ralph Moore, the rains "made a mist round their feet" (297), and when Aziz rides with Fielding, "aware that they would meet no more" (310), "myriads of kisses" surround them "as the earth drew water in" (313). But after Aziz has completed his conciliatory letter to Adela Quested, "the mirror of the scenery was shattered" (314), and the symbols of harmony give way to the chasms of the quotidian: "the scenery, though it smiled, fell like a gravestone on any human hope" (315). As earth and rock, temple, tank and palace, horses, birds, and carrion—the material and cultural forms of an India resistant to British rule—intercede against a premature concordance, "No, not yet.... No, not there" now signifies in a political as well a cognitive register the impossibility of the journey promised by the novel and withdrawn in the narration.

When Forster is relegated as a bloodless liberal, whose understanding of and opposition to empire was circumscribed, or whose affection for the East is suspect because it provided him with opportunities for sexual adventures, his considerable distance from the prevalent ideological positions of his day is occluded. For although his deviations were performed with discretion, his transgressive sexuality at a time when homosexuality was officially outlawed and publicly disapproved in Britain, his socialism in a period of bourgeois hegemony, and his anti-colonialism in an age of residual imperial enthusiasm converged in a stance, which if not radical was dissident.[21] It is often forgotten that in 1935 Forster attended a meeting in Paris of the International Association of Writers for the Defence of Culture organized by the Popular Front to unite communists, socialists, and liberals in defense of "the cultural heritage." In retrospect it is possible to be cynical about the conciliatory politics which the Congress opportunistically advocated, and to observe that Forster would have been quite at home in such a gathering. Yet his participation was surely an act of political integrity by an untheoretical socialist demonstrating his opposition to fascism and commitment to internationalism.

In his address to the Congress, Forster used the vocabulary of liberalism—justice, culture, liberty, freedom—and conceded that the times demanded another and more inclusive language which he could speak:

> *I know very well how limited, and how open to criticism, English freedom is. It is race-bound and it's class-bound ... you may have guessed that I am not a Communist, though perhaps I might be one if I was a younger and a braver man, for in Communism I can see hope. It does many things which I think evil, but I know that it intends good. (Abinger 62–63)*

Forster's nonconformist dispositions enabled him to write a self-reflexive fiction where the recourse to received themes and rhetorics is sublated in an engagement with a colonial world as an agent of knowledge and an adversary to imperial rule. The complex registers of a metropolitan novel, whose emergent modernism is inseparable from its unreached narrative destination in a colonial world, require that critics writing in a post-imperial era go beyond castigating its vestiges of orientalism, whether sexually or culturally accented, and recognize also the extent to which both the textual India of British writing and the empire of British self-representation are disorientated.

NOTES

My thanks to Derek Attridge, Laura Chrisman, John Fletcher, and Neil Lazarus for comments on a draft, and to Michael Sprinker for his unshakable skepticism about my "too tender" reading of the novel.

1. See, for instance, Coombes, MacKenzie, McClintock, Pieterse, and Said.

2. As demonstrated in, for example, Ferguson, Fraiman, Heller, Lineham, and Meyer.

3. Stepan has argued that because interactive metaphors shape our perceptions and actions while at the same time neglecting or suppressing information that does not fit the similarity, "they tend to lose their metaphoric nature and be taken literally" (52).

4. For an extensive and thoughtful examination of Said and Jameson in this context, see Chrisman.

5. This is a proposition I advance in "Narrating Imperialism: *Nostromo's* Dystopia."

6. Against this trend, Armstrong contests charges of epistemological and narrative naiveté, while the volume *A Passage to India*, edited by Davies and Wood, seeks to reexamine the novel in the light of contemporary critical paradigms.

7. See, for example, Sharpe, Silver, Suleri, Bakshi, Lane, and Bristow. For Sharpe the racial significance of rape in the novel requires that it be read "according to the narrative demands of the Mutiny reports," where "a discourse of rape" was used in the management of anti-colonial rebellion (237–38). In Silver's view, the book's deployment of sexuality within a discourse of power makes it possible to understand that to be *rapable* is "a social position" cutting across "biological and racial lines" (88). Addressing the novel's attempt to reconfigure colonial sexuality into "a homoeroticization of race," Suleri argues that this translation of an imperial erotic revises "the colonialist-as-heterosexual-paradigm," presenting instead an alternative colonial model in which "the most urgent cross-cultural invitations occur between male and male, with racial difference serving as a substitute for gender" (*Rhetoric* 139, 133). In more general terms, Bakshi has placed the fiction within a well-established narrative mode of an Orientalism imbued with homoerotic desire, while Lane considers that Forster transposed the problem of homosexuality onto race and colonialism, the shift in locale from England to colonial India alleviating his difficulty in writing about same-sex relationships at home, and Bristow finds that for Forster "the desire for connection between colonial rulers and subaltern peoples" is "indissociable from fantasies of dominative violence" ("Passage" 140).

8. Forster's shame at availing himself of sexual power over Indians is registered in his memoir, probably written in 1922. He was at this time employed as Private Secretary to the Maharajah of Dewas Senior, who in a gesture joining the abuse of his social authority with the tolerance of a committed heterosexual for a friend's incomprehensible urges, procured servants of his court to assuage Forster's lust, quaintly blamed by Forster on the heat. See the section "Kanaya," in *The Hill of Devi*. As Lane points out, this memoir records Forster's disgust with those servicing his sexual needs; as evident is his self-disgust.

9. The foremost exponent was E.J. Thompson, whose *A Farewell to India* was at the time of its publication (irrelevantly) compared to Forster's novel.

10. On this history of insurgency, see the work of the Subaltern Studies Group, a selection of which appears in Guha and Spivak.

11. Silver's reading misconstrues Adela Quested's charge of rape as an act of resistance against the silencing of women and Indians. It proceeds from conflating distinct and specific forms of oppression in the interest of appropriating all discourses of discrimination, as well as the counter-discourses these engender, to a feminist critique. Hence Silver privileges Quested's exercise of female autonomy over Quested's exercise of white authority, a move which seriously distorts the fiction's exposure of Anglo-Indian racialized sexual anxieties.

12. The telepathic Mrs. Moore "knows" that the accident to the Nawab Bahadur's car was caused by an apparition, "[b]ut the idea of a ghost scarcely passed her lips" (111); Adela hears what has not been spoken affirming Aziz's innocence (209); in the interstices of a chant to Krishna, Aziz recognizes "the syllables of salvation that had sounded during his trial" (308); the punkah-wallah is perceived as "a male fate, a winnower of souls" (221), and Ralph Moore is manifest as "a guide."

13. In an essay on Carpenter, Forster wrote: "As he had looked outside his own class for companionship, so he was obliged to look outside his own race for wisdom" (*Two* 207). Bristow has remarked that "[A]lthough Whitman's 'Passage to India' has frequently been mentioned in commentaries on *A Passage to India* ... the dissident homosexual politics implied in this choice of title have generally gone unrecognized (*Effeminate* 86).

14. Although Forster was not a scholar of Hindu philosophies, he was familiar with

the myths, epics, and iconography of India's varied cultures, and he found the dialectical style of Hindu thought congenial. On re-reading the *Bhagavad-Gita* in 1912 before his first visit to India, Forster observed that he felt he had now got hold of the structure of its thought: "Its division of states into Harmony Motion Inertia (Purity Passion Darkness)" (qtd. in Furbank 216).

15. A post-Vedic heterodoxy of the fifth Century B.C. but like Buddhism, with which it has historical and theoretical affinities, rooted in the ancient metaphysics of Dravidian India.

16. Dellamora has noted the coded homoerotic inflection which the word *friend* carried for Forster (159).

17. Godbole encounters the recalcitrance of stone during his religious observances when, in imitating God, he attempts and fails to impel it to "that place where completeness can be found" (283).

18. See Bakshi on Carpenter's preoccupation with the nakedness of natives: "Repeatedly in the Ceylon section of *From Adam's Peak to Elephanta*, the narrator dwells on the physique and nakedness of the natives.... Again, a *yogi* in Benares is approvingly described as 'a rather fine-looking man' with 'nothing whatever on but some beads round his neck and the merest apology for a loin-cloth'" (62).

19. For Bristow this transfer which represents Aziz's sexual potency and erotic power also represents his servility within an exploitative imperial situation: "This incident assuredly points to the ambivalent manner in which homophile longing and dreams of empire meet and part. Without doubt, Aziz's body provides the template for the highly conflicted desires experienced by the European liberal author whose homoeroticism often must have felt uncomfortably close to the dominative violence meted out by imperial rule" (*Effeminate* 87).

20. Lane contends that "the ending refuses to develop or curtail Aziz and Fielding's intimacy; geography intervenes, bringing their contact to a provisional halt without irreparable damage. The novel's closing sentences foreground a drama about the men's sexual intimacy and the abstract forces that keep them apart" (155). See also Bristow, who traces the novel's tension in striving to realize homophile intimacy while acknowledging "how comradeship—between men and between nations—can only come about with the end of empire" (*Effeminate* 86).

21. In "The Birth of an Empire" (1924), an account of a visit to the British Empire Exhibition at Wembley, Forster mocks the rhetoric of "a high imperial vision" (*Abinger* 44–47); and in "The Challenge of our Times" (1946), he applauds the colonial people kicking against their masters (*Two*).

WORKS CITED

Ahmad, Aijaz. "Indian Literature." *In Theory: Classes, Nations, Literatures*. London: Verso, 1992.

Armstrong, Paul. "Reading India: E.M. Forster and the Politics of Interpretation." *Twentieth Century Literature* 38.4 (1992): 365–85.

Bakshi, Parminder. "Homosexuality and Orientalism: Edward Carpenter's Journey to the East." *Edward Carpenter and Late Victorian Radicalism*. Ed. Tony Brown. London: Cass, 1990.

Barrell, John. *The Infection of Thomas De Quincy: A Psychopathology of Imperialism*. New Haven: Yale UP, 1991.

Bristow, Joseph. *Effeminate England: Homoerotic Writing After 1885*. Philadelphia: Open UP, 1995.

———. "Passage to E.M. Forster: Race, Homosexuality, and the 'Unmanageable Streams' of Empire." *Imperialism and Gender: Constructions of Masculinity*. Ed. C.E. Gittings. West Yorkshire: Dangeroo, 1996.

Burke, Kenneth. "Social and Cosmic Mystery: *A Passage to India*." *Language as Symbolic Action*. Berkeley: U of California P, 1966.

Calinescu, Matei. *Five Faces of Modernity: Modernism Avant-Garde Decadence Kitsch Postmodernism*. Rev. ed. Durham: Duke UP, 1987.

Carpenter, Edward. "India, The Wisdom-Land." *Toward Democracy*. London: Swan, 1911.

Chrisman, Laura. "Unhappy Dialogue? Socialism and Post-colonial Cultural Theory." *New Formations*. Forthcoming.

Coombes, Annie. *Reinventing Africa: Museums, Material Culture and the Popular Imagination in Late Victorian and Edwardian England*. New Haven: Yale UP, 1994.

Davies, Tony, and Nigel Wood, eds. *A Passage to India*. Philadelphia: Open UP, 1994.

Dellamora, Richard. "Textual Politics/Sexual Politics." *Modern Language Quarterly* 54.1 (1990): 155–64.

Drucker, Peter. "'In the Tropics There Is No Sin': Sexuality and Gay-Lesbian Movements in the Third World." *New Left Review* 218 (1996): 75–101.

Ferguson, Moira. "*Mansfield Park*: Slavery, Colonialism and Gender." *Oxford Literary Review* 13.1–2 (1991): 118–39.

Forster, E.M. *A Passage to India*. 1924. New York: Penguin, 1979.

———. *Abinger Harvest*. 1936. New York: Penguin, 1967.

———. *The Hill of Devi and Other Indian Writings*. Ed. Elizabeth Heine. London: Arnold, 1983.

———. *Two Cheers for Democracy*. 1951. London: Arnold, 1972.

Fraiman, Susan. "Jane Austen and Edward Said: Gender, Culture and Imperialism." *Critical Inquiry* 21.4 (1995): 805–21.

Furbank, P.N. *E.M. Forster: A Life*. Vol. 1. London: Secker, 1977.

Guha, Ranajit, and Gayatri Chakravorty Spivak. *Selected Subaltern Studies*. New York: Oxford UP, 1988.

Heller, Tamar. *Dead Secrets: Wilke Collins and the Female Gothic*. New Haven: Yale UP, 1992.

Jameson, Fredric. *Modernism and Imperialism*. Derry: Field Day, 1988.

———. *The Political Unconscious: Narrative as a Socially Symbolic Act*. London: Methuen, 1981.

Kazan, Francesca. "Confabulations in *A Passage to India*." *Criticism* 29.2 (1987): 197–214.

Lane, Christopher. *The Ruling Passion: British Colonial Allegory and The Paradox of Homosexual Desire*. Durham: Duke UP, 1995.

Lineham, Katherine Bailey. "Mixed Politics: The Critique of Imperialism in *Daniel Deronda*." *Texas Studies in Literature and Language* 34.3 (1992): 325–46.

Macherey, Pierre. "Georges Bataille: Materialism Inverted." *The Object of Literature*. Trans. David Macey. Cambridge: Cambridge UP, 1995.

MacKenzie, John M. *Orientalism: History, Theory and the Arts*. Manchester: Manchester UP, 1995.

McClintock, Anne. *Imperial Leather: Race, Gender and Sexuality in the Colonial Contest*. London: Routledge, 1995.

Metcalf, Thomas R. *Ideologies of the Raj*. Cambridge: Cambridge UP, 1995.

Meyer, Susan. *Imperialism at Home: Race and Victorian Women's Fiction*. Ithaca: Cornell UP, 1996.

Moore-Gilbert, Bart. "'The Babel of Tongues': Reading Kipling, Reading Bhabha." *Writing India: 1757–1990*. Ed. Moore-Gilbert. Manchester: Manchester UP, 1996. 111–38.

———. Introduction. *Writing India: 1757–1990*. Ed. Moore-Gilbert. Manchester: Manchester UP, 1996. 1–29.

Parry, Benita. *Delusions and Discoveries: Studies on India in the British Imagination 1880–1930*. 1972. London: Verso, 1998.

———. "Narrating Imperialism: *Nostromo*'s Dystopia." *Cultural Readings of Imperialism: Edward Said and the Gravity of History*. Ed. Keith Ansell-Pearson, Benita Parry, and Judith Squires. New York: St. Martin's Press, 1998.

Pathak, Zakia, Saswati Sengupta, and Sharmila Purkayastha. "The Prisonhouse of Orientalism." *Textual Practice* 5.2 (1991): 195–218.

Pieterse, Jan Nederveen. *White on Black: Images of Africans and Blacks In Western Popular Culture*. New Haven: Yale UP, 1992.

Said, Edward. *Culture and Imperialism*. London: Chatto, 1993.

———. *Orientalism*. London: Routledge, 1978.

———. "Orientalism Reconsidered." *Europe and its Others*. Vol. 1. Ed. Francis Barker, Peter Hulme, Margaret Iversen, and Diana Loxley. Colechester: U of Essex P, 1985.

———. "Representing the Colonized: Anthropology's Interlocutors." *Critical Inquiry* 15.2 (1989): 205–25.

Sharpe, Jenny. "The Unspeakable Limits of Rape: Colonial Violence and Counter-Insurgency." *Colonial Discourse and Post-colonial Theory*. Ed. Patrick Williams and Laura Chrisman. London: Harvester, 1992. 221–43.

Silver, Brenda. "Periphrasis, Power and Rape in *A Passage to India*." *Novel* 22.1 (1988): 86–103.

Sinha, Mrinalini. *Colonial Masculinity: The "Manly Englishman" and the "Effeminate Bengali" in the Late Nineteenth Century*. Manchester: Manchester UP, 1995.

Stallybrass, Oliver. Introduction. *A Passage to India*. By E.M. Forster. New York: Penguin, 1979.

Stepan, Nancy. "Race and Gender: The Role of Analogy in Science." *Anatomy of Racism*. Ed. David Theo Goldberg. Minnesota: Minneapolis UP, 1990.

Suleri, Sara. "The Geography of *A Passage to India*." *Modern Critical Views: E.M. Forster*. Ed. Harold Bloom. New York: Chelsea, 1987. 169–75.

———. *The Rhetoric of English India*. Chicago: U of Chicago P, 1992.

Whitman, Walt. "Passage to India." 1871. *Leaves of Grass and Selected Prose*. New York: Modern Library, 1950.

ELIZABETH MACLEOD WALLS

An Aristotelian Reading of the Feminine Voice-as-Revolution in E. M. Forster's A Passage to India

"But the crisis was still to come."
—E. M. Forster, *A Passage To India*

A Passage To India is a novel about moments, those both historical and topical, within which the immediate context of an utterance develops meaning and power. As an historical novel, *Passage* is mired in and defined by competing voices concerning the British Empire at the end of the nineteenth century. In 1924, when *Passage* was published, the imperial situation in India was at best "irreconcilable" and at worst ignitable.[1] E. M. Forster positioned himself as a kind of humanist barometer between points East and West, predicting and at times cautioning against British ignorance and pretentiousness as the imperial machine faced mounting threats of insurrection among the colonies. Forster viewed Britain's audacious political stance as emblematic of its ongoing blindness toward this tension. In various essays written around the time of publication of *A Passage To India*, Forster frequently characterized Britain's attitude toward its struggling colonies as pedantic and dangerous; in *Salute To The Orient!* Forster suggested, for example, that Britain's imperial motto was akin to "Johnny'd rather have us than anyone else" when in fact "Johnny'd like to see the death of the lot," according to Forster (*Abinger Harvest* 269).[2]

Despite his sardonic commentaries on Anglo-India, there was nothing glib about the depths to which these divisive events affected the author

---

From *Papers on Language and Literature* 35, no. 1 (Winter 99), © 1999 by the Board of Trustees, Southern Illinois University Press.

personally. India reflected more than Forster's own past: Forster's life in India
was integral to his literary and private personae. *A Passage To India* is, in
consequence, part and parcel of his attempt to articulate conflicts raging
among nations and civilizations while perpetuating the collective ethos of
Anglo-India in the 1920s. The crux of Forster's effort is an interrogation of
hegemonic rhetoric; *Passage* is an attempt both to criticize and, more
covertly, to stifle the authoritative voice of British rule. Forster achieves his
profound critique of imperial rhetoric subtly through a tender exploration of
cross-cultural friendship, and overtly through an imperial legal crisis
precipitated by the intangible experiences of the newly-arrived Briton, Adela
Quested. It is this civic crisis,[3] fueled by Adela Quested's gender and
nationality, that is the catalyst for anti-imperial consciousness between the
novel's male protagonists, Cyril Fielding and Dr. Aziz.

In *A Passage to India* Adela Quested, described by the narrator as a
"priggish" New Woman driven by personal/marital and cultural/national
identity crises to "see the real India," becomes a vehicle of linguistic,
legalistic, and eventually cultural subversion (*A Passage To India* 22).[4] From
the moment that Adela is retrieved from the Marabar hills after her
unsettling ordeal there, the official narrative of guilt begins to form within
the British camp. It is clear from the outset that gender is to be their rallying
point. For instance, the truth, as Fielding sees it, is immediately waylaid by
the Englishmen at the Club "speaking of 'women and children'—that phrase
that exempts the male from sanity when it has been repeated a few times"
(184). Thus upon Dr. Aziz's return to Chandrapore from the Marabar the
British have already devised an emotionally charged story of what happened
based upon sketchy reports from Adela.

The reliability of Adela's memory is questioned by Fielding and,
accordingly, by the reader. Yet despite Adela's apparent infirmity, the British
act on the assumption that their account of the events is true. I want to focus
here on the significance of the fact that in the end Adela does not comply
with this contrived official story. She chooses instead to denounce the
charges levied against Aziz, thereby reducing the primacy and stature of the
British legal system and giving impetus to a wave of riots following the
announcement of the verdict. During this moment of cultural crisis in the
novel, Forster uncovers the fallacy of imperial Britain's univocality by
converting British legal speech into a *techne* of anti-imperial rhetoric through
Adela's disruptive testimony.[5]

Aristotle's theory of rhetoric, written to comply with male-oriented
civic systems, provides sensitive heuristics for understanding Adela's
manipulation of androcentric rhetoric in the courtroom. Recognizing that
the *Rhetoric* was important to the development of British jurisprudence, we

see in *A Passage to India* that the feminine[6] utterance is revolutionary in that it renegotiates Victorian social spheres by employing a woman's voice to disrupt the chauvinistic and racist legal traditions undergirding the British Empire. Most significantly, Adela's rhetorical autonomy and her inversion of Aristotelian discourse at the trial become by association part of Forster's own narrative apparatus for criticizing the ethnocentricity and misogyny he sees as imbued in the British imperial legal system.

I

It is not enough to calculate Adela's *kairos*[7] in the witness box as rhetorical, revolutionary, or even Aristotelian without first capturing, at least cursorily, the historical moment that informed the writing and publication of *A Passage To India*. Between March of 1921 and January of 1922, Forster was for the second time a lone Englishman traveling Anglo-India.[8] Prior to and during this visit, nationalist agitation, spearheaded by Gandhi's civil disobedience movement, had begun to threaten the British machine in India. Concerns over Indian nationalism had occupied the British imperial psyche since the 1857 Mutiny. Yet the subsequent impossibility of English/Indian relations mirrored, as Forster describes so adroitly in *Passage*, the actions of two flames that "strive to unite, but cannot, because one of them breathes air, and the other stone" (125). In other words, Forster was sadly aware that tensions between the occupiers and the occupied would remain, with terrific tension, as long as Britain's "eclipse of power" progressed throughout the interwar imperial world.

The British Raj was instructed to placate the nationalists, though they were warned against underestimating the political power of the movement. The post-war climate was such that the Empire hardly could retain a tyrannical presence in India. What it could and did do, however, was encourage an attitude among Anglo-Indians not unlike that articulated by Mrs. Turton at the "Bridge Party" in *Passage*, who claims that "'you're superior to everyone in India except one or two of the Ranis, and they're on an equality'" (40). Forster's own insights into the *topoi*[9] or social and legal strategies of the Raj were more sophisticated than those supplied by the Burra Sahib's wife. Shortly after returning from India in January of 1922, Forster wrote: "Excluded from our clubs, [the Indian] has never been introduced to the West in the social sense, as to a possible friend. We have thrown grammar and neckties at him, and smiled while he put them on wrongly—that is all" (qtd. in Das 21). The cultural and political divisions imbibed in India, then, were for Forster beyond that which "Bridge Parties" could possibly mend.

Kieran Dolin suggests that Forster in *A Passage to India* undermines the myopic posture of Anglo-India by offering, as the title of her article suggests, a "critique of imperialist law." I want to follow through with Dolin's assertion and argue that although Forster himself knew little about British legal processes and even less of imperial law, he nonetheless married British law with British society in generating the climax of the novel. Indeed, according to Dolin, just as the "gaps in Adela's story are readily filled by the community around her," so "the narrative presented by the prosecution at the subsequent trial is a collective one" (339). The reader who is initially unaware of the actual occurrences at the Marabar watches, as Fielding does, from an estranged and helpless position as rash accusations, informed by virulent anti-Indian sentiment among the Raj, surge through the British camp. Adela's gender—rather than the basic violation of her personhood—makes her predicament valuable to the Raj: the narrator reminds us that Adela's "position and not her character" garners her sympathy from the British; after all, "she was the English girl who had had the terrible experience ... for whom too much could not be done" (212). Therefore, Anglo-India's explanation of Adela's situation lends support to the gendered constructs of Empire, reifying "all that is worth fighting and dying for" among the English gentry holed up at the Club—or, British cultural indelibility symbolized by the refined and chaste (white, upper class) British woman.[10]

Commensurate with the overblown chivalry of the Raj is their equally idealistic legal strategy against Aziz. In formulating their evidence against Aziz, the British, including Adela's fiancé and Chandrapore Magistrate Ronny and the Chandrapore Superintendent Mr. McBryde, believe that Adela's testimony offered at trial as proof will condemn Aziz, quell revolt, and provoke sterner measures against intercultural mingling. But early in the novel Fielding and the Indian contingent are skeptical as to whether Adela's words in the witness box will be her own. Fielding demands to speak with Adela to assuage his worries but is told by Mr. McBryde that Adela will remain secluded until after the trial. Mr. McBryde reminds Fielding that Adela "'tells her own story'" (171) and that her testimony should therefore not be doubted. To this Fielding retorts prophetically, "'I know, but she tells it to you'" (171), thereby rebuking McBryde's belief that Adela's views coincide with those projected uniformly by the Anglo-Indians. In conceiving of Adela's words and thoughts as they do, the Raj act on the assumption that Adela's Britishness and gender will compel her to corroborate the erroneous story crafted furiously by her compatriots.

Forster's narrative moves methodically from Fielding's anxiety to the Indians' fury to the Britons' pugnacity, resting finally with the ambiguous

Adela herself. Here the novel breaks from detailing the intricacies of imperial legal maneuvers and focuses on Adela's faltering cultural identity. As Adela's concept of her own Britishness crumbles, as the very essence of her identity alters, her disenfranchisement in Anglo-India calcifies; armed only with her own voice, Adela goes to trial.

II

While Adela is yet in the hands of her English supporters, the bewildered tourist "vibrate[s] between hard commonsense and hysteria" (194), vacillating, in other words, over what to believe and how to behave. Like Fielding, the reader is never party to all of Adela's thoughts and conversations after the cave experience. Instead one suspects as Fielding does that at some level her words cannot "be her own," since her story becomes a valuable legal and cultural bulwark against which the Indians can do little more than sling thin accusations of falseness. After all, the Raj, though detested by many, still wield authority in Chandrapore, and their indignation carries with it the credibility of the powerful. So Aziz's camp have few allies among the Anglo-Indians save for Fielding and a largely disinterested Mrs. Moore, while Adela is pitied by a network of strange allies working en masse on her behalf.

Adela is converted initially by the fury surging throughout the imperial community; she does not immediately denounce her caretakers' claim that she is in fact the victim of attempted rape. Accordingly, in chapter twenty-two Adela confirms that a "sort of shadow" accosted her and that, fleeing from its suffocating grasp, she lashed out with her field glasses and then escaped down the thorny hill. Even here, as she is encircled by sympathetic Club members, Adela does not accuse a man but indicts a shadow—she does not describe an attack per se (as she says, "He never actually touched me once"), but merely a pulling, "bottling" force (194). Yet in this novel of enigmatic opposites, where humble punkah wallahs are gods and subalterns fraternize with supposed Indian reprobates, it seems fitting that this shadowy tale is wrought from the same mind that had once so eschewed irrational fictions.

The narrative also tells us that in the care of the McBrydes Adela's "natural honesty of mind" has been subdued and that she is "always trying to 'think the incident out'" rather than face the empty reality of the persistent echo (194). Thus in Adela's pre-trial psyche the mysterious binaries common to the novel are perhaps best represented. Adela's conscious understanding, for instance, emulates the logic contrived by McBryde et al., while her private insights deceive her with uncharacteristic uncertainty: at moments

"She felt that it was her crime, until the intellect, reawakening, pointed out to her that she was inaccurate here, and set her again upon her sterile round" (195). The "intellect" as it is presented here conforms to British rationale, which suggests that a native Indian is the necessary culprit against the signifying body of British culture. Unfortunately, this same intellectual consciousness is informed as well by wild mistruths, prejudices, and sexist conflations of woman and nation that spring up following Dr. Aziz's arrest.

These prejudices become apparent when the Major, addressing Club members, claims that Adela's chaperone Mohammed Latif had been bribed by the "prisoner" to shirk his duty, and the dawdling Godbole had staged his own tardiness to facilitate Aziz's planned attack (187–88). Through the dissemination of these and other stories, cynicism prevails in the Anglo-Indian Camp. In their hyperbolic state, the McBrydes and Ronny, the principal guards of Adela's health and safety, wait until Adela is barely well to prime her for trial. The guardians' caustic view of British/Indian relations is conveyed to Adela at this precarious moment during her recovery: she learns of the near-riot, the threat posed to the civil station and, finally, the intricacies of her upcoming court appearance, each of which results from her accusation against Aziz. As Adela weeps helplessly before them, struck by the massive implications of her vague assertion, Mr. McBryde informs Adela casually of a letter addressed to her from Fielding which he admits to opening during her illness. Although McBryde has violated the sanctity of Adela's private correspondence, he excuses the "peculiar circumstances" behind his appropriation of the letter by condemning Fielding's behavior to Ronny at the Club (198). Adela, incensed by this new but decontextualized information, is compelled to reaffirm her commitment to the official story and, regretting all he "had already to bear ... for my sake," begs Ronny's forgiveness for the disastrous circumstances she has brought upon both him and the Raj (198).

As her rushed recovery unfolds before us, it becomes apparent that Adela's crowded mind is hindered from calmly rehearsing the confusion at the Marabar. Moreover, Adela begins to ask for Mrs. Moore who, it seems, is the only potential fail-safe to her addled conscience. Adela's desire to commiserate with Mrs. Moore, the only other victim of the Marabar's indiscriminate echo, is important to Adela's mental state because her longing signifies her need for empathetic guidance outside of, and emotional escape from, the Anglo-Indian contingent. But in fact Adela's confinement to "this atmosphere of grief and depression" (195) is left unabated by her attempted discourse with Mrs. Moore, whose apathetic greeting of both Ronny and Adela bewilders and dismays the couple.

But Adela's uncomfortable interaction with Mrs. Moore is surprisingly cathartic since Mrs. Moore's ambivalence actually prompts Adela's true memories partially to return. For instance, Ronny, who is blinded to Adela's needs by his own mounting anxieties about the trial, demands of his mother that she testify alongside Adela, "'to confirm,'" he says, "'certain points in our evidence'" (201). Yet Mrs. Moore responds indignantly to this idea. While she claims "'I'll have nothing to do with your ludicrous law courts'" and dismisses her son as petty and misinformed, Mrs. Moore inadvertently draws Adela's support in refuting Ronny's ill-timed demands. In a pivotal moment of self-awareness, Adela inserts herself suddenly between mother and son, declaring that Mrs. Moore's "'evidence is not the least essential'" even though, in his ignorance of Adela's true feelings, Ronny is sure that "'she would want to give it'" (201). At this important but nonetheless understated juncture in the novel, Adela asserts Aziz's innocence to Ronny, realizing the extent to which her trauma, masked by hazy memories and emotions, has been appropriated by and manipulated within the Anglo-Indian community in order to reinforce British rule in Chandrapore. Not surprisingly, Adela's claims are consistently undermined by Ronny who counters her logic by questioning her state of mind: "'I don't quite know what you're saying, and I don't think you do,'" he assures his fiancé abruptly (203). Yet Ronny is not the only one perplexed by Adela's sudden and emotional renunciation of Aziz's guilt. In reaching her conclusions about Aziz, Adela herself conflates Mrs. Moore's opinion of Aziz's innocence with exonerating statements from Fielding's letter. Here the narrative discloses Adela's susceptibility to outside influence, noting that Adela is quite "open to every suggestion" from anyone—from Mrs. Moore, her son, Fielding, and other members of the Raj (204). It is not until Adela is actually in the witness box and able to speak for herself that her authentic memory of the events is permitted to surface.

The trial itself is decidedly polemical. Das presides, to the dismay of "the ladies of Chandrapore" who find his power over Adela unpropitious (207); Amritrao is dramatic; the onlookers for both parties ejaculate inciteful commentary throughout. In Aristotelian terms, we might say that the rhetor at trial is Mr. McBryde, who becomes a representative of all things British, opposing the Indian defendant and his radical nationalist lawyer. McBryde—who, we are told, "left eloquence to the defense" (219)—signifies the "collective narrative" described by Dolin and consecrated by Anglo-Indian society. Put simply, he approaches Adela's testimony from his position as "spokesman ... for the public [imperial] domain," to co-opt Lloyd Bitzer's notion of the public spokesperson (74). Invention does occur between the rhetor and his auditor, Adela, at trial, but their interaction does not supply the useful testimony that McBryde expects it will. Rather, Adela is the one to invent meaning and judgment from proof, ambushing Anglo-India by inverting McBryde's legal discourse to procure judgment. against him and his Empire.

McBryde fails not only to predict Adela's response, but also to influence her recollection of the supposed attack made against her inside the caves. McBryde has no innate sense of the "inventional situation" occurring between himself and Adela as he asks her questions about the incident at the Marabar.[11] And because to Aristotle "moral character, so to say, constitutes the most effective means of proof" (1.2.4), Adela's version of the events becomes all the more threatening to the imperial establishment once she is presented with McBryde's authoritative rhetoric. The imperial rhetoric fails when the Superintendent assumes rather than persuades; in essence, McBryde sees Adela's situation as important but her humanity as trivial to his desired set of legal proofs. In fact, part of what Forster is illuminating with the trial scene is the dehumanizing effect of imperial systems and the extent to which women and other underlings of Empire are viewed as little more than buttresses to the colonial paradigm of virtues. Accordingly, McBryde understands Adela's own story as secondary to his overall argument against Aziz, and he is unable to cull significant parts of Adela's epistemology in order to generate the needed verbal evidence to convict the defendant (using, in Aristotle's terms, "atechnic" or inartistic proof, or *pistis*, do so).

Here McBryde reveals not only his indifference toward a British woman's viewpoint, but also his ignorance (or, at the very least, forgetfulness) of basic public, Aristotelian discourse, the legalistic *techne* which has influenced to its core British rhetoric. According to Aristotelian theories of rhetoric, being aware of an auditor's *topoi* is essential for the rhetor to create "lines, or strategies, of argument" in a trial (Kennedy 190). Lacking this awareness, McBryde unwittingly provides Adela with the rhetorical agency she needs to negate imperial rhetoric, legal, and cultural dominance at trial. And significantly, McBryde is the first among the Anglo-Indians to ask Adela outright and in a public setting about what actually occurred in the caves.

Adela is not technically an auditor; rather, she is a witness, a proof for the prosecution. However, her refusal to appease McBryde and the cadre of Anglo-Indians effectively exonerates Aziz the way a jury might acquit a defendant at a trial, simultaneously vilifying the Empire and McBryde's verbal strategies in court. Moreover, Adela becomes an auditor in the Aristotelian sense in that her testimony also judges British legal superiority to be fraudulent and unstable.[12] McBryde's lengthy association with the chauvinistic Raj precipitates his failure to persuade Adela, whose epistemology he has at once ignored and underestimated. And if, as Lloyd Bitzer has argued, a rhetor personifies "the public's fluid of knowledge" and echoes "[its] maxims ... honors its heroes; rehearses its traditions, performs its rituals," then McBryde represents the ethos of the Empire itself to Adela, which is revealed to her its a pretentious institution based in inequality (74). McBryde's errors in judgment provide Adela with the impetus she needs to shatter the lie against Aziz and falsify the underlying lie of imperialism in India. Adela bristles against McBryde's assumptive examination of her, and as she begins to speak, she "arms" herself, so the narrative says, against the sure destruction her words will produce, both in her own life and in that essentialist world of her compatriots' making:

> As soon as she rose to reply, and heard the sound of her own voice ... A new and unknown sensation protected her, like magnificent armour. She didn't think what had happened or even remember in the ordinary way of memory, but she returned to the Marabar Hills, and spoke from them across a sort of darkness to Mr. McBryde. The fatal day recurred, in every detail.... Questions were asked, and to each she found the exact reply. (228)

The exactness of Adela's reply is also key, since McBryde's unwitting verbal prompts at the trial apparently free Adela from her troubling self-doubt and shadowy memories of the caves.

Having exposed the Empire's fund of knowledge to be a series of weak connections among nationalistic myths, Adela proves despite her unsteadiness that the feminine utterance and the knowledge of one British woman are more viable than the Raj had ever supposed. At the same time "Miss Quested had renounced her own people" (232), in effect siding with the Indians, inverting Aristotelian precepts of judgment, and upsetting the indemnity of British Rule in Chandrapore.

III

It is telling that Forster allows the events at the Marabar and Adela's processing of them to remain ambiguous throughout *A Passage To India*. This ambiguity was intentional. The extant manuscripts of *Passage* reveal that explicit details of Adela's assault have been omitted from the final published version of the novel. In one of the unpublished manuscripts, Adela's assailant is described as grabbing Adela's hands and "forcing her against the wall" where "The strap of her field glasses ... was drawn across her throat" (qtd. in Levine 89).[13] June Perry Levine has read Forster's omission of the attack as a narrative technique meant to generate and maintain suspense in the novel. I maintain, rather, that among Forster's reasons for concealing the truth at the Marabar is to strengthen the potency of the novel's climax: the trial of Aziz and, implicitly, of the British Empire through Adela's timely recollections and devastating admissions in court.

The mystery of Adela's cave trauma gives exigency to Adela's testimony insofar as McBryde's ill-conceived questions force Adela to retrace the true occurrences inside the cave evidenced by Adela's verbal progression toward the truth during the trial scene. "'You went alone into one of those caves?'" he asks her, to which she replies, "'That is quite correct'" (226); McBryde follows Adela's answer, however, with an assumption of fact: "'And the prisoner followed you,'" he says (226). At this point Adela hedges her words, remembering that "her vision was of several caves" and, failing "to locate [Aziz]" in her memory, she reacts by saying "'I am not quite sure'" (226). This moment of instability offers the first public signal by Adela that her memory of the events at the Marabar does not mirror the explanation put forward by the British at court. Befuddled by a response he does not expect, McBryde becomes direct and urgent, demanding to know Adela's position. "'What do you mean, please?'" he persists (230). When pressed, Adela remembers that Aziz was in fact not the culprit at the caves and answers, finally, "'No' ... in a flat, unattractive voice... 'Dr. Aziz never followed me into the cave'" (230). From Adela's stunning affirmation of Aziz's innocence, the reader can infer both that Aziz is honorable and that Adela's own notion of the truth had been significantly affected by her own confusion and Anglo-Indian biases presented to her prior to the trial. The reader, meanwhile, becomes certain that in one instant Adela has succeeded in unraveling Britain's legal authority in Chandrapore and, more significantly, that her success is public, indiscriminate, and devastating.

The feminine voice, previously spoken over or dismissed by Anglo-India before the trial, has a profound effect on British pride, one woman's life, and the relationship between two men—indeed, two whole societies of thought—in this graceful political novel. In exploring Forster's use of voice in his fiction and essays, Jan Gordon claims that "it is in *A Passage To India* that voice is finally endowed with an independent ethical function" and that reminiscent of Bitzer, the utterance in *Passage* is given import through the sharing of "communal voice" (326). Gordon does not isolate any one voice within the larger community of voices in *Passage* as being *the* voice to initiate an awareness of public ethics. However, to the extent that Adela's transgression mirrors the subversiveness of Mrs. Moore's changing spirituality and Godbole's universalism,[14] by answering "no" in court Adela wields a kind of "community of ethics" against Anglo-India consistent with the almost mystical connection formed among these characters in *A Passage to India*. To be sure, Adela's race and nationality give her the latitude in the witness box to turn the tools of imperial civic discourse in on themselves. But Adela is able to reverse the expectations of her testimony during the few moments afforded her to "tell her own story" because, simply, no one believes that she will say anything other than what the Raj expect.

In giving her own version of the events at the Marabar (or the strange story of transgressive truths and inexplicable events), Adela actually invents a *techne* for her own experience that, in Aristotle's terms, is itself artfully concerned with "how to bring into existence a thing which may either exist or not, and which lies in the marker and not in the thing made" (*Nicomachean Ethics* 6.4.4). Adela also employs invention and memory as epistemological tools for rewriting the sociopolitical and sociolinguistic identities prescribed for her by the English community.[15] And it must be stressed that Adela's femininity, her status as a subordinate and companion in the world of Anglo-India, is ironically that aspect of Adela's ethos which underscores the powerful effect of her voice in a public arena. McBryde never imagines that Adela, who is a witness for the British prosecution, will invent her own proof in the witness box or draw upon a "fund of knowledge" (Bitzer 68) that only she as the injured woman can know and articulate. Yet it seems that Adela is the sole person in the novel who can reformulate her memory into proof for Dr. Aziz and, ultimately, into a discourse which proves publicly that the subjugated feminine voice is made more powerful by the dominant culture's insistence that it is a mysterious, unknowable, and unimportant factor within the civic hierarchy.

Through Adela, Forster renegotiates what Bitzer views as "private knowledge made general," giving voice to political ideas that, "lacking a public, have no status, no authorization, indeed no existence" (84). This public germination of knowledge continues as Adela maintains her relationship to other Anglo-Indians despite her expatriation to England after the trial. From her unseen position in Europe, Adela manipulates the reconciliation years later between Fielding and Aziz in India, and so becomes the motivation for the underlying pathos of the novel: that friendship between India and Britain will somehow exist, but ultimately "not yet" and "not there" (325). In one sense, then, Adela is Forster's unacknowledged representative of modernity in the novel; her private insights, brought to public fruition at trial, disengage from and dislodge Victorian social constraints concerning gender, race and class in imperial India by operating from a subordinate position inside the dominant legal structure engendered by the Raj. Within his sabotage of Victorian morality, Forster, himself "the spiritual heir of Blake" (Beer 15), constructs Adela's fate in *A Passage To India* with earnest purpose: the implications of the feminine voice transmitted through Adela reveal that, like Blake, Forster's social sympathies were as immense as his modern vision of women and his insight into the historical, momentary relationships of imperial India was revolutionary.

NOTES

I would like to thank Dr. Anne Cognard, Dr. Roger Cognard, and Dr. Linda Hughes for their valuable editorial suggestions. I would especially like to thank Dr. Richard Leo Enos under whose expert tutelage this essay was produced.

1. See G. K. Das: "Through 'The Ruins of Empire': *A Passage To India* And Some Later Writings About India," in *E. M. Forster's India*, 75–92. Das explains that the novel itself responds to the "main political issue of the time": the "irreconcilable challenge to the Empire" instigated by "politically awakened Indians" (86). This period in India saw such events as the massacre at Amritsar (1919), a boycott of British educational systems by the Indian National Congress, and the Khilafat movement among Indian Moslems, all of which lent support to Gandhi's civil disobedience and affected, in turn, Forster's writing of *A Passage To India* (see Das, chapter four).

2. *Abinger Harvest* was originally published in 1936, twelve years following the publication of *A Passage To India*; however, Forster, whose love and concern for India was immense, continued to comment upon imperial politics in India throughout the interwar period. By the time this quotation was penned, India was eleven years from receiving independence, and Britain was by and large committed to holding onto whatever vestiges of Empire it had left.

3. It is interesting to note that the root of the modern word "crisis" is the Greek term *krisis*, meaning "judgment," and used by Aristotle in the *Rhetoric* to signify the climactic act of adjudicating bodies (see Kennedy, 317).

4. *A Passage to India* is more renowned for developing a loving friendship between its protagonists, Cyril Fielding and Dr. Aziz. This essay does not suggest that Adela Quested, though a key character in the novel, is of central importance in *Passage*. Rather, I argue that Adela's testimony during the trial is indispensable to the novel's overall didacticism.

5. Since Aristotle's theory of civic rhetoric impacts with my reading of Adela's testimony, I have found it useful to refer to some terms taken directly from the *Rhetoric* to describe certain events and ideas surrounding the trial. *Techne* is one such term. According to George Kennedy's translation, *techne* (*teckhne*) is an "art, a reasoned habit of mind in making something" (320), translated commonly into "methodology" or "technique." For another translation, see John Henry Freese's *Aristotle, "The 'Art' of Rhetoric"* (1926).

6. I am using the term "feminine" rather than "female" to aid my argument concerning the power of Adela Quested's voice at court in accordance with Elaine Showalter's useful distinctions among the terms "Feminine," "Feminist," and "Female" articulated in *A Literature of Their Own*. Showalter suggests that these terms correspond not only to the rise of women's political consciousness in British literary history, but also with specific historical ideologies concerning gender and culture. Although she is speaking of women authors, I find that Showalter's description of the "feminine" is an embodiment of "repression, concealment, and self-censorship" (25) in Victorian society an apt corollary to the Anglo-Indian precepts of womanhood projected onto Adela (and explored at length in the Mosque chapters especially), but finally rejected by her during the trial scene.

7. *Krisis* is a Sophistic term, "pointing to the contingent relationship between truth and circumstances," or the contextual situations information a specific rhetorical moment (Bizzell and Herzberg 23).

8. Forster had been composing *Passage* since late 1913 by the time his second trip to India commenced. Quoted by K. Natwar-Singh in *E. M. Forster: A Tribute*, Forster says that during the 1921 trip, "I took the opening chapters with me," yet "The gap between India remembered and India experienced was too wide" (107). It wasn't until Forster returned to England that "the gap narrowed, and [he] was able to resume" (107).

9. *Topos*, pl. *topoi*, is a "topic ... a mental 'place' where an argument can be found or the argument itself" resides, according to Kennedy (320).

10. Indeed, the more precise image evoked by Forster here illuminates the extent to which Adela is useful because of her gender and race. The full quotation is as follows: "One young mother ... sat on a low ottoman in the smoking-room with her baby in her arms ... The wife of a small railway official, she was generally snubbed; but this evening, with her abundant figure and masses of corn-gold hair, she symbolized all that is worth fighting and dying for; more permanent a symbol, perhaps, than poor Adela" (181).

11. Richard Leo Enos and Janice Lauer's assertions concerning Aristotelian heuristics and the co-creation of meaning in rhetoric and writing ascribe revelatory power to public rhetoric. Enos and Lauer suggest that "rhetoric can not only be a way of arguing but can also generate its own way of knowing, its own kind of epistemic process" leading from "inventional situations between rhetor and audience" (83).

12. William Grimaldi suggests that the auditor is a "nonspeaking partner" (67) in the rhetorical exchange between rhetor and auditor (in this slightly different example, between McBryde and Adela). Grimaldi stresses, however, that if the rhetor neglects to familiarize him or herself with the auditor's ethos, then the rhetor "effectively negates or weakens the force of his own ethos as entechnic *pistis*" (1174).

13. There are three extant manuscripts of *A Passage to India* used by Levine, all of which were sold to the University of Texas by Forster on behalf of the financially troubled London Library in 1959 for $18,200.

14. Godbole, a Hindu mystic, is both comic relief and moralistic foil to the characters in *A Passage to India*. His "Universalist" worldview reminds the reader of the overall futility of human systems and prompts him to tell Fielding after Aziz's arrest that "'the action was performed by Dr. Aziz' ... "It was performed by the guide" ... 'It was performed by you' ... [and with] an air of coyness, 'It was performed by me'" (178).

15. Lisa Ede, Cheryl Glenn and Andrea Lunsford's article, "Border Crossings: Intersections of Rhetoric and Feminism," aided my reading of Adela's use of memory as a tool for rhetorical invention in the witness box. Ede, Glenn, and Lunsford write that "invention and memory constrain and shape both who can know and what can be known," which is of particular importance to women operating rhetorically within patriarchal (and traditionally Aristotelian) modes of civic discourse (295).

WORKS CITED

Aristotle. *The "Art" of Rhetoric*. Trans. John Henry Freese. London: Heinemann, Ltd., 1926.

———. *The Nicomachean Ethics*. Trans. H. Rackman. 2nd ed. London: William Heinemann, Ltd., 1933.

Beer, J. B. *The Achievement of E. M. Forster*. New York: Barnes, 1962.

Bitzer, Lloyd F. "Rhetoric and Public Knowledge." *Rhetoric, Philosophy, and Literature: An Exploration.* Ed. Don M. Burks. West Lafayette: Purdue UP, 1978, 67–93.

Bizzell, Patricia, and Bruce Herzberg, eds. *The Rhetorical Tradition: Readings from Classical Times to the Present.* Boston: Bedford, 1990.

Das, G. K. *E. M. Forster's India.* Totowa, NJ: Rowman, 1977.

Dolin, Kieran. "Freedom Uncertainty, and Diversity: *A Passage To India* as a Critique of Imperialist Law." *Texas Studies in Language and Literature* 363 (1991): 328–52.

Ede, Lisa, Cheryl Glenn, and Andrea Lunsford, "Border Crossings: Intersections of Rhetoric and Feminism," *Rhetorica* 13.3 (1995): 285–325.

Enos, Richard Leo, and Janice Lauer. "The Meaning of *Heuristic* in Aristotle's *Rhetoric* and Its Implications for Rhetorical Theory." *A Rhetoric of Doing: Essays on Discourse in Honor of James L. Kinneavy.* Eds. Stephen P. White, Neil Nakadate, and Roger G. Cherry. Carbondale: Southern Illinois UP, 1992. 79–87.

Forster, E. M. *Abinger Harvest.* London: Edward Arnold, 1953.

———. *A Passage To India.* London: Edward, Arnold, and Co., 1939.

Gordon, Jan B. "The Third Cheer 'Voice' in Forster. *Twentieth Century Literature* 32.2.3 (1985): 315–28.

Grimaldi, S.J., William M. A. "The Auditors' Role in Aristotelian Rhetoric." *Oral and Written Communication: Historical Approaches.* Ed. Richard Leo Enos. Newbury Park: SAGE, 1990, 65–81.

Kennedy, George, trans. and ed. *On Rhetoric.* By Aristotle. New York: Oxford UP, 1991.

Levine, June Perry. *Creation and Criticism: A Passage to India.* Lincoln: U of Nebraska P, 1971.

Natwar-Singh, K. *E. M. Forster: A Tribute.* New York: Harcourt, 1961.

Showalter, Elaine. *A Literature of Their Own.* Princeton, NJ: Princeton UP, 1977.

MARIA M. DAVIDIS

Forster's Imperial Romance: Chivalry, Motherhood, and Questing in A Passage to India

W hen Adela Quested enters *A Passage to India*, it becomes immediately apparent that she has entered an Anglo-Indian world both Victorian and modern, imperialist and anti-imperialist.[1] This Anglo-Indian society's spatial remove from the metropolis is simultaneously signified temporally: the narrator tells us that aspects of "feminist England" have not yet made their way to this part of the empire, and we see Anglo-Indians of the early 1920s perform or plan to perform plays such as *Cousin Kate* (1903), *Quality Street* (1901), and *The Yeomen of the Guard* (1888).[2] Traditional chivalry guides the community, which holds onto its rule by appealing to the protection of women, a notion made popular after the 1857 Mutiny.[3] At the same time, we see stirrings of modernity and nationalism in the book: the Indian characters protest the "Turtons and Burtons" and their racism, and Aziz and Fielding move towards an ostensibly liberating politics of race.

In this setting, Adela Quested is unique among the characters in that she maintains both Victorian and modern aspects in herself and therefore disrupts both elements of Anglo-Indian society rather than fitting in. For example, when Adela says that she wishes to "'see ... the real India,'" she seems modern and progressive—a type of New Woman—in comparison to the Englishwomen already in India, who attempt to recreate England in their houses and the Club rather than adapt to their new country (pp. 24–25). At the same time, Adela's wish to see India seems curiously retrogressive; when

From *Journal of Modern Literature* 23, no. 2, Winter 1999, © 1999 by Maria M. Davidis.

Fielding suggests that she should "'[t]ry seeing Indians,'" he implies that meeting the indigenous people is more important (and progressive) than simply seeing the land (p. 25). Adela's desire for romance—her wish to explore the landscape—harkens back to male explorer figures of the past, who traditionally penetrate a fecund feminine landscape in order to bring forth its fruits for the British empire. At this point in imperial history, Adela is a reminder that the time of great imperial questing is over; the empire has been mapped and civilized enough so that even women can enter, transforming adventure into tourism. But it is also clear, perhaps contradictorily, that a woman who wants to explore is overly masculine and either sexually aggressive or undesirable; from a narrative perspective, she is an almost impossible figure, preferring imperial romance, as she does, over the usual desire of unmarried women, the heterosexual romance that results in marriage. Her yearning for imperial romance thus challenges both Victorian and modern sensibilities.

The traditional chivalric model followed by the Victorian segment of this imperial society, represented by most of the Anglo-Indian characters, stresses heterosexuality, the rules of public school, the powerlessness of women, and continued British rule in India; the more modern and ostensibly forward-thinking characters, Aziz and Fielding, follow a seemingly antithetical model, the "new chivalry." This new movement substitutes a homoerotic relationship for the heterosexual one in traditional chivalry and looks forward to the end of British rule over the colonies. The imperial romance desired by the novel is thus that between Indian and Anglo-Indian men, but the relationship is destined to fail, if only because of the power disparity inevitable in a still-existing Anglo-India.[4]

Although the old chivalry and new chivalry may be opposed politically (heterosexual opposed to homoerotic, imperialist to anti-imperialist), they agree on one point at least: the men in both believe that the once or future perfect relationships between Indian and Anglo-Indian men have been damaged. Textual evidence might suggest bad government or the men's own racism as the likely causes of these problems, but at a time in which masculine adventure seems to be vanishing and male power is being challenged—for example, by female travellers in the empire, and women agitating for suffrage and equal access to education and employment at home—the men in the novel place the blame for deteriorating relationships with native Indians on the Anglo-Indian women in the sexual economy, that is, women who are married or "on the market."[5] By extension, heterosexual romance becomes problematic, the implication being that it separates men from one another. Adela Quested, in particular, becomes the chief scapegoat in the novel as she seeks types of romance denied to British women in India. Her inability to conform to the dictates of either brand of chivalry threatens this most masculine and homosocial world, and results in physical and psychological trauma, social castigation, and narrative expulsion from India. Only a British woman beyond sex, the maternal Mrs. Moore, can enable Indian and Anglo-Indian men to come together. Rather than being a force of separation, she acts as a type of mirror, illuminating or facilitating the relationships between men, but never becoming romantically involved.

*   *   *   *

In *A Passage to India*, the system of old chivalry, represented by the mainstream Anglo-Indian community, comes into relief at a revealing moment of crisis. After Adela is "insulted" in the caves, all look, not to her, but to "[o]ne young mother—a brainless but most beautiful girl.... The wife of a small railway official, she was generally snubbed; but this evening, with her abundant figure and masses of corn-gold hair, she symbolized all that is worth fighting and dying for; more permanent a symbol, perhaps, than poor Adela" (p. 200). Unlike Adela, who is not very attractive to the Anglo-Indians, either in character or in looks, this young mother symbolizes the empire. Class concerns are discarded by the Anglo-Indians in favor of nationalism, and the Anglo-Indians appropriate and mobilize around an image of beauty, fertility, and powerlessness, displacing the more substantive principle of justice, in order to maintain their rule of India. The practitioners of this brand of chivalry use women only as a tool and thereby create a governmental ideology that bolsters its power over an presumably inferior race by using the so-called inferior sex.

The possibility of a more mature and intimate relationship between men of different races exists in the friendship between Aziz and Fielding. This emphasis on a different kind of friendship between men is constitutive of the New Chivalry, taking hold in England at the beginning of the century along with the rise of the idea of the New Woman. The idea behind the new chivalry, according to Mark Girouard's *The Return to Camelot*, was that "the exaltation of women in mediaeval chivalry was essentially bound up with the need to procreate; now that the world was sufficiently well populated, women should be replaced by young men. Another feature of the new chivalry was that it was to be democratic: beauty and spiritual quality, not birth, were to be the passports to entry."[6] As late as 1918, this chivalric spirit was evident, for example, in the poems of Edwin Emmanuel Bradford, who published a volume entitled *The New Chivalry*:

Nay, boys need love, but not the love of women:

Romantic friendship, passionate but pure,

Should be their first love ...

And linked in love the knight and squire shall run

To seek adventures ...

But earth is earth—not heaven: well I know

Full many a squire will fail to win his spurs

    Woman will call him, and the lad will go.[7]

The adventures that these men and boys seek as their ideal depart not only sexually, but ideologically, from those of the old chivalry. As Linda Dowling writes in her excellent study, *Hellenism and Homosexuality in Victorian Oxford*, in schemata such as Bradford's or those of Charles Kains-Jackson, in his own *New Chivalry* (1894), "Greek love is able ... to be represented ... as the animating spirit of a new chivalry, a warfare to be fought out not amid the blood and clamor of actual battlefields but on a higher plane of ideas."[8] In this way, English civilization might be rejuvenated.

The new chivalry, as it appears in Forster's India, adapts the political undertones of the domestic new chivalry for anti-imperial purposes. Rather than allying itself with the simultaneous defense and oppression of women and a strong allegiance to nation and imperialism, as the old chivalry does, this movement represented by Aziz and Fielding is associated with the end of imperialism, the birth of Indian nationalism, and the links between Indian and Anglo-Indian men.[9] Despite the liberating potential in the movement, the relationship itself does not quite promise the equality that Aziz is seeking: the age differential in the Platonic relationship figured by Bradford appears as a race differential in India, with Aziz taking on the subordinate position of squire to Fielding's knight.[10]

Initially meeting on what seems to be an equal footing, Aziz and Fielding begin a personal relationship that becomes the most significant in the novel. When Aziz is the first to arrive at Fielding's bungalow for tea, the effortlessness with which the two men become acquainted prompts Fielding to think that he is "not surprised at the rapidity of their intimacy" (p. 68). The heterosexuality of the old chivalry gives way to the homoeroticism of the new as Aziz chivalrously offers his only collar stud to his new friend in a scene which Sara Suleri describes as "the most notoriously oblique homoerotic exchange in the literature of English India" (pp. 67–68).[11] "Ben[ding] his neck," Fielding allows Aziz to insert the stud from his own shirt collar into the back hole of Fielding's collar (one of the few times we see an Indian touch an Anglo-Indian in this novel) (p. 69). Aziz thus becomes intimate with Fielding in a way that does not conform to the practices of mainstream Anglo-India.

The homoerotic trust they establish is cemented, much like older forms of male bonding, over a woman; but, the great ritual of the exchange of women becomes a mere formality as Aziz requests that Fielding examine, not his wife, who is dead, but her picture.[12] He allows Fielding the honor, not because she is so important, for she is "'nothing, she was not a highly educated woman or even beautiful,'" but because showing her is the action of one brother to another (p. 125). The action of showing takes on a greater importance than the substance shown, allowing Aziz to reveal his love for, and trust in, Fielding; the fact of his wife's existence only as a photograph, silent and still, allows these men an even closer bonding than they would otherwise experience.

The intimate undertones and familiarities become more explicit as the novel continues, but they also become more disturbing, for Aziz is depicted as Victorian racial theory describes the black man, as a child if not an animal. Aziz's reaction to Fielding and Godbole's narrowly missing the train on the way to the Marabar Hills is not to scream for both of them, but only to "howl" for his English friend after he "leap[s] on to the footboard of a [train] carriage" and reassures onlookers of his safety, saying, "'We're monkeys, don't worry'" (p. 144). His desire to please the English causes him to transform himself into precisely that which the majority of Anglo-Indians believe him to be. His desire and debasement only increase with his frustration as, in a last desperate gesture, he screams to Fielding, "'Jump on, I must have you,'" a possession he is destined to lack (p. 144). Like the Marabar Hills, Fielding's figure recedes even as Aziz tries to grasp him.

Yet only this frustration of union, the time away from Fielding, leads to Aziz' self-empowerment and change in social position as he leads the expedition; had Fielding come, "he himself would have remained in leading-strings" (p. 145). The elevated position in which Aziz finds himself permits him to approach Mr. Fielding with something that approaches equality:

> [T]he colour and confusion of his little camp soon appeared, and in the midst of it he saw an Englishman's topi, and beneath it— oh joy!—smiled not Mr. Heaslop, but Fielding.
>
> "Fielding! Oh, I have so wanted you!" he cried, dropping the "Mr." for the first time. (p. 172)

This expression of desire would not be possible were it not for the responsibility taken by Aziz and his belief in his own success, a belief that lasts until he disembarks from the train in Chandrapore on the return trip.

While still at the Marabar Caves, Aziz revels in assuming his own imperial role, that of the "Mogul emperor who had done his duty" (p. 176). Aziz' self-depiction as an Oriental conqueror makes him feel superior to the conquering English of the twentieth century, who are blatant outsiders, but also allows him to adopt a chivalric role analogous to that of the present colonizers of the country. His roles as Mogul emperor and host allow him to feel "unassailable" and intimate with the English whom he loves: Mrs. Moore, who sleeps, and "by his own side ... Fielding, whom he began to think of as 'Cyril'" (p. 177). This eventual arrival at calling Mr. Fielding by his first name implies an intimacy between the two but never quite implies equality. Aziz' role of Mogul emperor cannot erase the fact that India is still dominated, at least in this novel, by an Anglo-Indian old chivalry.

* * * *

The crossover between the old and new chivalries occurs as the narrative point of view allies itself with Aziz and Fielding, the New Chivalry, while the characters of the old order, those who remain in military service, slowly face the fact that both their brand of chivalry and their system of imperial rule do not work and may never have. Although the Anglo-Indian men are cruel to the Indians, most of the blame for cruelty falls upon women, who are seen, more often than not, as forces separating the men of the two races.[13] For example, the Indians in the novel agree that "granted the exceptions, all Englishwomen are haughty and venal" (p. 9). McBryde, the "most reflective and best educated of the Chandrapore officials," evolves a "complete philosophy of life" based on the oppression of Indians only because of a "somewhat unhappy marriage" (p. 184). Major Callendar thinks, "'After all, it's our women who make everything more difficult out here,' ... as he ca[tches] sight of some obscenities upon a long blank wall, and beneath his chivalry to Miss Quested resentment lurk[s], waiting its day—perhaps there is a grain of resentment in all chivalry" (p. 237). The juxtaposition of obscenities and chivalry toward women underscores the feeling of ill-omen and filth, of *obcaenum*, that comes to exist in relation to the status of these women in the India of the novel.

Both chivalric orders share territory in blaming the white female for the failed relationship between Indians and Anglo-Indians yet neglect the fact that the structures which they have established in Anglo-India place the white woman in India into an unfortunate liminal position.[14] The fact of her sex permits men to silence her, victimize her sexually, and use her as a justification for imperial rule; but the fact of her race confers a status superior to that of the native population, and she can therefore speak about them, often disparagingly. As Mrs. McBryde states in her conversation with the Englishwomen,

> "I was a nurse before my marriage, and came across them a great deal, so I know. I really do know the truth about Indians. A most unsuitable position for any Englishwoman—I was a nurse in a Native State. One's only hope was to hold sternly aloof."

> "Even from one's Patients?"

> "Why, the kindest thing one can do to a native is to let him die," said Mrs. Callendar.

> "How if he went to heaven?" asked Mrs. Moore, with a gentle but crooked smile.

> "He can go where he likes as long as he doesn't come near me. They give me the creeps." (pp. 25–26)

This reaction by an Anglo-Indian woman is against what she has been taught to believe is obscene. Possessing no real power in Anglo-Indian society and threatened by what she perceives as potential contamination, that is, the presence of Indians, Mrs. McBryde reacts with hostility and ignorance. Like the ideal Victorian woman, she has therefore taken refuge in marriage and the domestic sphere, protected by her husband and other Englishmen from the alleged dangers presented by Indian men in the public sphere.

What happens when a New Woman enters the picture is a different matter. In wanting to know the country she visits, she threatens to discard the feminine role expected of her and to usurp the position of the traditional male explorer. In wanting to know the indigenous people in the country she visits, she becomes a sexual threat to the progress of new chivalry in the novel, that is, to Aziz and Fielding. A more extreme example of this kind of intrusion, and the solution to it, occurs in Forster's unpublished play of 1911, "The Heart of Bosnia."[15] In that work, which also takes place very much away from home, Mirko, a Bosnian of the best blood, and Nicolai, Mirko's "intimate friend," fall in love with Fanny Stevens, daughter of the British consul to Bosnia. Although her father warns her not to play with the feelings of men whose culture and chivalry she cannot understand, she states her determination to carry on with her "conquests" in this land of "orientals" and flirts with both men, neither of whom she intends to marry ("Heart," p. 8). Mirko's and Nicolai's revelations to each other that they have fallen in love with the same woman cause them to become distressed and then to propose a duel. As they are fighting Fanny walks in, only to announce that their dueling is ridiculous and that she intends to marry neither man. As P. N. Furbank, Forster's biographer, relates the rest of the plot, "She confiscates their knives and returns into the inner room, leaving Mirko and Nicolai staring at each other in despair. All is over for them, they realize, and kissing each other once more—this time with the kiss of blood—they follow the only course left, which is to murder her. The servants look on impassively."[16]

*   *   *   *

Such a dramatic solution does not, of course, befall Adela Quested. Nonetheless, her intrusion is every bit as disruptive to the masculine world in *A Passage to India* as Fanny Stevens' in "The Heart of Bosnia." Like the Miss Quested in *Howards End*, who attends a luncheon at which are discussed Thought and Art and the rights of women,[17] *A Passage to India*'s Miss Quested appears as a type of New Woman, here wholly at odds with the specimens of femininity already residing in Chandrapore and is, as David Lean reads her, "'a prig and a bore.'"[18] Her desires to know India and to set about meeting Indians jar the Anglo-Indians; unwilling to be a Victorian "angel in the house," she represents an intrusion from the future. At the same time, this New Woman is not the "woman who did," as Grant Allen terms it in his 1895 novel of that title, but a woman who is not sure if she wants to, and certainly not with Ronny, supposedly the man she has come out to India to marry.[19] Her sexual desires seem inextricably bound to her discoveries on this journey, as they are for so many men before her, both fictional and non-fictional.

Part of Quested's desire for women's progress seems to be a desire to seize male roles of the past, particularly that of explorer. In the India of the 1920s, though, it seems that no place for exploring exists. The British projects for the mapping of India had been completed for many years, leaving bureaucracy to command a gridded colony, one that has no blank spaces to fill in. Nonetheless, for a New Woman fresh from England, filled with progressive and ostensibly liberal ideas about the colonies, India presents itself as a place that can be explored on a new level. Adela's statement that she wants to see the "'real India'" implies her awareness that she sees a British India created by the white powers that be; the statement also reveals, of course, her mistake in believing that there can be a single real India at all, rather than one of a "hundred mouths" (p. 25, p. 150).

In narrative or generic terms, this impulse to explore can be termed the desire for imperial romance. Both Miss Quested and Mrs. Moore want it, but it is prohibited to the British women in the novel: "They had made such a romantic voyage across the Mediterranean and through the sands of Egypt to the harbour of Bombay, to find only a gridiron of bungalows at the end of it.... Life never gives us what we want at the moment that we consider appropriate. Adventures do occur, but not punctually" (p. 23). Romance can be found elsewhere for them, but it is impossible for them to find it in Chandrapore. The "gridiron of bungalows" suggests a place already mapped and therefore not open to exploration. The components of the term further suggest the inflexibility and hardness of a prison.

The absence of romance makes it clear that the heterosexual plot no longer works; its impossibility is clarified even more in the viewing of the "false dawn" before they reach the caves. The description of the dawn, which links the domestic and imperial senses of romance, makes both appear completely negative:

> [T]he sky to the left turned angry orange. Colour throbbed and mounted behind a pattern of trees. grew in intensity, was yet brighter, incredibly brighter, strained from without against the globe of the air. They awaited the miracle. But at the supreme moment, when night should have died and day lived, nothing occurred. It was as if virtue had failed in the celestial fount. The hues in the east decayed, the hills seemed dimmer though in fact better lit, and a profound disappointment entered with the morning breeze. Why, when the chamber was prepared, did the bridegroom not enter with trumpets and shawms, as humanity expects? The sun rose without splendour. He was presently observed trailing yellowish behind the trees, or against the insipid sky, and touching the bodies already at work in the fields. (pp. 151–52)

Heterosexuality clearly fails in this passage, seeming especially draining for the masculine sun. In a setting of expectation of a heterosexual union, the bridegroom becomes diminished and impotent, appearing only reluctantly and trailing the color associated since the *fin de siècle* with male decadence. "Virtue" seems to have failed, and rather than fertilizing the feminine earth—previously described as draining whatever comes in contact with it— the masculine sun touches the presumably male bodies working in the fields.

This frustration of romance appears not only in the landscape of the novel, but in Miss Quested's name as well. The surname suggests the form that romance always takes, that of the quest; but having "quested" does not necessarily imply having found anything. The question of whether it is feasible in fiction for women to explore is answered for us in the scene in which Adela visits the Marabar Caves. The expedition that Quested undertakes sounds hauntingly reminiscent of some tactics used by previous explorers: become acquainted with the "natives"; hear them talk about a supposedly magical place in their country; and persuade them to guide one to the place so that the explorer can enter it and subsequently report on it to his or her own people. Yet Adela's being a woman challenges the customary trope of Victorian imperial exploration, that of male penetration of a feminine landscape. Female exploration of a feminine space therefore implies abnormality, if not outright perversity in its challenge to gender (and sex) roles, and is virtually unthinkable.[20]

Adela's entrance into the caves is her first experience alone in India; elsewhere, as befits a young Englishwoman, she has been attended by an Englishman or by Mrs. Moore, there to protect her from unwanted attentions. As an adventure, this outing permits her to ponder sexual issues, which women in Anglo-India, in keeping with their Victorian present, seem not to do. For Adela to be able to think, "'What about love?'" breaks all the rules and opens up treacherous paths for her mind to follow (p. 168). The rock she is climbing, "nicked by a double row of footholds," suggests to her an arduous road for her impending marriage. That, however, is not all, for the tracks which she sees on the road to the caves "were the pattern traced in the dust by the wheels of the Nawab Bahadur's car"; both the path to the cave and the marriage path promise, like the tracks of the car (which is involved in an accident earlier in the novel), to lead to disaster and illusion or hallucination (p. 168).

Disaster and hallucination are triggered not only by penetrating the cave, but also by considering an alternative forbidden to Ronny. About Aziz, Adela thinks, "What a handsome little Oriental he was.... [S]he guessed he might attract women of his own race and rank..." (p. 169). Her attraction is tempered by the feeling that "[s]he did not admire him with any personal warmth, for there was nothing of the vagrant in her blood ..." (p. 169). Adela's thoughts transgress the boundaries delimiting sexual relations to partners of the same race, but she resembles Anglo-Indian women and belongs more to Anglo-India than she supposes: for she scrutinizes Aziz almost scientifically, dehumanizing and objectifying him in the process, and detaching herself from him by placing herself above "vagrancy."

Whereas Adela's romantic/sexual meditations are followed by her actual rape in the manuscript of *Passage*, the published version leaves us uncertain as to what actually occurs in the cave.[21] It may be that Adela comes face to face with what it means to be a woman in this imperial economy. Several critics have interpreted the caves as representing female sexuality and written that frigid Adela's confrontation with that sexuality scares and repels her.[22] Whether she is actually attacked or not, it is after the awareness of sexuality and her own invasion of an empty space that she is, herself, violated. Rather than reading this as a reaction to her fear of sex, I read it as a penalty for having refused to operate within the gendered discourses of imperialism. As Adela recalls after the incident, "'I remember scratching the wall with my finger-nail, to start the usual echo, and then as I was saying there was this shadow, or sort of shadow, down the entrance tunnel, bottling me up'" (p. 214). Not only does she enter into a feminine space; she acts upon it, scratching the surface as explorers have done in other spaces entered. Unlike those explorers, though, this woman is "bottled up" as a consequence of her actions.

Walking into a stereotypically female space and being violated effectively pushes Adela into the framework of femininity by which women in Anglo-India operate in the novel. The cactus spines upon which she falls as she runs down the hill painfully prick her flesh, and then,

> Miss Derek and Mrs. McBryde examined her through magnifying glasses, always coming on fresh colonies, tiny hairs that might snap off and be drawn into the blood if they were neglected. (p. 214)

Adela's plight seems to bear out the Anglo-Indians' fear of what will occur if their women exceed the bounds of the feminine domestic sphere. Her penetration of part of the Indian colony causes her to be penetrated by elements of the colony itself, which cause pain and threaten to contaminate the blood of the Englishwoman, even though its signs are almost imperceptible. The imperceptibility makes the issue even worse, as it calls to mind the invisible signs of another kind of entry and the suspicion of Victorian race theorists that miscegenation results in degeneration of the white woman. This fear materializes most obviously in Mrs. Turton's violent reaction before the trial,

> "Why, they ought to crawl from here to the caves on their hands and knees whenever an Englishwoman's in sight, they oughtn't to be spoken to, they ought to be spat at, they ought to be ground into the dust, we've been far too kind with our Bridge Parties and the rest." (p. 240)

Her reaction refers to the "crawling orders" enacted after the riots of 1919 in Amritsar, in which Indians were forced to crawl down a street on which an

Englishwoman had been assaulted. In this system, Indian men are perceived as sexually voracious and therefore need to be restrained through surveillance and humiliation.[23]

By exploring, Adela has left what McBryde calls the "line" of united Anglo-India and has therefore left "a gap in the line" (p. 190). As Ronny's fiancée, she is supposed to conform to the ranks, and she cannot escape, no matter how much she strives to break through the ranks. As Miss Derek and Mrs. McBryde remove the cactus thorns, their fingers, rather than soothing it, "develop the shock that had begun in the cave" (p. 214). That shock binds her further into Anglo-Indian society as it makes her more fragile and more of a victim than she had initially appeared. Her inclusion into the ranks of Anglo-Indian wives thus seems assured: "Mrs. McBryde wished her an affectionate good-bye—a woman with whom she had nothing in common and whose intimacy oppressed her. They would have to meet now, year after year, until one of their husbands was superannuated" (p. 219). Along with her inclusion comes an acceptance of her lot and a message of self-blame that verges on conformity to the ideology of the old chivalry: "Truly Anglo-India had caught her with a vengeance and perhaps it served her right for having tried to take up a line of her own" (p. 219). The refrain from Anglo-India, like the echo in the cave, sounds the same no matter what the original sound. A woman intending to marry one of the men serving there cannot take up any role but that already assigned by the system. Either the women already there or the land itself ensures it.

The walls of the caves themselves represent the divisive nature of females in this novel, and their description foreshadows the events surrounding Aziz and Fielding's relationship. Like the "broad channels of the plain," depressions in the earth that separate each hill from "his neighbour," the walls frustrate the attempt of two like beings or souls to come into contact with each other (p. 151). The first description of the flame from the match of a visitor to the caves presages the frustrating outcome of the relationship between Aziz and Fielding (p. 137); the caves, a space womblike and empty, are penetrated by the visitor, who

> arrives for his five minutes, and strikes a match. Immediately another flame rises in the depths of the rock and moves towards the surface like an imprisoned spirit: the walls of the circular chamber have been most marvelously polished. The two flames approach and strive to unite, but cannot, because one of them breathes air, the other stone. A mirror inlaid with lovely colours divides the lovers, delicate stars of pink and grey interpose, exquisite nebulae, shadings fainter than the tail of a comet or the

midday moon, all the evanescent life of the granite, only here
visible. (p. 137)

This passage resonates strongly if we consider the novel's conclusion, in
which Aziz and Fielding want to be together but cannot. The two flames
strive to unite, but they are of fundamentally different natures, that is, Indian
and British. The mirror, a female mirror inlaid with lovely colours and
associated with the female domain of the nighttime and the moon, does not
reflect one flame, but rather divides two, just as Adela does with men in the
space of the novel. Rather than helping Aziz and Fielding come together, she
forces them apart, most notably by bringing charges against Aziz for having
"insulted" her in the caves.

* * * *

Even so, an alternative mirror exists to bring together the Indian and
Anglo-Indian men in the novel: Mrs. Moore, whose presence stills and even
erodes the progress of the old chivalry. Mrs. Moore, a maternal woman "past
marrying.... even unhappily" (and therefore not having to compete for men),
acts as a bridge over the gulf between men of different races, a gulf that the
men who are there are unable to bridge alone (p. 102). She originally appears
to Aziz not as one involved in Anglo-Indian life, but as one outside:

> He repeated the phrase with tears in his eyes, and as he did so one
> of the pillars of the mosque seemed to quiver. It swayed in the
> gloom and detached itself. Belief in ghosts ran in his blood, but
> he sat firm. Another pillar moved, a third, and then an
> Englishwoman stepped out into the moonlight. (p. 17).

Aziz' perception of her, a vision distorted by his tears, makes her part of his
personal India, that of the temple and Islam. She is also perceived, though,
as a ghost, the spirit of a dead woman, a perception which links her with the
Indian belief in the potency and permanence of spirits. (Later, when Ronny,
Adela, and the Nawab Bahadur are involved in the car accident, only Mrs.
Moore does not promptly dismiss the idea that a ghost might have caused the
accident.) Only after waiting does Aziz see that she is an Englishwoman, and
even so, she has followed the rules for being in a mosque by taking off her
shoes. Her having "'two sons and a daughter,'" her being a widow, and her
not having remarried reflect the characteristics of Aziz' own life (p. 20). She
further proves her connections to him by sympathizing about the Anglo-
Indians:

He was excited partly by his wrongs, but much more by the knowledge that someone sympathized with them. It was this that led him to repeat, exaggerate, contradict. She had proved her sympathy by criticizing her fellow countrywoman to him, but even earlier he had known. The flame that not even beauty can nourish was springing up, and though his words were querulous his heart began to glow secretly. Presently it burst into speech.

"You understand me, you know what others feel. Oh, if others resembled you!"

Rather surprised, she replied: "I don't think I understand people very well. I only know whether I like or dislike them."

"Then you are an Oriental." (p. 21)

Unlike Adela, Mrs. Moore works as a mirror that nourishes the flame inside Aziz, allowing the emergence of an aspect of himself that he has not previously revealed to any Englishman or -woman. The flame that in the cave can be seen only divided and in the dark here "spring[s]" into light, a hidden glow allowing Aziz to speak in a way that he cannot to the other Britons he has met. The intuition and sensitivity to people that Aziz and Mrs. Moore mirror in each other lead to new connections between Indian and Anglo-Indian, for this meeting with Mrs. Moore will lead to Aziz' first tea with Fielding.

Mrs. Moore's joining of Indian and Anglo-Indian men can be initiated but clearly cannot be effected completely within the confines of the old order of imperialism; when Mrs. Moore accuses Ronny of possessing sentiments that are "'those of a god'" and thus provokes the response, "'India likes gods,'" she clearly touches on another element of the old chivalry, marked by divine rule and "'Englishmen ... posing as gods'" (p. 51). Her attempt to supersede his gods by asserting her own makes organic and whole whatever it is that requires fragmentation if Englishmen are to rationalize their rule of this place: "'India is part of the earth. And God has put us on the earth in order to be pleasant to each other. God ... is ... love.' She hesitated, seeing how much he disliked the argument, but something made her go on. 'God has put us on earth to love our neighbours and to show it, and He is omnipresent, even in India, to see how we are succeeding'" (p. 53). In putting forth values that are not compatible with the Victorian sense of manifest destiny, however, Mrs. Moore opens herself up to being discounted as a superstitious old woman: Ronny "knew this religious strain in her, and that it was a symptom of bad health; there had been much of it when his stepfather died. He thought, 'She is certainly ageing, and I ought not to be vexed with anything she says'" (p. 53).

It is not what she says that vexes the old chivalry, but what she does not say. Even after the "spiritual muddledom" envelops her following her visit to the caves, Mrs. Moore's spirit works against the imperial ideology that separates Indian and Anglo-Indian men, most notably by influencing Adela to recant her testimony:

> When he returned, she was in a nervous crisis, but it took a different form—she clung to him, and sobbed, "Help me to do what I ought. Aziz is good. You heard your mother say so."
>
> "Heard what?"
>
> "He's good; I've been so wrong to accuse him."
>
> "Mother never said so."
>
> "Didn't she?" she asked, quite reasonable, open to every suggestion anyway.
>
> "She never mentioned that name once."
>
> "But, Ronny, I heard her."
>
> "Pure illusion. You can't be quite well, can you, to make up a thing like that."
>
> "I suppose I can't. How amazing of me!"
>
> "I was listening to all she said, as far as it could be listened to; she gets very incoherent."
>
> "When her voice dropped she said it—towards the end, when she talked about love—love—I couldn't follow, but just then she said: 'Doctor Aziz never did it.'"
>
> "Those words?"
>
> "The idea more than the words." (p. 226)

The invisible text, the silence that is neglected by the powers that be (the petty bureaucracy of Anglo-India personified by Ronny), is precisely the text that begins to influence the transformation of the social structure. Even after Ronny dissuades her, Adela's thoughts are re-confirmed by Mrs. Moore: "'Of course he is innocent'" (p. 227). The judicious interpretation of Mrs.

Moore's silences begins to place the races on an equal footing, even if equality is never fully achieved.

This textual lacuna, a function of absence and memory, continues to work to right wrongs at the trial. Mrs. Moore exits at the point at which she can do nothing more for Aziz, for in the world of British rationality, her belief that it is not in Aziz' character to commit a crime would not hold. Nonetheless, her presence and her absence, which, as Godbole would say, are part of the same pattern, prove to be magical. Adela believes that the echo she is hearing in her head could be alleviated by Mrs. Moore, that "[o]nly Mrs. Moore could drive it back to its source and seal the broken reservoir" (p. 215). Significantly enough, this "broken reservoir" is yet another rounded female space; this site of excess, like female sexuality as it has been (mis)shapen by societal pressures, threatens to drown civilization if left unchecked, and it seems that only Mrs. Moore can heal Adela and stem the flow of the evil. During the trial, it is only after the chanting begins that Adela feels well enough to testify about the truth:

> "Esmiss Esmoor
>
> Esmiss Esmoor..."
>
> "Ronny ..."
>
> "Yes, old girl?"
>
> "Isn't it all queer."
>
> "I'm afraid it's very upsetting for you."
>
> "Not in the least. I don't mind it."
>
> "Well, that's good."
>
> She had spoken more naturally and healthily than usual. Bending into the middle of her friends, she said: "Don't worry about me, I'm much better than I was; I don't feel the least faint; I shall be all right, and thank you all, thank you, thank you for your kindness." She had to shout her gratitude, for the chant, Esmiss Esmoor, went on.
>
> Suddenly it stopped. It was as if the prayer had been heard, and the relics exhibited. (p. 251)

The prayer to the new Hindu goddess seems to work, although again not in the precise way expected, for the goddess never comes, as in Godbole's song. In fact, the victory in this trial depends on the goddess' never coming.

Her presence would imply consent to conducting the trial according to the rules of the detective story, which can deduce only by rational means, as opposed to Godbole's explanation of the crime, which frustrates the impulse to find a scapegoat, for "[a]ll perform a good action, when one is performed, and when an evil action is performed, all perform it" (pp. 196–97). Mrs. Moore's absence is crucial for Aziz' acquittal; those who know her persist in remembering her as she was before the incident in the caves, and her absence allows her transformation into a text that may be written upon, a name that does not rhyme with Turton and Burton and that can be mobilized in the service of a political action. The name, which "burst[s] on the court like a whirlwind," gathers force as it goes (pp. 248–49). Seemingly made of nothing, its force is strengthened by the material it collects, its sweeping binding together disparate elements and making out of them a force that no one of them would possess in isolation.

The evocation of Mrs. Moore allows Adela to "hear the sound of her own voice.... [A] new and unknown sensation protect[s] her, like magnificent armour" (p. 253). Departing from the role assigned to her—that of the maiden in distress—and taking on the armor of the more active role in the traditional romance—that of the knight—Adela uses the moment to rebel against the imposition of a rehearsed story and to tell what she remembers. Telling her story, she no longer lies "passive beneath ... fingers, which developed the shock that had begun in the cave" (p. 214). No longer is her brain weak; nor is she confused or in darkness. Rather, she speaks from "across a sort of darkness" to Mr. McBryde (p. 253). This speech reveals between Quested and McBryde an obscurity that may not be illuminated because the experience undergone by Quested is one that McBryde cannot bring himself to imagine; the gap between them grows wider as Adela finds herself closer to the position of Mrs. Moore. Like Mrs. Moore, Quested has a "double vision" (p. 230), but her vocalization of her experience allows her to be both "of it [the "fatal day"] and not of it at the same time, and this double relation [gives] it indescribable splendour" (p. 253). Her romance is found in reliving the situation as she experienced it, but with the safety of being removed from the scene.

*　*　*　*

Once Adela returns to the present reality, she suffers yet again for having refused to conform to the role prescribed by the old chivalry and is shunned by Anglo-Indians and Indians alike. Drained by her experience on the stand, and, as Fielding perceives, about to "have a nervous breakdown," she now falls back into the role of maiden in distress (p. 255). Despite Aziz' cry, "'Cyril, Cyril, don't leave me'" (p. 258), Adela's need to be taken care of forces Fielding into the old chivalric code even as he desires to move beyond it: "[I]f some misunderstanding occurred, and an attack was made on the girl by his allies, he would be obliged to die in her defence. He didn't want to die for her, he wanted to be rejoicing with Aziz" (p. 260). Adela's deeds once again separate the two men just when they believe that they will be able to be together.

Even after the day of the trial, when Aziz hopes to be reunited with Fielding, Miss Quested is again connected with the reasons that Fielding cannot "'give in to the East,' ... and live in a condition of affectionate dependence upon it," as Aziz wants him to do (p. 289). Although the text states that "something racial intrude[s]" in Fielding's objection to submitting to his surroundings, what emerges in the argument between the friends is put in terms of gender and economics: "Aziz would conclude: 'Can't you see that I'm grateful to you for your help and want to reward you?' And the other [Fielding] would retort, 'If you want to reward me, let Miss Quested off paying'" (p. 290). The issue of Miss Quested once again separates them and prevents Fielding from uprooting himself from English ways. Fielding's statement about being rewarded operates on a transitive principle: he will consider himself rewarded if Adela is rewarded.

This equation of himself with Quested, though, cannot but lead to Aziz' suspicion of a prospective marriage between the two; where gender, money, and race are grouped together, thoughts of marriage cannot be far behind: "Cyril would marry Miss Quested—he grew certain of it, all the unexplained residue of the Marabar contributing. It was the natural conclusion of the horrible senseless picnic, and before long he persuaded himself that the wedding had actually taken place" (p. 313). In this novel, however, marriage does not occur on Indian soil, an imaginative space unlike and even opposed to the space of the domestic novel, the traditional site of wedded bliss for English readers. The spectre of Fielding's journey to England is thus doubly frightening for Aziz, as it puts Fielding far away from him and at home. There, not only are Fielding and Quested racially equivalent, they are complementary in the heterosexual economy of the domestic marriage plot on which Forster had concentrated in his previous novels. Aziz' eventual feeling that the wedding between Fielding and Miss Quested "ha[s] actually taken place" conforms to a generic expectation of conventional closure, but, contrary to his expectations, the cycle of events is not completely ruled by the domestic romance.

*   *   *   *

The cycle that begins with Mrs. Moore's and Adela's journey to India must end not with the return home, but with another passage to India—that of Fielding, his wife, Stella, and her brother, Ralph Moore. In this second passage, taking place in the section of the novel dominated by the Hindu festival of Gokul Ashtami, Mrs. Moore's spirit acts once again to assist the new chivalry. Aziz' anxieties about and resentment toward the English are allayed when Mrs. Moore's name is mentioned: "It had been an uneasy, uncanny moment when Mrs. Moore's name was mentioned, stirring memories. 'Esmiss Esmoor ...'—as though she was coming to help him" (pp. 339–40). The help she provides this time comes in the form of her son, Ralph, who appears as almost an incarnation of his demi-goddess mother. Alone with Ralph while examining his bee stings, Aziz experiences a repetition, with some differences, of his first meeting with Mrs. Moore. Young but appearing "prematurely aged" and wise beyond his years, Ralph can feel not only Aziz' continued resentment toward the English—"'Your hands are unkind,'" he tells Aziz; he can also perceive through touch when that resentment has passed (p. 347):

> [Aziz] remembered how detestable he had been, and said gently, "Don't you think me unkind any more?"
>
> "No."
>
> "How can you tell, you strange fellow?"
>
> "Not difficult, the one thing I always know."
>
> "Can you always tell whether a stranger is your friend?"
>
> "Yes."
>
> "Then you are an Oriental." (p. 349)

Although Aziz' reiteration of his words "to Mrs. Moore in the mosque in the beginning of the cycle" cause him to "shudder" (p. 349) for fear that the events of the previous cycle will recur, they also establish Ralph as a similar type of kindred and guiding spirit as his mother (p. 349). Indeed, when Aziz pays "homage to Mrs. Moore's son" by taking him onto the water to view the Gokul Ashtami celebrations, Ralph's seemingly magical powers emerge as he leads Aziz to a spot the doctor has never before been able to reach—where they can look "straight into the chhatri of the Rajah's father through an opening in the trees.... There was only one spot from which it could be seen, and Ralph had directed him to it. Hastily he pulled away, feeling that his companion was not so much a visitor as a guide" (pp. 351–52). Like Mrs. Moore, Ralph is an agent of revelation for Aziz.

Not only does Aziz experience previously hidden phenomena when he is with Ralph; this tour during Gokul Ashtami, a time of death and rebirth, allows the spirit of a dead Mrs. Moore to be recalled in another way: "'Radhakrishna Radhakrishna Radhakrishna Radhakrishna Krishnaradha,' went the chant, then suddenly changed, and in the interstice he heard, almost certainly, the syllables of salvation that had sounded during his trial at Chandrapore" (p. 352). As during the trial, the spirit of "Esmiss Esmoor" emerges during the silence between words, and the message accords with the spirit of the celebration of Krishna's birth. Explicitly compared to Christ in the novel (p. 322), Krishna is also subject to a cruel king and is a god who, as Mrs. Moore would say, "is love." This love again works to bring men of different races together, here not only Ralph and Aziz, but Aziz and Fielding. As Aziz says to Fielding, "'I partly love him [Ralph] because he brought me back to you ...'" (p. 357).

But the return to Fielding is not a final coming together. Instead, it is a prelude to "say[ing] good-bye" (p. 357). Despite her removal to another continent and despite her remaining an "odd woman" in England, Adela still has the power to come between Fielding and Aziz, not by being married to Fielding, but by introducing him to his future wife. By virtue of his marriage, Fielding has effectively joined Anglo-India and therefore cannot reunite with Aziz:

> [T]his was their last free intercourse. All the stupid misunderstandings had been cleared up, but socially they had no meeting-place. He had thrown in his lot with Anglo-India by marrying a countrywoman, and he was acquiring some of its limitations, and already felt surprise at his own past heroism. Would he to-day defy all his own people for the sake of a stray Indian? Aziz was a memento, a trophy, they were proud of each other, yet they must inevitably part. (pp. 357–58)

The Indian man, replaced by a wife, can now function only as a more passive commodity than the white woman does. As a "trophy," Aziz functions as an object only to be looked at by Fielding and merely commemorates a triumph or memory in Fielding's life. Because of Fielding's entry into the heterosexual marriage plot and regression into a type of old chivalry, the relationship between him and Aziz cannot progress. Rather, friendship must be postponed for a time when all are equal, as Aziz states:

> "Down with the English anyhow. That's certain. Clear out, you fellows, double quick, I say. We may hate one another, but we hate you most. If I don't make you go, Ahmed will, Karim will, if

it's fifty-five hundred years we shall get rid of you, yes, we shall drive every blasted Englishman into the sea, and then"—he rode against him furiously—"and then," he concluded, half kissing him, "you and I shall be friends."

"Why can't we be friends now?" said the other, holding him affectionately. "It's what I want. It's what you want."

But the horses didn't want it—they swerved apart; the earth didn't want it, sending up rocks through which riders must pass single file; the temples, the tank, the jail, the palace, the birds, the carrion, the Guest House, that came into view as they issued from the gap and saw Mau beneath: they didn't want it, they said in their hundred voices, "No, not yet," and the sky said, "No, not there." (pp. 361–62)

Aziz' kiss is only half one, and his desire is mixed with aggression. Unlike Fielding, he cannot be purely affectionate, and the import of the inability to unite makes itself evident not only on a personal, but on a cosmic level. The earth and sky, woman and man in the Hindu marriage ceremony, do not want them to unite just yet; the voices of the other forces in the scene number the same as the mouths of the female India (described elsewhere in the novel), always postponing promise as they appeal. The conclusion makes it clear that men can come together with other men only when Indians are equal to Englishmen and when the history of colonial India is rewritten. This novel looks forward to a time when neither Englishman nor Englishwoman will want to see the "'real India,'" which, as Aziz notes, is only another "form of ruling India" (p. 343), when India will achieve nationhood, and when there is a chivalry that no longer misshapes societal roles and relationships. In consonance with the last section of the novel and as in Forster's unpublished short stories, there must be death, in some form, before men can realize "the life to come."

NOTES

1. For another, fuller discussion of the Victorian and modern aspects of this novel, see Malcolm Bradbury, "Two Passages to India: Forster as Victorian and Modern" in *E.M Forster's A Passage to India*, ed. Harold Bloom (Chelsea House, 1987), pp. 29–44.

2. E.M. Forster, *A Passage to India* (1924; Harcourt, Brace, Jovanovich, 1952), p. 40. Hereafter, this work will be referred to parenthetically in the text.

3. See Jenny Sharpe, *Allegories of Empire: The Figure Woman in the Colonial Text* (University of Minnesota Press, 1993) .

4. See also Elaine Freedgood, "E. M. Forster's Queer Nation: Taking the Closet to the Colony in *A Passage to India*," in *Genders 23: Bodies of Writing, Bodies in Performance*, eds. Thomas Foster, Carol Siegel, and Ellen E. Berry (New York University Press, 1996), pp. 123–44.

5. Freedgood, p. 129.

6. Quoted in Mark Girouard, *The Return to Camelot: Chivalry and the English Gentleman* (Yale University Press, 1981). pp. 217–18.

7. Girouard, p. 218.

8. Linda Dowling, *Hellenism and Homosexuality in Victorian Oxford* (Cornell University Press, 1994), pp. 30-31.

9. Like *A Passage to India*, both "The Feminine Note in Literature" and Forster's unpublished novel, *Arctic Summer*, are concerned with chivalry. P.N. Furbank notes that in "The Feminine Note in Literature," Forster "put the case against chivalry and sexual 'chauvinism'" (p. 209). In *Arctic Summer*, the character Martin Whitby states that men practicing a "new chivalry" must be "'worthy of [women] in the way they wish, not in the way we wish'" (in *Arctic Summer and Other Fiction*, Abinger Edition of E.M. Forster, vol. 9, eds. Elizabeth Heine and Oliver Stallybrass (London: Edward Arnold, 1980), p. 194). The manuscript is principally occupied, though, with the relationship that begins after Clesant (or Cyril) March, a young soldier, chivalrously saves Martin, an older clerk, from an accident. Implied rather than overtly discussed in *Arctic Summer*, the issue of men's chivalry toward other men emerges much more fully in *A Passage to India*.

10. The relationship between Aziz and Fielding resembles Forster's own romantic relationships with, for example, his Indian barber, and with Mohammed El Adl, an Egyptian train conductor: like Aziz, the objects of Forster's affections were subordinate because of either race or class (or both), and darker than he, whether because of racial difference or because they were outdoor laborers. See P.N. Furbank, *E.M. Forster: A Life*, Vol. 2, *Polycrates' Ring (1914–1970)* (London: Secker & Warburg, 1978), pp. 35, 91, See also Forster's *Maurice* for a fictional depiction of such a dynamic.

11. Suleri, *The Rhetoric of English India* (University of Chicago Press, 1992). p. 138.

12. See Freedgood, p. 133.

13. See Freedgood, p. 129.

14. Forster notes in the novel that Anglo-India is not yet "feminist England" (p. 165), a society that by this time includes women in the workforce and allows some women to vote. In the society of this novel, the restrictions on women's behavior (including economic behavior), make the possibility of "feminism" in India seem remote.

15. E.M. Forster. "The Heart of Bosnia," ts., E. M. Forster Collection, King's College, Cambridge, England, 7. Hereafter, this work will be referred to parenthetically in the text.

16. P.N. Furbank, *E.M Forster: A Life*, Vol. 1, *The Growth of the Novelist (1879–1914)* (London: Secker & Warburg, 1978), p. 201.

17. E.M. Forster, *Howards End* (1910; Vintage, 1921), pp. 76ff.

18. Salman Rushdie, "Outside the Whale," *Crania* 11, p. 128. Quoted from *The Guardian*, 23 January 1984.

19. Grant Allen, *The Women Who Did* (London: Jonathan Lane, 1895).

20. British women who did explore in the empire were often careful to appear as feminine as possible (at least to their readers at home). Mary Kingsley, exploring West Africa in the 1890s, wore full skirts, and Gertrude Bell, exploring the Syrian desert just after the start of the century, often sent requests to her stepmother for frocks from London.

21. E. M. Forster, *A Passage to India*, ms., E.M. Forster Collection, King's College, Cambridge, England, B48.

22. See Wilfred Stone, *The Cave and the Mountain: A Study of E.M. Forster* (Stanford University Press, 1966), pp. 335–37; Valerie Broege, "The Journey Toward Individuation of Adela Quested in E.M. Forster's and David Lean's *A Passage to India*," in *Heroines of Popular Culture*, ed. Pat Browne (Bowling Green State University Popular Press, 1997), pp. 41–53, esp. 48–49; Louise Dauner, "What Happened in the Cave? Reflections on *A Passage to India*," in *Perspectives on E. M. Forster's A Passage to India*, ed. V.A. Shahane (Barnes & Noble, 1968), pp. 51–64, esp. 61; and Benita Parry, *Delusions and Discoveries: Studies in India in the British Imagination 1880–1930* (University of California Press, 1972), pp. 294–95.

23. Brenda Silver goes a step further, seeing Ariz as "absorbed into a discourse that simultaneously defines him as penis and castrates him, equaling castration and rape." See "Periphrasis, Power, and Rape in *A Passage to India*," *Novel*, XXII (1988), p. 97.

Chronology

1879	Edward Morgan Forster born in London on January 1. His father, an architect of Anglo-Irish descent, dies the following year. His mother is descended from the Thornton family, of "Clapham Sect" fame.
1883–93	Forster lives in Hertfordshire at Rooksnest, the home that will be the prototype of *Howards End*.
1887	Forster favorite aunt, Marianne Thornton, dies, leaving him a legacy of £8,000.
1893	Forster's family moves to Tonbridge, where he attends Tonbridge School as a day boy. His unhappiness there will later help him to write of Sawston School in *The Longest Journey*.
1897	Enters King's College, Cambridge where he studies Classics (B.A., 1900) and History (B.A., 1901, M.A. 1910). Among the teachers who influenced Forster: Goldsworthy Lowes Dickinson, J.M.E. McTaggert, Roger Fry, and Nathaniel Wedd. Through his friendship with H.O. Meredith, the prototype for Clive Durham in *Maurice*, Forster joins the Cambridge Conversazione Society aka the Apostles, where he meets Leonard Woolf, Lytton Strachey, John Maynard Keyes, Desmond MacCarthy and Saxon Sidney-Turner. A select group of these young men would later form part of the Bloomsbury group, with whom Forster associates throughout his life.

1901	Forster travels to Italy and Greece; lives there until 1902, when he moves to Arbinger Hammer, Surrey.
1902	Forster teaches at the Working Men's College where he will continue to teach periodically until 1922.
1903	Forster's first short story, "Albergo Empedocle," is published in in *Temple Bar*. Several of his Cambridge friends, including Dickinson, G.M. Trevelyan, Wedd and Edward Jenks, found the *Independent Review*, to which he will contribute.
1905	*Where Angels Fear to Tread* published.
1907	*The Longest Journey* published.
1910	*Howard's End* published.
1911	*The Celestial Omnibus and Other Stories* published.
1912–13	Forster takes his first trip to India with Dickinson and R.C. Treveylan. The visit, lasting from October until March, includes a stay with the Maharajah of Dewas Senior.
1914	Essays and reviews for *New Weekly*.
1915–1919	Forester volunteers with the Red Cross in Alexandria, Egypt.
1919	Forster becomes literary editor of the *Daily Herald*, a Labour publication.
1920	"The Story of a Siren" is published as a Hogarth Press booklet by Leonard and Virginia Woolf.
1921	Forster returns to India as the private secretary of the Maharajah of Dewas Senior. At the end of the stay, he is presented with the Tukyjirao Gold Medal, the highest honor possible for a Westerner.
1922	*Alexandria: A History and a Guide* is published.
1923	A collection of essays and sketches, *Pharos and Pharillon*, is published.
1924	*A Passage to India* is published.
1925	Forster receives the Femina Vie Heureuse and James Tait Black Memorial Prizes for *A Passage to India*.
1927	*Aspects of the Novel*, a lecture series presented at Cambridge during this year, is published. Forster is elected a fellow at King's College.
1928	*The Eternal Moment and Other Stories* is published.
1934	Forster's first biography, *Goldsworthy Lowes Dickinson*, is

published. *The Abinger Pageant*, one of several dramatic efforts, is produced at Abinger Hammer. Forster becomes the first president of the National Council for Civil Liberties. He is elected again in 1942 and resigns in 1948.

1936 A collection of essays, *Abinger Harvest: A Miscellany*, is published.

1939 *What I Believe* is published.

1940 *Nordic Twillight* and *England's Pleasant Land, A Pageant Play* are published.

1941 Forster delivers the Rede Lecture on Virginia Woolf.

1943 The first major critical work on Forster is published by Lionel Trilling (*E.M. Forster*), accompanied by the republication of all of Forster's novels. This initiates a Forster revival in the United States.

1945 Forster makes his third visit to India for a conference in Laipur. After his mother's death, Forster accepts an honorary fellowship at King's College, Cambridge, his chief residence for the rest of his life.

1947 At Harvard University symposium on music criticism, Forster gives the lecture "The Raison d'Etre of Criticism in the Arts." *Collected Tales* published in the United States.

1948 *Collected Short Stories* published in England.

1949 "Art for Art's Sake" given as lecture at the American Academy of Arts and Letters.

1951 *Two Cheers for Democracy*, a collection of essays, is published. Receives an honorary degree from Nottingham University. *Billy Budd*, an opera written in collaboration with Eric Crozzier and Benjamin Britten, is produced at Covent Garden.

1953 Forster is awarded membership in the Order of Companions of Honor to the Queen by Elizabeth II. *The Hill of Devi*, a memoir of his first two India trips, is published.

1956 *Marianne Thornton*, a biography of Forster's aunt, is published.

1961 Forster is named Companion of Literature by the Royal Society of Literature.

1969 Forster is awarded the Order of Merit.

1970 Forster dies on June 7, at the age of 91.

Contributors

HAROLD BLOOM is Sterling Professor of the Humanities at Yale University and Henry W. and Albert A. Berg Professor of English at the New York University Graduate School. He is the author of over 20 books, including *Shelley's Mythmaking* (1959), *The Visionary Company* (1961), *Blake's Apocalypse* (1963), *Yeats* (1970), *A Map of Misreading* (1975), *Kabbalah and Criticism* (1975), *Agon: Toward a Theory of Revisionism* (1982), *The American Religion* (1992), *The Western Canon* (1994), and *Omens of Millennium: The Gnosis of Angels, Dreams, and Resurrection* (1996). *The Anxiety of Influence* (1973) sets forth Professor Bloom's provocative theory of the literary relationships between the great writers and their predecessors. His most recent books include *Shakespeare: The Invention of the Human* (1998), a 1998 National Book Award finalist, *How to Read and Why* (2000), and *Genius: A Mosaic of One Hundred Exemplary Creative Minds* (2002). In 1999, Professor Bloom received the prestigious American Academy of Arts and Letters Gold Medal for Criticism, and in 2002 he received the Catalonia International Prize.

LIONEL TRILLING was a Professor of English at Columbia University. He is the author of two influential books of critical essays: *The Liberal Imagination* and *The Opposing Self*. He also wrote a book of criticism on E.M. Forster and a novel, *The Middle of the Journey*.

SIR MALCOLM BRADBURY was a Professor of American Studies at the University of East Anglia. Bradbury is an author of both critical and creative works, including novels and television scripts.

MICHAEL ORANGE has taught at the University of Sidney, and has contributed several pieces to *Sydney Studies in English*.

CHAMAN L. SAHNI wrote his Ph.D. thesis on "E.M. Forster and Indian Thought" at Wayne State University. He has taught at Wayne State University, and served as Chair of the English Department at Boise State University.

WENDY MOFFAT is Associate Professor of English at Dickinson College. She has written on Forster, Conrad, and Austen.

WILFRID R. KOPONEN, Ph.D., is an Albuquerque-based freelance writer and editor.

LELAND MONK is an Associate Professor of English at Boston University. He has written many articles on British novels of the late nineteenth-century and the early twentieth-century.

YONATAN TOUVAL studied at Rutgers University and participated in the 1997 Narrative Conference.

DEBRAH RASCHKE teaches at Southeast Missouri State University, where she has served as Director of Graduate Studies. In addition to Forster, she has also written on Doris Lessing, William Faulkner, and Margaret Atwood.

BENITA PARRY is Honorary Pofessor, Department of English and Comparative Literary Studies, University of Warwick. Her Books include *Delusions and Discoveries: Studies on India in the British Imagination* (1972) and *Conrad and Imperialism: Ideological Boundaries and Visionary Frontiers* (1984).

ELIZABETH MACLEOD WALLS is a doctoral candidate at Texas Chistian University. In 2000, she won the Walter L. Arnstein Prize for Dissertation Research in Victorian Studies.

MARIA M. DAVIDIS has served as a Mellon Postdoctoral Fellow at Wellesley College and currently teaches at Cornell University where she is an Assistant Dean.

Bibliography

Allen, Walter. *The English Novel*. New York: Dutton, 1955.

Ault, Peter. "Aspects of E.M. Forster." *Dublin Review* 219 (October 1946): 109–34.

Bakshi, Parminder Kaur. *Distant Desire: Homoerotic Codes and the Subversion of the English Novel in E.M. Forster's Fiction*. New York: Peter Lang Publishing, Inc., 1996.

Barratt, Robert. "Marabar: The Caves of Deconstruction." *Journal of Narrative Technique* 23:2 (1993): 127–35.

Bedient, Calvin. *Architects of the Self: George Eliot, D. H. Lawrence, and E.M. Forster*.

Berkeley and Los Angeles: University of California Press, 1972.

Beer, Gillian. "Negation in *A Passage to India*." *Essays in Criticism* 30, no. 2 (April 1980): 151–66.

Beer, John B. *The Achievement of E.M. Forster*. New York: Barnes & Noble, 1962.

———. *A Passage to India: Essays in Interpretation*. London: Macmillan, 1970.

Bell, Quentin. *Bloomsbury*. London: Weidenfeld & Nelson, 1968.

Bodenheimer, Rosemarie. "The Romantic Impasse in *A Passage to India*." *Criticism* 22, no. 1 (Winter 1980): 40–56.

Bowen, Elizabeth. "E.M. Forster." In *Collected Impressions*, 119–126. London: Longmans Green, 1950.

Bradbury, Malcolm, ed. *E.M. Forster: A Passage to India*. London: Macmillan, 1970.

Bower, Reuben Arthur. "The Twilight of the Double Vision: Symbol and Irony in *A Passage to India*." In *The Fields of Light*. New York: Oxford University Press, 1951.

Brown, E.K. *Rhythm in the Novel*. Toronto: University of Toronto Press, 1950.

Buhariwala, Shernavaz. *Arcades to a Dome: Humanism in Forster's Novels*. Bombay: Somaiya, 1983.

Burke, Kenneth. "Social and Cosmic Mystery: *A Passage to India*." In *Language as Symbolic Action: Essays on Life, Literature and Method*, 223–39. Berkeley: University of California Press, 1968.

Burra, Peter. "The Novels of E.M. Forster." *Nineteenth Century and After* 116 (November 1935): 581–94.

Buzard, James Michael. "Forster's Trespasses: Tourism and Cultural Politics." *Twentieth Century Literature* 34:2 (1988): 155–79.

Cammarota, Richard S. "Musical Analogy and Internal Design." *English Literature in Transition* 18, no. 1 (1975): 38–46.

Cheng, Sinkwan. "Crossing Desire and Drive in *A Passage to India*: The Subversion of the British Colonial Law in the 'Twilight Zone of Double Vision.'" *Literature and Psychology: A Journal of Psychoanalytic and Cultural Criticism* 47:3 (2001):1–24.

Colmer, John. *E.M. Forster: The Personal Voice*. London and Boston: Routledge & Kegan Paul, 1975.

Crews, Frederick. *E.M. Forster: The Perils of Humanism*. Princeton: Princeton University Press, 1962.

Daleski, H.M. "Rhythmic and Symbolic Patterns in *A Passage to India*." In *Studies in English Language and Literature*, edited by Alice Shalvi and A.A. Mendilow. Jerusalem: Hebrew University, 1966.

Das, G.K. and John Beer, eds. *E.M. Forster: A Human Exploration: Centenary Essays*. London: The MacMilliam Press Ltd., 1979.

Davidis, Maria M. "Forster's Imperial Romance: Chivalry, Motherhood, and Questing in *A Passage to India*." *Journal of Modern Literature* 23:2 (1999/2000) 259–76.

Davies, Tony and Nigel Wood, eds. *A Passage to India*. Buckingham: Open University Press, 1994.

Dawson, Jennifer. "Reading the Rocks, Flora and Fauna: Representation of India in *Kim*, *A Passage to India*, and *Burmese Days*." 28:1/2 (1993): 1–12.

Dolin, Kieran. "Freedom, Uncertainty, and Diversity: *A Passage to India* as a Critique of Imperialist Law." *Texas Studies in Literature and Language* 36:3 (1994): 328–52.

Dowling, David. *Bloomsbury Aesthetics and the Novels of Forester and Woolf.* London: Macmillan, 1985.

Faulkner, Peter. *Humanism in the English Novel.* London: Elek/Pemberton, 1976.

Finchman, Gail. "Arches and Echoes: Framing Devices in *A Passage to India.*" *Pretexts: Studies in Literature and Culture* 2:1 (1990) 52–67.

Friend, Robert. "The Quest for Rondure: A Comparison of Two Passages to India." *The Hebrew University Studies in Literature* 1, no. 1 (Spring 1973): 76–85.

Furbank, P.N. *E.M. Forster: A Life.* 2 vols. London: Secker & Warburg, 1977.

Ganguly, Adwaita P. *India: Mystic Complex and Real: A Detailed Study of E.M. Forster's A Passage to India: His Treatment of India's Landscape, History, Social Anthropology, Religion, Philosophy, Music and Art.* Delhi: Motilal Banarsidass Publishers Pvt., Ltd., 1990.

Gardner, Philip, ed. *E.M. Forster: The Critical Heritage.* London and Boston: Routledge & Kegan Paul, 1973.

Gillie, Christopher. *A Preface to Forster.* London: Longman Group, 1983.

Gransden, K.W. *E.M. Forster.* Edinburgh and London: Oliver & Boyd, 1962.

Hardy, Barbara. *The Appropriate Form.* Evanston, Ill., Northwestern University Press, 1971.

Heath, Jeffrey. "A Voluntary Surrender: Imperialism and Imagination in *A Passage to India.*" *University of Toronto Quarterly* 59:2 (1989/1990): 287–309.

Herz, Judith Scherer. *A Passage to India: Nation and Narration.* New York: G.K. Hall, 1993.

Italia, Paul G. "Under the Rules of Time: Story and Plot in E.M. Forster's *A Passage to India.*" *English Language Notes* 27:3 (1990) 58–62.

Johnstone, J.K. *The Bloomsbury Group: A Study of E.M. Forster, Lytton Strachey, Virginia Woolf, and Their Circle.* New York: Noonday Press, 1954.

Kermode, Frank. "The One Orderly Product (E.M. Forster)." In *Puzzles and Epiphanies: Essays and Reviews 1958–1961.* New York: Chillmark Press, 1962.

Koponen, Wilfrid R. "Krishna at the Garden Party: Crisis of Faith in *A Passage to India.*" *International Fiction Review* 20:1 (1993): 39–47.

Lago, Mary. *E.M. Forster: A Literary Life.* New York: St. Martin's Press, 1996.

Langbaum, Robert. "A New Look at E.M. Forster." *Southern Review* 4 (Winter 1968): 33–49.

Leavis, F.R. "E.M. Forster." *Scrutiny* 7 (September 1938): 185–202.

Levine, June Perry. *Creation and Criticism: A Passage to India*. Lincoln: University of Nebraska Press, 1971.

Lin, Lidan. "The Irony of Colonial Humanism: *A Passage to India* and the Politics of Posthumanism." *Ariel* 28:4 (1997): 133–153.

Macauley, Rose. *The Writings of E. M. Forster*. New York: Harcourt Brace, 1938.

Martin, Robert K. and George Piggford, eds. *Queer Forster*. Chicago, University of Chicago Press, 1997.

Marx, John. "Modernism and the Female Imperial Gaze." *Novel: A Forum on Fiction* 32:1 (1998): 51–75.

May, Brian. *The Modernist as Pragmatist: E.M. Forster and the Fate of Liberalism*. Columbia: University of Missouri Press, 1997.

McConkey, James. *The Novels of E. M. Forster*. Ithaca: Cornell University Press, 1957.

McDowell, Frederick P. W. *E. M. Forster*. Revised edition. Boston: Twayne, 1982.

Medalie, David. *E.M. Forster's Modernism*. Chippenham: Antony Rowe, Ltd., 2002.

Messenger, Nigel. "Imperial Journeys, Bodily Landscapes and Sexual Anxiety: Adela's Visit to the Marabar in *A Passage to India*." *Journal of Commonwealth Literature* 33:1 (1998): 99–110.

Meyers, Jeffrey. "The Politics of *Passage to India*." *Journal of Modern Literature* 1, no. 3 (March 1971): 329–38.

Moffat, Wendy. "*A Passage to India* and the Limits of Certainty." *Journal of Narrative Technique* 20:3 (1990): 331–41.

Monk, Leland. "Apropos of Nothing: Chance and Narrative in Forster's *A Passage to India*." *Studies in the Novel* 26:4 (1994): 392–403.

Moore-Gilbert, Bart. *Writing India 1757-1990: the Literature of British India*. Manchester: Manchester University Press, 1996.

Natwar-Singh, K., ed. *E. M. Forster: A Tribute*. New York: Harcourt, Brace & World, 1964.

Page, Norman. *E.M. Forster*. New York: St. Martin's Press, 1987.

Parry, Benita. "Materiality and Mystification in *A Passage to India*." *Novel: A Forum on Fiction* 31:2 (Spring 1998): 174–94.

Pintchman, Tracy. "Snakes in the Cave: Religion and the echo in E.M. Forster's *A Passage to India*." *Soundings: An Interdisciplinary Journal* 75:1 (1992): 61–78.

Pradhan, S.V. "*A Passage to India*: Realism Versus Symbolism, A Marxist Analysis." *Dalhousie Review* 60, no. 2 (Summer 1980): 300–317.

Proctor, Margaret. "Possibilities of Completion: the Endings of *Women in Love* and *A Passage to India*." *English Literature in Transition* 34:3 (1991): 261–280.

Rahman, Tariq. "The Significance of Oriental Poetry in E. M. Forster's *A Passage to India*." *Durham University Journal* 81:1 (1988): 101–110.

Rahman, Tariq. "Syed Ross Masood and E.M. Forster's *A Passage to India*." *ANQ* 4:2 (1991): 78–81.

Raschke, Debrah. "Forster's Passage to India: Re-envisioning Plato's Cave." *Comparatist* 21 (1997): 10–24.

Rapport, Nigel. *The Prose and the Passion: Anthropology, Literature and the Writing of E.M. Forster*. New York: St. Martin's Press, 1994.

Richards, I. A. "A Passage to Forster." *Forum* 78 (December 1927): 914–29.

Riddy, John. "Courtesy in Conflict: Indian and Pakistan English Fictions." *Ariel* 29:1 (1998): 67–87.

Rosecrance, Barbara. *Forster's Narrative Vision*. Ithaca: Cornell University Press, 1982.

Rutherford, Andrew, ed. *Twentieth Century Interpretations of* A Passage to India: *A Collection of Critical Essays*. Englewood Cliffs: Prentice-Hall, Inc., 1970.

Schwarz, Daniel R. "The Originality of E.M Forster." *Modern Fiction Studies* 29, no. 4 (Winter 1983): 623–41.

Shahane, V.A., ed. *Perspectives on E.M. Forster's* A Passage to India: *A Collection of Critical Essays*. New York: Barnes & Noble, 1968.

———, ed. *Focus on Forster's* "A Passage to India" Bombay: Orient Longman, 1975.

Sharpe, Jenny. "The Unspeakable Limits of Rape: Colonial Violence and Counter-insurgency." *Genders* 10 (1991): 25–46.

Shusterman, David. *The Quest for Certitude in E.M. Forster's Fiction*. Bloomington: Indiana University Press, 1965.

Spender, Stephen. "Personal Relations and Public Powers." In *The Creative Element: A Study of Vision, Despair and Orthodoxy Among Some Modern Writers*. London: Hamish Hamilton, 1953.

Summers, Claude J. *E.M. Forster*. New York: Frederick Ungar, 1966.

Stallybrass, Oliver, ed. *Aspects of E. M. Forster: Essays and Recollections Written for His Ninetieth Birthday, January 1, 1969*. New York: Harcourt, Brace & World, 1969.

Stewart, Garrett. "The Foreign Offices of British Fiction." *Modern Language Quarterly* 61:1 (2000): 181–206.

Stone, Wilfred. *The Cave and the Mountain: A Study of E.M. Forster*. Stanford: Stanford University Press, 1966.

Thomson, George H. *The Fiction of E.M. Forster*. Detroit: Wayne State University Press, 1967.

Thumboo, Edwin. "E.M. Forster's *A Passage to India*: From Caves to Court." *Southern Review* 10, no. 4 (December 1978): 386–404.

Trilling, Lionel. *E.M. Forster*. Binghamton, NY: New Directions, 1943.

Turk, Jo M. "The Evolution of E.M. Forster's Narrator." *Studies in the Novel* 5, no. 4 (Winter 1973):428–39.

Walls, Elizabeth MacLeod. "An Aristotelian Reading of the Feminine Voice-as-Revolution in E.M Forster's *A Passage to India*." *Papers on Language and Literature* 35:1 (1999): 56–73.

Warren, Austin. "The Novels of E.M. Forster." In *Rage for Order*, 119–41. Chicago: University of Chicago Press, 1948.

Wilde, Alan. "Depths and Surfaces: Dimensions of Forsterian Irony." *English Literature in Transition* 16, no. 4 (1973): 257–73.

———, ed. *Critical Essays on E.M. Forster*. Boston: G.K. Hall & Co., 1985.

Winn, Harbour. "English Inward Journeys: *A Passage to India* and *St. Mawr*." *English Language Notes* 31:2 (1993): 62–6.

Acknowledgments

"*A Passage to India*" by Lionel Trilling from *E.M. Forster*: 136–161. Copyright © 1943, 1964 by New Directions Publishing Corp. Reprinted by permission of New Directions Publishing Corp.

"Two Passage to India: Forster as Victorian and Modern" by Malcolm Bradbury from *Aspects of E. M. Forster*: 123–142. Copyright © 1969 by The Malcolm Bradbury Estate. Reprinted by permission of Curtis Brown on behalf of The Malcolm Bradbury Estate.

"Language and Science in *A Passage to India*" by Michael Orange from *E.M. Forster: A Human Exploration*, eds. G.K. Das and John Beer: 142–160. © 1979 by New York University Press. Reprinted by permission.

"The Marabar Caves in the Light of Indian Thought" by Chaman L. Sahni from *Focus on Forster's* "A Passage to India": *Indian Essays in Criticism*, ed. V.A. Shahane: 105–114. © 1975 by Orient Longman. Reprinted by permission.

"*A Passage to India* and the Limits of Certainty" by Wendy Moffat from *The Journal of Narrative Technique* 20, no. 3, (Fall 1990): 331–341. © 1990 by Wendy Moffatt. Reprinted by permission.

"Krishna at the Garden Party: Crises of Faith in *A Passage to India*" by Wilfrid R. Koponen from *The International Fiction Review* 20, no. 1 (1993): 39–47. © 1993 by the International Fiction Association. Reprinted by permission.

"Apropos of Nothing: Chance and Narrative in Forster's *A Passage to India*" by Leland Monk from *Studies in the Novel* 26, no. 4 (Winter 1994):

392–403. Copyright © 1994 by the University of North Texas. Reprinted by permission of the publisher.

"Colonial Queer Something" by Yonatan Touval from *Queer Forster*, eds. R.K. Martin and G. Piggsford: 237–254. © 1997 by The University of Chicago Press. Reprinted by permission.

"Forster's *Passage to India*: Re-Envisioning Plato's Cave" by Debrah Raschke from *The Comparatist* XXI (May 1997): 10–25. © 1997 by Debrah Raschke. Reprinted by permission.

"Materiality and Mystification in *A Passage to India*" by Benita Parry from *Novel: A Forum on Fiction* 31, no. 2 (Spring 1998): 174–193. © 1998 by Benita Parry. Reprinted by permission.

"An Aristotelian Reading of the Feminine Voice-as-Revolution in E. M. Forster's *A Passage to India*" by Elizabeth MacLeod Walls from *Papers on Language and Literature* 35, no. 1 (Winter 1999): 56–73. © 1999 by the Board of Trustees, Southern Illinois University Press. Reprinted by permission.

"Forster's Imperial Romance: Chivalry, Motherhood, and Questing in *A Passage to India*" by Maria M. Davidis from *Journal of Modern Literature* 23, no. 2 (Winter 1999/2000): 259–276. © 1999 by Maria M. Davidis. Reprinted by permission.

Index

Abinger Harvest
  "The Abbeys' Difficulties" in, 13
  "Captain Edward Gibbon" in, 13
  "The Past" in, 13
  "Trooper Silas Tompkyns
    Comberbacke" in, 13
  "Voltaire's Laboratory" in, 13
  Lord Acton, 17
"Advance, India!"
  Indian life in, 12
Alexandria, 5–6, 9–10
Alexandria: A History and a Guide
  contempt for Christianity in, 12
  Egyptian book, 12
  Forster's years in Alexandria in,
    5–6
  love for the Hellenic and
    naturalistic in, 12
Ali, Mahmoud, 94, 153
"Allegory of the Cave"
  compared to *A Passage to India*,
    131–35, 137, 140–42
Allen, Glen O., 69
Allen, Grant, 192
Allen, Walter, 33
Aristotle, 172, 177–78, 181
Arnold, Matthew, 26, 32
Arnold, William Delafield, 26
Aspects of the Novel, 33, 74
Austen, Jane, 33

Aziz in *A Passage to India*, 16, 24,
    194
  and accusations, 19, 25, 52,
    76–77, 80, 89–90, 93–95, 112,
    114–15, 117–19, 136–37, 152,
    172, 174–76, 178–79, 181,
    197, 200
  aspirations of, 57, 95–96, 135,
    189
  belief in friendship, 87, 90,
    92–93, 100–1, 107, 121, 124,
    165
  and the caves, 51, 58–59, 87–89,
    94, 103, 141, 201
  civilization of, 17–18, 38
  dislike of the British, 87, 94–95,
    153, 203
  and Fielding, 17, 19–21, 25–26,
    49, 52–53, 56, 58, 62, 81, 83,
    90–91, 93, 100, 106–7,
    116–17, 121, 123–24, 153–54,
    160, 163–65, 172, 181,
    185–91, 196–98, 201–2, 204–5
  innocence of, 25, 77, 115–16,
    133, 135, 142, 172, 177, 180,
    201
  and irony, 57
  lack of conscious will in, 2, 55
  and marriage, 95, 125
  misery of, 18, 82

and Mrs. Moore, 18–19, 39, 79,
    89–90, 92, 94, 100, 106, 121,
    132, 138–39, 141, 153, 190,
    197–201, 203
and Moslem ideal, 21, 38, 58, 89,
    93, 95, 100, 104, 152
nature of, 21, 39, 49, 57, 81, 135
passage of, 10
queerness of, 112
sexuality of, 111, 120–21,
    123–24, 137–41, 202–3
silence of, 56–57, 156
vision of, 139–40
Azmi, Shabna, 119

Barrell, John, 157
Bataille, Georges, 154
Beaumont, Ernest, 70–71
Beer, Gillian, 89
    "Negation in *A Passage to India*,"
    101–3
Bharucha, Rustom, 90
Bitzer, 179–80
Blake, William
    compared to Forster, 1
    influence on Forster, 181–82
Bloom, Harold, 213
    introduction, 1– 10, 90
Bradbury, Malcolm, 29–44, 213
    on cosmological implications in
A Passage to India, 36–38, 40
    on Forster compared to Melville,
    44
    on the modern values in *A
    Passage to India*, 30–32, 34
    on the Victorian values in *A
    Passage to India*, 30–31, 33–34
Bradford, Edwin Emmanuel,
    187–88
Bristow, Joseph, 151, 158
Brown, E.K., 35

Burke, Kenneth, 153, 161
Burrough, William, 109
Butler, Samuel, 12, 33, 137

Campbell, Joseph, 48
Carpenter, Edward, 157
"Cave" section in *A Passage to India*,
    9, 151, 153, 158–59
    Fielding's rational view in, 81
    heart of darkness in, 104, 108
    Indian theory in, 66, 71, 100
    narrative mode of, 100, 102–3,
    108
    nothingness theme in, 101–3
Coleridge, Samuel Taylor, 13, 32
Commonplace Book
    compared self to Eliot in, 2
Conscious will concept, 1–2
"Consolations of History, The"
    persistent fault of taste in, 13
Conrad, Joseph, 30, 62, 103, 148
    Forster on, 5
Cortázar, Julio
    Hopscotch, 109
Cousin Kate, 185
Craft, Christopher, 112
Crews, Frederick, 80

Das, G.K. in *A Passage to India*, 20,
    87, 93, 158, 177
King David, 3–4
Davidis, Maria, M., 214
    on romance elements of the
    quest in *A Passage to India*,
    185–207
Dickinson, Emily, 82
Dickinson, G. Lowes, 155
    Forster's biography on, 13, 47
    journey to India, 3, 11–12, 18
    political life of, 13
Dolin, Kieran, 174, 177

"Doll Souse, The"
    political piece on the Queen's
Doll House, 15
Drew, John, 92

Eliot, T.S., 47, 129–30
    compared to Forster, 1–2
"Empire Is Born, An"
    political piece on the British
Empire Exhibition at Wembley, 15
English Officials in *A Passage to
India*
    Mr. Callendar in, 190
    portrayal of, 16–18

Fielding in *A Passage to India*, 75, 77,
    80, 88
    and Aziz, 17, 19–21, 25–26, 49,
        52–53, 56, 58, 62, 81, 83, 90,
        92–93, 100, 106–7, 116–17,
        121, 123–24, 153–54, 160,
        163–65, 172, 181, 185–91,
        196–98, 201–2, 204–5
    belief of Aziz's innocence, 19, 50,
        53–54, 90–91, 115–16, 172,
        174–77
    and the beauty of form, 10
    and the echo, 40, 162
    and Hinduism, 49, 56, 60, 156
    honesty of, 52–53, 55–56, 58, 60,
        81, 104
    hopes of, 36
    humanity of, 52
    limitations of, 52–53, 55–57, 94,
        106
    and marriage, 124–25
    passage of, 10, 39
    queerness of, 116
    as renegade, 16–17, 39
    sexuality of, 111, 122–24, 202
    spirituality of, 52, 54

and Stella, 21, 25–26, 95, 124,
    203
values of, 82
vision of, 9
Finkelstein, Bonnie, 136
Forster, E.M.
    and Alexandria, 5–6, 12
    ambiguities of, 74, 82–83, 179
    and Arian heresy, 6–7
    compared to Blake, 1
    chronology, 209–11
    and conscientiousness, 74
    criticism of, 1, 30–31
    and the *Daily Herald*, 14
    death of, 163
    and development of *A Passage of
        India*, 74–77
    on the difference between life
        and art, 73, 82
    compared to Eliot, 1–2
    and England, 14
    and Hinduism, 3, 5, 7, 25–26, 45,
        92
    and India, 3, 11–12, 16, 26, 99,
        149, 154, 157–58, 162,
        172–73, 188
    liberal imagination of, 1, 16–17,
        29–31
    on literary freedom, 15, 166
    compared to Melville, 44
    and Modernism, 30–32, 34
    moral world of, 77
    compared to Morris, 1
    passion of, 29
    political concerns of, 12–15, 166,
        171, 173–74
    praise of, 29
    predilection for mysteries in, 156
    and public affairs, 13
    as private secretary to Maharahah
        of Dewas State Senior, 3

and religion, 3–4, 91, 93
sexuality of, 6, 83, 95, 130, 151, 165
and the story, 33
and tolerance, 83
and Victorian, 30–31, 33 –34
vision of, 32, 34–35
writing style of, 45, 60, 62
Forster, E.M., influences of
Blake, 181–82
Plato, 129–35, 137, 140–42
Marcel Proust, 3
John Rushkin, 3
Walt Whitman, 157
Four Quarters, The (Eliot), 130
Frieländer, 134
Furbank, P.N., 192

Gandhi, Prime Minister Indira, 113
Gandhi, Mahatma, 113
Girouard, Mark, 187
God Krishna in A Passage to India, 3–4, 10, 22, 25, 59, 72, 92–93, 95, 104, 151, 157, 159, 161, 164, 204
Godbole, Professor in A Passage to India, 5, 19, 23, 72, 152, 189
and the caves, 58–59, 88, 92, 137
and his "completeness," 41–42, 54, 60
consciousness of, 22, 39, 55
epiphany of, 9–10
faith of, 60
and the Hindu vision, 25, 49, 58, 60, 82–83, 87, 92–93, 104–5, 107–8, 135, 151, 159, 162, 180, 200–1
judgment of, 56
lack of conscious will in, 2
queerness of, 116
revelation of, 41, 50, 95
silence of, 156, 164

and the wasp, 22, 25
"Gods of India, The," 83
Gordon, Jan, 180
Government of Egypt, The
pamphlet of the International Section of the Labor research Department, 13

Harvest of Hellenism, The (Peters)
Alexandria as precursor to all culture in, 6
"Heart of Bosnia, The," 11, 191–92
Heart of Darkness (Conrad), 5, 103, 148
Heimann, Betty, 66–67
Heaslop, Ronny in A Passage to India, 16, 59, 80, 153
point of view of, 18, 20, 25, 38–39, 90–92, 94, 114, 134, 136–37, 140, 160, 174, 198
and Adela, 19–20, 22, 51, 92, 94–95, 105, 107, 132–33, 135–37, 141–42, 174, 176–77, 192, 194, 197–200
Heidegger, Martin, 102, 109
Hellenism and Homosexuality in Victorian Oxford (Dowling), 188
Herz, Judith, 91
Hill of Devi, The
letters from India in, 3
Maharajah in, 3–5
mystical apprehension in, 3
publication of, 3
Hinduism
and Forster, 3, 5, 7
in A Passage to India, 2, 7–9
Howards End, 1, 130, 192
city as a metaphor in, 36
class attitude in, 45
conflict in, 48
Germany's growing strength in, 11

Helen in, 11, 24
Margaret in, 11, 79
powers and forces in history in,
    32
Mr. Schlegal in, 11
urbanization and industrialism in,
    32, 148
Mrs. Wicox in, 2, 79
Huysmans, J.K.
    compared to Forster, 1
Huxley, Aldous, 47

India
    Forster's journeys to , 3, 11–12
Irigaray, Luce, 131, 133–35, 139
Isherwood, Christopher, 29

James, Henry, 2, 36, 102
Jameson, Fredric, 129, 148
Joyce, James, 2, 30, 129

Kahn, Albert, 11
Kains-Jackson, Charles, 188
Katrak, Ketu H.
    "Indian Nationalism, Gandhian
        'Satygraha,' and Representations
        of Female Sexuality," 113
Keats, Fanny, 13
Keats, John, 13
Kermode, Frank, 35
Koponen, Wilfrid, R., 214
    on Forster's judgment of India
        and the spiritual crises in A
        Passage to India, 87–97
Kosinski, Jerzy
    Being There, 109

Lacan, Jacques, 108
Lawrence, D.H., 30
Leavis, F.R., 82
Levine, June Perry, 76, 179

Lewes, George Henry, 12
Lindsey, Joan, 162
Longest Journey, The, 130
    Gerald in, 79
Lukács, Georg, 129

Macherey, Pierre, 154
Maharajah of Chhatarpur, 12
Maharajah of Dewas State Senior, 3
    death of, 3
    Forster's portrayal of in The Hill
        of Devi, 3–5
Mandela, Nelson, 119
Mayo, Katherine
    Mother India, 114
McConkey, James, 69
McDowell, Fredrick P.W., 92
"Me, Them, and You"
    political piece, 14–15
    review of the Sargent exhibition
        of 1925, 14–15
Melville, Herman, 4–5
    compared to Forster, 44
Moby Dick (Mellville), 44
Moffat, Wendy, 214
    on the ambiguous genre in
        A Passage to India, 78–82
    on the writing of the cave scene
        in A Passage to India, 74–77
    on Forster's conviction in
        A Passage to India, 73–85

Monk, Leland, 214
    on the three narrative modes in
        A Passage to India, 99–110
Moore Mrs. in A Passage to India,
    16–17, 20
    and Aziz, 18–19, 39, 79, 89–90,
        92, 94, 100, 106, 121, 132,
        138–39, 141, 153, 190,
        197–201, 203

beliefs of, 87, 91, 136, 140, 192
and the caves, 59, 65–66, 68–70,
    77–78, 88, 91, 101, 103,
    132–33, 135, 137, 156, 160,
    162, 176, 199
and the echo, 23–25, 39–40, 51,
    59, 68–69, 71, 91, 132
death of, 19, 24, 79–80, 106, 136,
    153
disillusion of, 57
figure of wisdom, 5–6, 49, 175
as heroine, 5, 80
and the Hindu theme, 21, 26,
    40–41, 60, 90, 105–7, 117,
    136, 161, 187, 200
humanity of, 18, 34, 39
intuition of, 19, 22, 38, 56, 62,
    106, 108
lack of conscious will in, 2, 22, 50
language of, 56
and love and marriage, 90, 95,
    125, 194, 197
and ostracized, 19, 25, 58, 117
panic of, 24
psychic paralysis of, 70, 82, 101,
    106
queerness of, 116
and the "racial secret," 22–23
rebirth of, 72
receptivity of, 9
religion of, 9, 22, 68–70, 87–88,
    91–92, 132, 135, 180
silence of, 200
spirit of, 25, 106–8, 116, 177,
    197–98, 200–4
vision of, 68, 71, 89, 93
and the wasp, 21–22, 24, 108
Morris, William
    compared to Forster, 1
"Mosque" section in *A Passage to
    India*, 135, 138, 151, 153, 158–59

Indian theory in, 100
Moslem ideas of friendship in,
    100
narrative mode of, 101, 104
"My Wood"
    growth of the property sense in,
    15

New Chivalry (Kains-Jackson), 188
New Chivalry, The (Bradford),
    187–88
Nostromo (Conrad), 5, 148

Oakfield: Or, Fellowship In The East
    (Arnold, W.)
    denouncement of England in
        India, 26
"On Tolerance," 73
Orange, Michael, 214
    on the language and silence in
        A Passage to India, 45–63

Parry, Benita, 214
    on Forster's own mystification of
        India, 88, 147–70
Passage to India, A
    Alexandrian philosophy in, 5–6,
        9–10
    compared to "Allegory of the
        Cave," 131–35, 137, 140–42
    beauty of form in, 10
    "Caves" section in. See "Caves"
        section in *A Passage to India*
    cave symbology in, 65–66, 68
    chance in, 100, 105–6, 108
    chivalry in, 186–90, 197, 203
    cohesion and intricacy in, 23
    consciousness of, 46, 52, 67, 94
    controversy of, 16–17
    corruption of power in, 17
    cosmological implications in,

criticism of, 16, 18, 35, 65, 69–71, 82, 87–89, 101–3, 108–9, 112, 150–51, 159, 164, 173–74, 194

cultural differences in, 21, 37–39, 46, 50, 94, 100, 151, 162–63, 165, 172–74, 176, 185, 188, 190

death in, 79, 205

disintegrating question of, 26

the echo in, 23, 25, 39–40, 49, 53, 58, 67–69, 71, 75, 77, 82, 87–89, 91, 94–95, 103, 115–16, 132, 151, 155–56, 161, 176, 195, 200

"essential life" in, 39

expulsion of the English in, 20, 36, 39, 49, 100, 111–12, 119, 150–52, 154, 171–72

flexibility of, 47

friendship theme in, 100–1, 153, 158, 163, 172, 181, 187, 204

genre of, 78–82, 137

Hinduism in, 2, 7–9, 19, 21, 25, 38, 56, 58–60, 62, 68, 70, 72, 87, 91–93, 95, 104–9, 120, 156, 158–59, 161, 164, 203

history in, 46

human relationships in, 36, 41, 50, 78, 80, 83, 160, 186–87, 190

imagery in, 46, 68, 88

imagination in, 17, 57, 114

India in, 2, 12, 16–17, 19, 22, 25–26, 36–39, 41, 46, 48–49, 51–52, 57, 66, 69, 71, 78–80, 82, 87–88, 90–91, 95–96, 107, 111, 116, 126, 132, 149–52, 154–56, 158, 160, 162, 166, 171–72, 181–82, 185, 187–88, 192, 194, 202, 205

Indian Thought in, 65–72, 88, 100, 104, 114, 158, 161

Indian Nationalism in, 20–21, 80, 112–13, 152, 173, 185, 188

irony in, 37, 47, 49–50, 57, 61

language in, 45–52, 57–59, 61–62, 76, 78, 116, 149, 151, 155–56, 162, 166

man and nature in, 35, 40, 79

Marabar Caves in, 19, 23–24, 37, 40–41, 43, 56, 58–59, 65–72, 74–75, 77, 82, 87–89, 92, 94–95, 101–4, 112–16, 131–37, 140–42, 152, 155, 159–62, 164, 172, 174–76, 178–80, 189–90, 194, 196, 202

marriage theme in, 78, 81, 90, 94–95, 125, 186, 191, 193, 202

metaphors in, 36, 50–51, 77, 132, 134

modernism in, 100, 102–4, 108–9, 149, 166, 182, 185–86

moral dimension of, 62, 83

"Mosque" section in. See "Mosque" section in A Passage to India

Moslem culture in, 21, 38, 58, 78, 89, 95, 100, 104, 107, 159, 163

mystical aspect of, 36, 38, 46, 48, 54, 105, 151, 160, 181

mythology in, 65–66, 103, 108, 158

narrative of, 2, 5, 50–52, 56–57, 76, 78–79, 99–109, 114, 119, 123, 136, 138, 149–51, 156, 162–63, 165–66, 172–76, 179–80, 185, 190, 192

nothingness theme in, 101–2, 104, 107–9

panic and emptiness in, 24

the passage in, 47
plot of, 18–19, 25, 37, 43, 49
poetic realm of, 41
politics of, 80, 90, 151–53, 162,
    164, 166, 173, 185–86
power in, 35–36
public and political nature of,
    16–17, 35–38, 42
"queerness" in, 111–28
religious theme of, 2, 22, 25, 36,
    51, 55, 58, 60, 65, 67, 72, 91,
    104, 119, 156–57, 159
remoteness of the characters in,
    21
romanticism in, 32, 37, 140, 193
self-consciousness in, 1
separateness theme in, 20–21, 38
silence in, 46–47, 54–59, 77, 89,
    91, 154–56, 159, 164
spiritual question of, 6–7
spirituality in, 5, 40–41, 89, 180
story of, 18, 23
symbols in, 42, 61, 67, 150
"Temple" section in. *See*
"Temple" section in *A Passage to
    India*
time and eternity in, 61–62, 66,
    68, 70–71
tone of, 46–47, 49–50, 61–62
unity of vision in, 34–35, 40
Victorian values in, 181, 185–86,
    189, 195
the wasp in, 21–23, 25, 105, 108
writing of, 74–77
Passage to India, A, characters in, 18
Aziz in. *See* Aziz in *A Passage to
    India*
the English officials in. *See* in
    A Passage to India
Fielding in. *See* Fielding in
    A Passage to India

Godbole in. *See* Godbole in
    A Passage to India
Graysford in, 50, 79, 83 Ronny
    Heaslop in. *See* Heaslop,
    Ronny in *A Passage to India*
Mohammed Latif in, 176
McBryde in, 91, 93, 95, 115–16,
    118–19, 121, 123, 174–76,
    178–81, 190–91, 196, 200
Mrs. Moore in. *See* Mrs. Moore
    in *A Passage to India*
Ralph Moore in, 25, 50, 89, 107,
    153, 156, 165, 203–4
Stella Moore in, 21, 25, 93, 107,
    124, 153, 156, 203
the Nawab Bahadur in, 50,
    105–6, 194, 197
Poldy in, 2
Adela Quested in. *See* Quested,
    Adela in *A Passage to India*
Mr. Sorley in, 41, 50, 79, 83
Turton in, 19–20, 90, 185, 201
Turton's wife in, 19–20, 173, 185,
    195
"Passage to India" (Whitman), 157
Peters, F.E., 6
Phaedrus (Plato), 130
Pharos And Pharillon
    Alexandrian history and local
        color in, 12–13
    irony in, 13
Picnic at Hanging Rock (Lindsay), 162
Plato
    influence on Forster, 129–35,
        137, 140–42
Popper, Karl, 30
Portrait of the Artist as a Young Man
    (Joyce), 129
Portrait of a Lady, The (James)
    Isabel Archer in, 2
Pride and Prejudice (Austen)

the Bennet family in, 78
Proust, Marcel, 33

Quality Street, 185
Quested, Adela in A Passage to India,
 16, 90, 121, 123, 157
 attack of, 75–76, 81, 89, 93, 115,
  117–18, 132, 135, 137, 152,
  172, 175–77, 187, 194–95
 desire of, 49, 51, 76–77, 82, 94,
  106, 115, 118–19, 136, 140,
  142, 176, 186, 192–93, 201
 and the echo, 87, 95, 115, 195,
  200
 experience in the caves, 87, 95,
  103–4, 114–15, 132–35, 137,
  141, 152, 162, 172, 175–77,
  179–81, 187, 194
 faith of, 41
 fears of, 77, 195
 hallucinations of, 17, 19, 23, 25,
  37, 39–40, 52, 54–55, 75,
  94–95, 106, 115, 133–34, 137,
  152, 165, 175–76, 187, 202
 and Ronny, 19–20, 22, 51, 92,
  94–95, 105, 107, 132–33,
  135–37, 141–42, 174, 176–77,
  192, 194–197–200
 humanity of, 18
 limitations of, 50–52, 54, 61, 87,
  93–95, 114, 175
 queerness of, 116
 rage of, 76, 115, 176
 Victorian and modern aspects in,
  185–86, 190, 195–96, 204
 vision of, 38
 voice of, 173–82, 199, 201

Raschke, Debrah, 214
 on the inversion of Adela's
  epiphany of the Marabar

Caves in A Passage to India,
 129–45
Return to Camelot, The (Girouard),
 187
"Rhapsody on a Windy Night"
 (Eliot), 129
Rosecrance, Barbara, 87, 93

Sahni, Chaman L., 214
 on Indian Theory in the Marabar
  Caves in A Passage to India,
  65–72, 88
Said, Edward, 147–49, 158, 164
Shakespeare, William, 102
Shelley, Percy Blysshe, 33
Socrates, 129–30, 134
Spencer, Herbert, 12
Spender, Stephen, 34
Stein, Gertrude, 47
Stone, Wilfred, 35, 103
Suleri, Sara, 87, 188
"Suppliant, The"
 Indian life in, 12
Symposium (Plato), 130

Tanner, Tony, 29
"Temple" section in A Passage to
India, 9, 72, 138, 151, 153, 158–59
 apotheosis in, 3, 108
 chance in, 106
 mysterious and chaotic festivals
  in, 82, 104, 133
 narrative mode in, 100, 104–5,
  109
 questions of genre in, 81
Timaeus (Plato), 137
Tinsley, Molly B., 89
To The Lighthouse (Woolf), 129
Tolstoy, Leo, 33
Touval, Yonatan, 214
 on the relation of homoeroticism

to colonialism in *A Passage to India*, 111–28
Trevelyan, R.C., 11
Trilling, Lionel, 213
   on Forster, 1, 5
   on *A Passage to India*, 11–27, 32, 35, 57, 80
Turn of the Screw, The (James), 102

Ulysses (Joyce), 2

Queen Victoria, Empress of India, 153

Walls, Elizabeth MacLeod, 214
   on Forster's use of Adela's voice, 171–84

Waste Land, The (Eliot), 47, 130
Weir, Peter, 162
Where Angels Fear to Tread
   Gino in, 79
Whitman, Walt, 37, 43–44, 157
Wilde, Alan, 72
Wilson, Angus, 29
Woolf, Virginia, 47, 129
Wordsworth, William, 32
World War I, 1, 11, 90

Yeats, William Butler, 130
   compared to Forster, 1
Yeomen of the Guard, The, 185